SAVING BELIEF

SAVING BELIEF

A Critique of Physicalism

Lynne Rudder Baker

PRINCETON UNIVERSITY PRESS

Published by Princeton University Press, 41 William Street,
Princeton, New Jersey 08540
In the United Kingdom: Princeton University Press, Guildford, Surrey

Library of Congress Cataloging in Publication Data will be
found on the last printed page of this book

ISBN 0-691-07320-1

Publication of this book has been aided by the Whitney Darrow Fund
of Princeton University Press

This book has been composed in Linotron Sabon and Serif Gothic

Printed in the United States of America by Princeton University Press,
Princeton, New Jersey

To
Virginia Bennett Rudder
James Maclin Rudder

CONTENTS

CONTENTS

PREFACE

This book is a critical examination of the dominant philosophical interpretation of cognitive science: physicalism. A physicalist holds either that nonintentional and nonsemantic sufficient conditions can be specified for intentional states like belief, desire, and intention, or that there really are no such states identified by content. The first approach is reductive; the second, eliminative.

Part I examines reductive positions, formulated by Jerry A. Fodor and others, that aim to provide nonintentional sufficient conditions for belief. With the aid of a series of thought experiments, I shall show (in Chapters Two, Three, and Four) the inadequacy of each such position, and then diagnose (in Chapter Five) the reason for the failure: Physicalists place incompatible constraints—one semantic and the other physical—on the concept of intentional content. Thus, I argue, no physicalistically acceptable notion of the content of a belief or other attitude will be forthcoming.

Part II examines eliminative positions, formulated by Stephen P. Stich, Paul M. Churchland, Patricia S. Churchland, Daniel C. Dennett, and others, that deny the existence of beliefs or other attitudes identified by content. In Chapter Six, I argue that the common-sense conception that invokes belief is not simply a theory subject to empirical disconfirmation, and in Chapter Seven, I argue that wholesale denial of the common-sense conception is self-defeating in various ways. After taking up Dennett's instrumentalistic construal of belief in Chapter Eight, I draw some modest conclusions in Chapter Nine. Prominent among these, I suggest that we may endorse naturalism without physicalism.

The upshot is that common-sense mentalistic and intentional notions need no foundation in physicalism. Their legitimacy is assured, not by any justification in nonintentional terms, but by their indispensable contribution to our cognitive enterprises.

This book is full of arguments, many of which raise hotly contested issues. Recognizing and even enjoying the controversial nature of the arguments, I have tried to make the book technically competent on the one hand, and lively and fun to read on the other. My hope is that many of those who profoundly disagree with my conclusions will find the argument clear enough and fair enough to be worth engaging seriously, if only to sharpen their own views.

Lynne Rudder Baker
May 14, 1987

ACKNOWLEDGMENTS

Many people read parts of the argument in preliminary form and made useful comments; I am grateful to Paul M. Churchland, Daniel C. Dennett, Jerry A. Fodor, and Stephen P. Stich, among others. The close and critical reading that Tyler Burge gave the entire manuscript prompted many improvements. The book has also benefited from responses by Alan Berger, Charles Chastain, Andrew Cling, Kathleen Emmett, Jay L. Garfield, John Heil, Hilary Kornblith, Joseph Levine, William G. Lycan, Gareth B. Matthews, and Jerry Samet, as well as by my colleagues at Middlebury College, Stanley P. Bates, Victor L. Nuovo, Michele LaRusch, and Kenneth Taylor. I owe a special debt to David F. Austin and to Derk Pereboom for their careful and continuing criticism.

Audiences at various universities and colleges where I have presented papers have been helpful as well, especially at: the University of Massachusetts, Amherst; the University of North Carolina, Chapel Hill; Oberlin College; the University of Rochester; Syracuse University; Vanderbilt University; the University of Vermont; Williams College; the National Humanities Center; and the Five-College Cognitive Science Group in Amherst.

Versions of arguments in Chapter Two come from "Just What Do We Have in Mind?" in *Studies in the Philosophy of Mind*, ed. Peter A. French, Theodore E. Uehling, Jr., and Howard K. Wettstein, Midwest Studies in Philosophy, 10 (Minneapolis: University of Minnesota Press, 1986), 25–48; in Chapter Three, from "A Farewell to Functionalism," *Philosophical Studies* 48 (1985), 1–13 (© 1985 by D. Reidel Publishing Company); in Chapters Four and Five, from "Content by Courtesy," *Journal of Philosophy* 84 (1987), 197–213; in Chapters Six and Seven, from "Cognitive Suicide," *Contents of Thought: Proceedings of the 1985 Oberlin Colloquium in Philosophy*, ed. Robert H. Grimm and Daniel D. Merrill (Tucson: University of Arizona Press, forthcoming); in Chapter Eight, from "Instrumental Intentionality," *Philosophy of Science*, forthcoming. I am grateful to the editors of these publications for permission to reprint parts of the articles.

Work on this project has been supported by a Fellowship from the National Humanities Center (1983–1984), by a Fellowship for College

Teachers from the National Endowment for the Humanities (1983–1984), and by a grant from the Middlebury College Faculty Research Fund. Thanks are due to these sources of support.

Finally, I wish to thank Tom Baker, whose ready wit helped to see me through this venture.

SAVING BELIEF

· 1 ·

COMMON SENSE AND
PHYSICALISM

Psychology still awaits its Newton. Even so, many philosophers and others are confident that the human mind, in principle no more unruly than the rest of nature, is soon to be harnessed by science. The long history of success in explaining phenomena in one domain after another gives reason to think that nothing—not even the human mind—will long remain beyond the reach of scientific theory. Against this background, a certain urgency attends the question: What are the relations between emerging scientific concepts of the mind and the familiar, everyday concepts in terms of which we see ourselves and others as acting on beliefs, desires, and intentions?

In some of the areas within the purview of scientific psychology (for example, the discovery of how one learns a language or how one stores telephone numbers in long-term memory), there are no widely held pretheoretical views. In other areas, however, pretheoretical opinions are well entrenched (for example, the supposition that human beings sometimes act from reasons). The question of the relation between the deliverances of the science and pretheoretical views, then, is unavoidable, as it is with any science of some domain on which there are already established opinions.

To make the general question more manageable, I shall divide it: Will there be a science that incorporates concepts like those of belief, desire, and intention, and hence renders them scientifically respectable? If not, will such concepts be exposed as illegitimate? Will scientific psychology conflict with the ordinary framework for explaining behavior in terms of, say, beliefs and intentions?

Of course, the answers to these questions will depend in part on what scientific psychology ends up saying about the mind. Without trying to predict the actual course of science, I shall investigate versions of the dominant philosophical interpretation of psychology and their implications for what I call 'the common-sense conception of the mental,' a conception to be sketched shortly. What characterizes the dominant philosophical interpretation of psychology is a thoroughgoing commitment to physicalism.

Physicalism

Physicalism, as I construe it, has two components, and rejection of either component is rejection of physicalism. Physicalism is the product of a claim about science together with a particular conception of science. The claim is that science is the exclusive arbiter of reality. This scientific realism is captured nicely by Wilfrid Sellars, who transforms the aphorism attributed to Protagoras to fit the current intellectual temper: "in the dimension of describing and explaining the world, science is the measure of all things, of what is that it is, and of what is not that it is not."[1] On this view, scientific knowledge is exhaustive.

The particular conception of science embedded in physicalism is that physically indistinguishable individuals with physically indistinguishable histories are to be assigned the same states. Applied to psychology, the physicalistic conception is that individuals in the same physical, functional, and dispositional states at least make the same contributions to their psychological states; and psychological states of such indistinguishable individuals in the same contexts must have the same truth conditions (or, more generally, satisfaction conditions). I shall use 'physicalistic psychology' to speak not of any particular psychological theory but of this physicalistic interpretation of psychology—an interpretation overwhelmingly endorsed, explicitly or implicitly, by philosophers concerned with cognitive science.

Physicalism has individualistic and nonindividualistic versions. I shall employ 'individualism' in the manner of Tyler Burge, who introduced the term in its current usage:

> Individualism is a view about how kinds are correctly individuated, how their natures are fixed. . . . According to individualism about the mind, the mental natures of all a person's or animal's mental states (and events) are such that there is no necessary or deep individuative relation between the individual's being in states of those kinds and the nature of the individual's physical or social environments.[2]

[1] Wilfrid Sellars, "Empiricism and the Philosophy of Mind," in his *Science, Perception and Reality* (London: Routledge and Kegan Paul, 1963), 173.

[2] "Individualism and Psychology," *Philosophical Review* 95 (1986), 4. See also Burge's "Individualism and the Mental," in *Studies in Metaphysics*, ed. Peter A. French et al., Midwest Studies in Philosophy, 4 (Minneapolis: University of Minnesota Press, 1979), 73–122. Burge has been the foremost critic of individualism. Philosophers with quite different sympathies use 'individualism' in a sense that coincides with its usage in this book. For example, as Ned Block puts it, "Let us say that a propositional attitude or meaning ascription is individualistic if it is supervenient on the physical state of the individual's body, where physical state is specified nonintentionally and independently of

Roughly, if psychological states are specified without presupposing anything about the character of the external environment, then the physicalism is individualistic; otherwise, it is not individualistic. Although other characterizations of individualism have been proposed, this one seems to have the greatest currency and to be the most intuitive.[3]

Thus, a physicalistic interpretation of psychology aims to provide nonintentional and nonsemantic sufficient conditions for psychological states, whether such conditions are construed individualistically or not. (I take the most important divide to be the one between the intentional/semantic and the nonintentional/nonsemantic, rather than that between the individualistic and the nonindividualistic.) The question for physicalists, then, is whether nonintentional and nonsemantic sufficient conditions can be specified for states with content, or representational states. As Jerry A. Fodor says, "The worry about representation is above all that the semantic (and/or the intentional) will prove permanently recalcitrant to integration in the natural order; for example, that the semantic/intentional properties of things will fail to supervene upon their physical properties."[4] If this worry is not dispelled, then a physicalist will have to reject belief/desire psychology.

Physicalists are committed to the following as a condition of adequacy on a scientific psychology: Molecular identity must suffice for psychological identity. Again, on the individualistic construal, psychological identity is to be guaranteed by molecular identity of individuals considered in isolation from their environments; but on the nonindividualistic construal, psychological identity is to be guaranteed by molecular identity of individuals together with their environments.

This widely shared physicalism will also allow us to locate the various positions to be investigated with regard to a simple, general argument. Since, for the time being, I shall not question the physicalistic assumption that an adequate scientific psychology assigns the same

---

physical and social conditions obtaining outside the body." Ned Block, "Advertisement for a Semantics of Psychology," in *Studies in the Philosophy of Mind*, ed. Peter A. French, Theodore E. Uehling, Jr., and Howard K. Wettstein, Midwest Studies in Philosophy, 10 (Minneapolis: University of Minnesota Press, 1986), 624.

[3] Jerry A. Fodor has proposed distinguishing individualism, which he takes to individuate mental representations in terms of their causal powers, from methodological solipsism, which individuates mental representations without regard to semantic evaluation. See Fodor, *Psychosemantics* (Cambridge, Mass.: MIT/Bradford, 1987), ch. 2. The arguments in Chapters Four and Five, which apply to what I call 'nonindividualistic physicalism,' also apply to what Fodor calls 'individualism.' As Fodor uses 'individualism,' I am not sure that there is any room for a nonindividualistic physicalism.

[4] Jerry A. Fodor, "Semantics, Wisconsin Style," *Synthese* 59 (1984), 232.

psychological states to molecular duplicates (at least in molecularly identical environments), it is appropriate to call this argument an 'Argument from Physicalism.'

ARGUMENT FROM PHYSICALISM

(1) Either physicalistic psychology will vindicate (in a sense to be specified) the common-sense conception of the mental, or the common-sense conception is radically mistaken.
(2) Physicalistic psychology will fail to vindicate (in the relevant sense) the common-sense conception of the mental.
Therefore,
(3) The common-sense conception of the mental is radically mistaken.

The first premise is simply a statement of physicalism. It is held, with a special qualification for Daniel C. Dennett, by both nonphilosophers and philosophers. For example, Stephen P. Stich endorses it explicitly when he says that either "folk psychology" will be "vindicated by scientific theory," which he clearly construes physicalistically, or "[s]tates and processes spoken of in folk psychology are . . . mythical posits of a bad theory."[5]

The second premise, on which much of the discussion here will focus, is a very general and vague prediction about the future of physicalistic psychology. The strongest sort of vindication of the common-sense conception would come from a theory whose generalizations apply to mental states by virtue of their contents; a minimal vindication would result even from a theory that held that, although common-sense concepts are incorrect, they are extensionally equivalent to correct ones.

So, physicalistic friends of content would hold (1) true but (2) and (3) false. Physicalists skeptical of the adequacy of any concept of content would hold (1) true and envisage either of two possibilities for (2): false if science minimally vindicates the common-sense conception; true otherwise. Either way, these physicalists voice suspicions that (3) is true. Yet another kind of physicalist would endorse (1), (2), and (3), but argue that the common-sense conception is to be retained for its heuristic value. The premise shared by all physicalists is (1): physicalism. It is this premise that will finally be called into question.

Since examination will reveal deep, apparently insuperable difficulties with all of these positions, we shall need an alternative to physicalism in both its reductive and its eliminative forms. There is a wide-

[5] Stephen P. Stich, *From Folk Psychology to Cognitive Science: The Case Against Belief* (Cambridge, Mass.: MIT/Bradford, 1983), 9-10.

spread assumption that the only alternative to physicalism is a kind of unpalatable mysticism. But this is only a metaphysical bias that has blinded philosophers to the nonmystical, even mundane, alternative to either rendering the common-sense conception physicalistically acceptable or eliminating it altogether. As a result of the bias, the project of giving a naturalistic account of mind has been conflated with the distinct project of providing a basis for a physicalistic science of the mind. Yet the fact that both Donald Davidson and Ludwig Wittgenstein, in the course of their impeccably naturalistic investigations,[6] raise doubts about the prospects for a physicalistic science of the mind suggests that naturalism does not require physicalism.[7]

WAYS TO REDUCE

The issue of theoretical reduction is a main topic in the philosophy of science. Although a kind of theoretical reduction will be considered in Chapter Six, the kinds of reduction most relevant to Part I are weaker forms that do not entail theoretical reduction. Nevertheless, let me pause for a word about theoretical reduction.

Theoretical reduction concerns a relation that may hold between two theories, called the reducing theory and the reduced theory. On the standard view, to put it extremely roughly, one theory reduces another if: (a) the reducing theory has predicates not contained in the reduced theory; (b) there are "bridge laws" connecting relevant terms in both theories; and (c) the reducing theory together with the bridge laws en-

[6] See, for example, Donald Davidson, "Mental Events," in *Experience and Theory*, ed. Lawrence Foster and J. W. Swanson (Amherst: University of Massachusetts Press, 1970), 79–101; "Thought and Talk," in *Mind and Language*, ed. Samuel Guttenplan (Oxford: Clarendon Press, 1975), 7–24; "Psychology as Philosophy," in Davidson, *Essays on Actions and Events* (Oxford: Clarendon Press, 1980), 229–244. And see Ludwig Wittgenstein, *Philosophical Investigations*, trans. G.E.M. Anscombe, 3rd ed. (New York: Macmillan, 1968), and *Remarks on the Philosophy of Psychology*, vols. 1 and 2, ed. G.E.M. Anscombe and G. H. von Wright (Chicago: University of Chicago Press, 1980).

[7] Some physicalistic philosophers—for example, Hartry Field and Alexander Rosenberg—are explicit in their aim to develop positions consistent with their prior metaphysical commitments. Field sees a major task of philosophy to be to construct an account of belief and desire adequate to materialism. Rosenberg takes stringent theses of physicalism and empiricism, with little argument, as assumptions in his study of sociobiology and the social sciences. See Alexander Rosenberg, *Sociobiology and the Preemption of Social Science* (Baltimore: Johns Hopkins University Press, 1980), 209–210; Hartry H. Field, "Mental Representation," in *Readings in the Philosophy of Psychology*, vol. 2, ed. Ned Block (Cambridge, Mass.: Harvard University Press, 1981), 78. Although other philosophers are less explicit, we shall see the effects of their ontological commitments on their attempts to develop a science of the mind.

tail all the consequences of the reduced theory and more. Theoretical reduction is thus a kind of explanatory reduction: every explanation in the reduced theory is in principle "translatable" into a (deeper) explanation in the reducing theory. The hypothesis of the unity of science is that all theories reduce in this sense to physics.

The ontological position most congenial to a standard theoretical reduction of psychology to a more basic science (say, neurophysiology) is "type-type" physicalism, according to which there is a type of physical state for each type of mental state. If attitudes attributed in intentional explanations of behavior matched up with, say, brain states in this systematic way, then we could formulate bridge laws: for example, x is a belief that snow is white if and only if x is a token of physical type T. Then, for any intentional explanation in terms of beliefs and desires, there would correspond a physical explanation in the vocabulary of neurophysiology, which, in principle, may replace the intentional explanation.

The physicalists considered in detail here do not envisage anything as strong as "translations" of belief/desire explanations into the vocabulary of neurophysiology or physics. (Although I shall not explicitly discuss claims of type-type physicalism, the arguments in Chapter Two apply straightforwardly to them.) For example, Fodor's representational approach is to explain behavioral phenomena by subsuming them under generalizations in the language of content, a language continuous with that of ordinary intentional explanations in terms of beliefs and desires. Fodor does not predict that intentional psychology will be replaceable by physics.[8]

Nevertheless, the positions endorsed by Fodor and others may be considered reductive in other ways. Construing token-token physicalism as "simply the claim that all the events the sciences talk about are physical events,"[9] Fodor takes the objects with which his science is concerned—that is, tokens of mental representations—to be physical tokens in the brain. Thus Fodor's intentional psychology, which quantifies only over ordinary physical objects, is designed to meet the demands of physicalism.

So, token-token physicalism is to be contrasted, on the one hand, with type-type physicalism[10] and, on the other hand, with a more ex-

---

[8] Jerry A. Fodor, "Special Sciences," in his *Representations: Philosophical Essays on the Foundations of Cognitive Science* (Cambridge, Mass.: MIT/Bradford, 1981), 127–145. Also, see Fodor's "Computation and Reduction," in ibid., 146–174.

[9] Fodor, "Special Sciences," 130.

[10] For further discussion of the distinction between type physicalism and token physicalism, see Ned Block, "What Is Functionalism?" in *Readings in the Philosophy of Psy-*

treme ontological position, a position to be considered in Part II: elimination of putative intentional phenomena altogether. The reductive and the eliminative approaches are similar in one respect: They share the view that there are no irreducibly intentional entities or properties.

A central issue for physicalists, then, concerns specifying conditions for a state's being the mental state that it is. This issue may be introduced by considering the problem of intentionality. For a long time, a main question in the philosophy of mind has been to understand how one thing (some mental item) can mean or represent or be about some other thing (for example, some state of affairs)—to understand how anything can have content. This is the question of intentionality. Eliminativists simply dissolve the difficulties by denying that there are any intentional phenomena to worry about. Reductive physicalists try to make a place for intentional phenomena in a wholly physical world by specifying nonintentional conditions for them.[11]

Reductive physicalists proceed in one of two broad ways: Either they take belief to be a relation to a mental sentence, or they do not. Although in Chapter Five I shall generalize the argument to apply to reductive physicalists who reject a linguistic picture in favor of a nonlinguistic, or pragmatic, picture (Robert Stalnaker's distinction), much of the detailed discussion here will concern physicalists who, like Fodor, subscribe to some version of the hypothesis of a language of thought.

Consider, for example, the two-step reduction of intentionality proposed by Fodor. The first step, schematically, is to hold that "for behavior to have such and such an intentional property involves its being caused by a mental state having the corresponding propositional content." The second step is to hold that "to have a mental state with the propositional content *that P* is to be related, in a certain way, to a mental representation which expresses the proposition *that P*."[12] Then, the issue is to give some substance to the claim that a mental representation expresses the proposition *that P*. As Fodor conceives the project,

What is required . . . is therefore, at a minimum, the framing of *naturalistic* conditions for representation. That is, what we want

chology, vol. 1, ed. Ned Block (Cambridge, Mass.: Harvard University Press, 1980), 171–184.

[11] I do not consider the possibility of a physicalist who holds that the intentional is fully determined by the nonintentional but who declines to give any indication of what nonintentional states are related to what intentional states, even in particular cases. Such a view, at least until developed further, seems to lack bite. Physicalism, as I am considering it, is either eliminative or (perhaps weakly) reductive.

[12] Jerry A. Fodor, "Cognitive Science and the Twin-Earth Problem," *Notre Dame Journal of Formal Logic* 23 (1982), 101.

at a minimum is something of the form '*R represents S' is true iff* C where the vocabulary in which condition C is couched contains neither intentional nor semantical expressions.[13]

A philosopher adopting such a reductive position takes the concept of mental states identified by content to be suitable, perhaps after regimentation, for incorporation into science; in consequence, he must assume the task of showing how a concept of content can be physicalistically respectable. This task is one of providing nonintentional and nonsemantic conditions for an individual to be in a given intentional state.[14] To say that the conditions C are nonintentional is to say that they are specifiable without attributions of 'that'-clauses and without semantic terms like 'denotes.' If instances of the schema

(N) *M* represents *S* if and only if *C* obtain,

(where C are conditions specified nonintentionally and nonsemantically, M is a mental item, and S is a state of affairs) supported counterfactuals, then intentionality—and with it, the common-sense conception of the mental—would pass muster and become available for physicalistic science. For purposes here, the most relevant kind of reduction concerns *specification of nonintentional and nonsemantic conditions for intentional states like belief, desire, and intention.*

Although I have made it sound as if eliminativism and reductivism exhaust the physicalistic field, there is an intermediate position, which I call 'weakly reductive.' Weakly reductive positions have been formulated, if not actually endorsed, in certain of the more optimistic writings of Stephen Stich and Paul Churchland. These positions, while denying a scientific role to content, take warranted attributions of content in some sense to correlate with statements derivable from truths of scientific psychology.

Speaking ontologically, weak reductivists are like eliminativists in holding that there are no genuine "contentful" phenomena. But I want to distinguish the weakly reductive positions from the eliminative positions, because the former, but not the latter, envisage a kind of matching up of common-sense and physicalistic psychology, which grants a measure of legitimacy to attributions of content. Such a correlation

[13] Fodor, "Semantics, Wisconsin Style," 232.

[14] Fodor is not alone in undertaking this task. See, for example, Fred I. Dretske, *Knowledge and the Flow of Information* (Cambridge, Mass.: MIT/Bradford, 1981); Dennis W. Stampe, "Toward a Causal Theory of Linguistic Representation," in *Contemporary Perspectives in the Philosophy of Language*, ed. Peter A. French, Midwest Studies in Philosophy, 2 (Morris: University of Minnesota at Morris, 1977), 81–102; Robert C. Stalnaker, *Inquiry* (Cambridge, Mass.: MIT/Bradford, 1984).

would be less threatening to our practices of attributing attitudes than would outright elimination. Stich states the position well: "If this view [that I am calling 'weakly reductive'] can be sustained, then perhaps we need not worry about our scientific psychology undermining the humanities, the social sciences, and the many social institutions which are so intimately interwoven with the conceptual framework of folk psychology."[15]

What distinguishes weak reductivism from eliminativism is that the eliminativists do not foresee a scientific psychology that even "cleaves reasonably closely to the general pattern presupposed by folk psychology."[16] Furthermore, the eliminativists divide into those (like Stich and Churchland in their more pessimistic moments) who conclude that the common-sense conception is bankrupt and therefore should be eliminated, and those (like Dennett) who conclude that the common-sense conception is practically indispensable and should not be deemed illegitimate.

Thus, the issue between reductivists and eliminativists is an ontological issue, distinct from the issue of the integrity of psychological explanations in a vocabulary irreducible to that of physics. All parties agree that physical objects exhaust reality; they disagree about the senses (if any) in which certain physical objects have content.

An Overview

Parts I and II, respectively, will attempt to answer these questions: Will physicalistic psychology save belief? Is belief obsolete? Many philosophers would say that belief is not obsolete if and only if a physicalistic psychology vindicates it. Such philosophers differ, however, about which of the questions deserves the affirmative answer and which the negative answer. Optimists about physicalistic psychology answer the first question in the affirmative and the second in the negative; pessimists give the opposite answers. Looking ahead, I should mention that, opposing both optimists and pessimists, I shall urge that neither question be answered affirmatively. In consequence, I expect the pessimists to agree with much of Part I and the optimists with some (but by no means all) of Part II.

Although the general target of the investigation here is physicalism as broadly construed above, I believe that the most useful way to proceed is to pay close attention to particular arguments advanced by

---

[15] Stich, *From Folk Psychology to Cognitive Science*, 224.
[16] Ibid., 222.

physicalists. Much of Part I is concerned with various views of Jerry A. Fodor, who is indisputably a leader in the effort to render the concept of attitudes with content usable by a psychology committed to physicalism. Nevertheless, since the ultimate concern of Part I is with all attempts to specify nonintentional and nonsemantic conditions for intentional states, I show in Chapter Five how the arguments apply to physicalism generally. Part II, which focuses on the views of Stephen Stich, Paul Churchland, and Daniel Dennett, considers whether or not the common-sense conception would be jeopardized by failure to formulate a concept of content adequate to the demands of physicalistic psychology.

I shall consider these possible outcomes of physicalistic psychology:

(i) First is the approach to physicalistic psychology most hospitable to the common-sense conception. On this approach, the common-sense concepts of belief and other attitudes are considered largely correct (by physicalistic standards) and able to be rendered suitable for the explanatory purposes of science. Since the common-sense concepts are too amorphous as they stand for the purposes of science, their vindication by science would require regimentation and perhaps paring. What is distinctive about this view is that scientific generalizations, as well as identifications of psychological states, are to be cast in the vocabulary of *content*; its chief task is to locate attitudes identified by content in the nonintentionally described world. An able exponent of this view in its several forms is Jerry A. Fodor.

(ii) An approach less hospitable to the common-sense conception, but one that still leaves room for particular attributions of attitudes— the approach I call 'weakly reductive'—holds that the common-sense concepts are incorrect but that they are extensionally equivalent to correct ones. That is, although a completed scientific psychology would be in a vocabulary that invoked no "contentful" states, there would be a correlation between (what we now describe as) believing that snow is white and being in a state recognized by the completed theory. 'S believes that p' does not attribute to S any property of believing that p; but, by virtue of its relation to some other sentence (for example, 'At t, S is in context C and state Q'), it may nonetheless express a truth. Paul M. Churchland's discussion of theoretical reduction and Stephen P. Stich's "modified Panglossian prospect" are examples of this approach.[17]

[17] Paul M. Churchland, "Reduction, Qualia, and the Direct Introspection of Brain States," *Journal of Philosophy* 82 (1985), 8–28; Stich, *From Folk Psychology to Cognitive Science*, ch. 11.

(iii) The third approach repudiates the common-sense conception altogether. According to it, common-sense concepts are incorrect and extensionally nonequivalent to the concepts in terms of which human behavior is truly explained, and the incompatibility between common-sense concepts and the correct scientific concepts renders the common-sense concepts illegitimate. On this view, no sentence of the form 'S believes that p' expresses, or has ever expressed, a truth, and no such sentences can explain anything. Paul Churchland and Stephen Stich have formulated this position, which they are prepared to endorse pending the outcome of physicalistic psychology.

(iv) The final, instrumentalistic approach deems the common-sense conception to be empirically false, yet worthy of retention. On it, common-sense concepts are incorrect and not even extensionally equivalent to the correct scientific concepts; but, because of their convenience and practical value, they retain a kind of legitimacy. The leading proponent of this instrumentalistic interpretation of the common-sense conception is Daniel C. Dennett, who emphasizes the moral dimension of the common-sense conception. A central issue, as he sees it, is whether or not intentional explanations, which invoke beliefs, desires, and other attitudes, can co-exist with scientific explanations, which do not invoke beliefs:

> [T]he validity of our conceptual scheme of moral agents having dignity, freedom, responsibility stands or falls on the question: can men ever be *truly* said to have beliefs, desires, intentions? If they can, there is at least some hope of retaining a notion of the dignity of man; if they cannot, if men never can be said truly to want or believe, then surely, they never can be said truly to act responsibly, or to have a conception of justice, or know the difference between right and wrong. . . . [C]an intentional explanations (citing beliefs, desires, etc.) on the one hand, and proper, ultimate, scientific explanations on the other hand, co-exist? Can they ever both be true, or would the truth of a scientific explanation always exclude the other?[18]

Dennett's position is a novel attempt to combine eliminative materialism with a verdict of innocent on common-sense intentional explanations.

Chapters Two and Three will consider individualistic construals of the moderately reductive view described in (i); Chapters Four and Five

---

[18] Daniel C. Dennett, "Skinner Skinned," in his *Brainstorms: Philosophical Essays on Mind and Psychology* (Montgomery, Vt.: Bradford, 1978), 63–64 (emphasis his).

will broaden the scope to nonindividualistic construals of the view described in (i). Chapter Six will consider the weakly reductive view described in (ii), Chapter Seven the eliminative view described in (iii), and Chapter Eight the instrumentalistic view described in (iv). Chapter Nine will draw together some of the lessons of the preceding chapters.

Part I shows that content—by which one belief is distinguished from another, one desire from another, and so on—is too elusive for physicalistic psychology. Part II shows that states identified by content are not dispensable for either everyday or scientific purposes, and it gives a preliminary assessment that, I hope, begins to make sense of the situation in which we find ourselves. The assessment is based on the observation that psychology as practiced is varied in its methods and its explanatory aims. Psychological explanation is a highly pragmatic and flexible notion; to harden it into a single model wedded to a particular theoretical outlook serves no good purpose, certainly not that of truth—or so I shall urge. What will remain is a kind of belief/desire psychology, but not one that conforms to the strictures laid down by those now proposing a science of the mind.

Philosophers are understandably wary of any discussion that suggests that something cannot happen or that makes bold to predict the future course of science. Since this book may be read in such a vein, let me say how I regard it. My primary interest is explicitly conceptual: I aim to investigate the relations between common-sense and physicalistic conceptions of the mind and of explanations of behavior. John Searle has warned against the prejudice of defining science in terms of features of existing scientific theories. He seems to prefer to take 'science' to be "the name of the collection of objective and systematic truths we can state about the world," or perhaps merely as "systematic investigation."[19] I am quite sanguine about the prospects for systematically investigating mental phenomena—intentionality, subjectivity, and the rest—regardless of the prospects for a scientific theory with standard physicalistic credentials. But since the broad philosophical consensus is that scientific psychology is physicalistic, I shall for now put aside the question of whether an investigation that violates the physicalistic requirement that molecular duplicates share psychological states is properly called "science."

Cognitive science, the locus of scientific concern for intentional explanations, is developing so fast that it is impossible always to be up to the moment. However, my argument is not just an argument "in prin-

[19] John Searle, *Minds, Brains and Science* (Cambridge, Mass.: Harvard University Press, 1984), 25.

ciple": I look in detail at various physicalistic approaches to belief that have been offered, and I try to identify the underlying reason for their failure. It turns out that the requisite concept of content is implicitly constrained by conditions of adequacy that cannot be jointly satisfied. And this, in turn, is traceable to the differences in identity conditions for items that are deemed theoretically acceptable and items that are attributable by 'that'-clauses. If I am right and the difficulty lies in differences of individuation, then the prospects for any concept of the content of attitudes to live up to the physicalistic demands on scientific theory are, in principle, dim.

Before turning to attempts to formulate a physicalistically adequate concept of content, it is worth trying to sharpen the common-sense side of the contrast between common-sense concepts and physicalistic ones. Just what is the common-sense conception of the mental, and how does content figure into it?

COMMON SENSE AND CONTENT

The common-sense conception of the mental comprises those complex patterns of beliefs, desires, intentions, and so on that are the basis of our everyday understanding of human behavior and experience. There are two points to emphasize at the outset. First, the issues concern the common-sense conception in a wholesale way. Called into question by physicalistic psychology are not the details of the common-sense conception, which, in any case, may be difficult to discern, but the entire framework in terms of which we describe ourselves and others as desiring, hoping, fearing, intending, supposing, speculating, imagining, hypothesizing, inferring, and so on. Since common-sense concepts are interrelated, what is at stake is the fate of the framework as a whole.

Second, I want to emphasize what propositional attitudes have in common. The key feature of the common-sense conception is that such attitudes have *content*; one believes that such-and-such is the case, intends to do one thing rather than another, fears that a particular state of affairs will come about, and so on. Propositional attitudes are sometimes said to be about or directed upon states of affairs; this feature, their intentionality, sets attitudes apart from other attributes that a person may have. Whether or not intentionality is a general criterion for demarcating the mental, we shall see that it generates interesting philosophical questions concerning the amenability of attitudes to physicalistic treatment.

The common-sense conception of the mental has come to be thought of as a kind of folk theory, dubbed 'folk psychology.' Since I shall question the construal of the common-sense conception as a would-be scientific, or protoscientific, theory, I shall avoid use of that term. Nevertheless, the core of what I am calling the common-sense conception coincides with the core of what others call 'folk psychology': definitive of each is the *network of attitudes identified by content.*

Content is typically attributed in English by 'that'-clauses, and this feature permits an ontologically and theoretically neutral way to distinguish one belief from another (or one desire from another, and so on). On the common-sense conception, one belief differs from another as the meanings of the 'that'-clauses of their attributions differ. The belief that snow is white differs from the belief that grass is green by virtue of the fact that what is expressed by the 'that'-clause of the former (that snow is white) is distinct from what is expressed by the 'that'-clause of the latter (that grass is green).[20]

Nevertheless, not every feature of the 'that'-clauses is relevant to intentional explanation or to practical reasoning. For example, that snow is white is true is irrelevant to whether or not a belief that snow is white plays a role in someone's practical reasoning. Of course, any belief that plays a role in practical reasoning is thought to be true by the reasoner. But no one is omniscient: A belief that Fleet O'Foot is sure to win the race may motivate someone to bet a lot of money, only to have the belief turn out to be false. Similarly, a child's desire to please Santa Claus may lead her to leave out cookies even though Santa Claus does not exist. Thus, for purposes of inquiring into practical reasoning, we may disregard the truth and reference to individuals of beliefs and other attitudes.

Moreover, we want to regard the hope that the most competent candidate win to be distinct from the hope that the shortest candidate win—even if the most competent candidate happens to be the shortest. Substitution of one expression for another in 'that'-clauses does not preserve the truth value of the attribution: One may believe (or hope, or whatever) that the most competent candidate will win without believing (or hoping) that the shortest candidate will win. In this case, the expressions 'the most competent candidate' and 'the shortest candidate' are said to occur obliquely. Obliquely occurring expressions are those for which co-extensive terms—such as 'the shortest candidate' and 'the most competent candidate' in the content clauses of the attributions above—may not be freely interchanged.

---

[20] From the fact that attitudes identified in English by 'that'-clauses are constitutive of the common-sense conception, it does not follow that the *objects* of those attitudes are sentences or other linguistic entities. Robert Stalnaker and David Lewis have emphasized this distinction.

Let me illustrate the matter of identifying, or individuating, beliefs. Suppose that there is someone who does not know that 'the largest U.S. state' and 'the northernmost U.S. state' designate the same state (Alaska). Such a person may assent to 'The northernmost U.S. state is sparsely populated' but not assent to 'The largest U.S. state is sparsely populated.' (Perhaps she thinks that Maine is the northernmost state and Texas the largest.) It would be natural, then, to attribute to the person a belief that the northernmost state is sparsely populated, but not a belief that the largest state is sparsely populated. In that case, we would be individuating beliefs in such a way that the belief that the northernmost state is sparsely populated and the belief that the largest state is sparsely populated count as different beliefs. (If we took them to be the same belief, we could not consistently say that someone believes the one but fails to believe the "other.") And we may further describe the difference in belief as a difference in representation: 'The largest state' and 'the northernmost state' are different representations of the same state.

To count beliefs this way is to take attributions of attitudes to be "opaque" or nontransparent. Nontransparent attributions are those in which singular terms, such as 'the northernmost state' and 'the largest state,' occur obliquely. For example, on a nontransparent interpretation, 'Sally believes that the northernmost state is sparsely populated' attributes to Sally a belief different from 'Sally believes that the largest state is sparsely populated,' even if Sally is an expert on geography. By contrast, on a transparent interpretation, the two ascriptions attribute to Sally a single belief—of a certain state that it is sparsely populated.[21]

Since beliefs and other attitudes are identified by the obliquely occurring expressions in the 'that'-clauses of their attribution, it will be useful to introduce a new term to refer to the content of the 'that'-clauses of attributions in a particular restricted sense: Let us say that two mental tokens (that is, occurrences or instances) are of different *restricted semantic types* if there are semantic differences (other than truth value or reference to individuals) in what is expressed by the obliquely occurring expressions in the 'that'-clauses attributing them.

The term 'restricted' in this context indicates that beliefs (and other attitudes) identified by restricted semantic type are characterized without regard to reference to any particular individuals and without regard to their truth or falsity. By contrast, a belief identified partly by

---

[21] Although I think that attributions in common-sense explanations of behavior are typically nontransparent (see my "*De Re* Belief in Action," *Philosophical Review* 91 [1982], 364–387), I do not believe that this view jeopardizes the ensuing arguments.

reference to a particular object other than oneself—such as my belief of my sister (of that particular person) that she is happy—is not identified by restricted semantic type.

The term 'semantic' in 'restricted semantic type' simply indicates that the belief is identified by a 'that'-clause. For example, a belief identified as 'the belief most frequently cited in philosophy' is not identified by semantic type; the same belief identified as 'the belief that snow is white' is identified by restricted semantic type. 'Semantic' is often contrasted with 'syntactic,' which refers to grammatical properties; more broadly, the term 'formal,' which encompasses not only syntactic but also functional and physical features, is opposed to the term 'semantic.' Although beliefs have syntactic and other formal properties, they are all semantic in the following sense: Anything that is a belief is coherently identifiable by a 'that'-clause.

The term 'type' indicates that what is at issue is classification (or identification or individuation) of particular items. By contrast, the term 'token' refers to the particular items or instances that are subject to classification according to various types.

More precisely, if 'A believes that p' is true and 'A believes that q' is false, and all the expressions in the 'that'-clauses occur obliquely, then tokens of the belief that p and of the belief that q are of different restricted semantic types. Although here 'p' abbreviates an English sentence S, to say that A believes that p is not to say that A would assent to the sentence S; A may not know English. Rather, for current purposes, a sufficient condition for A's believing that p is that there be some sentence S' in some language such that A would sincerely and comprehendingly assent to S', and S' has S as an adequate English translation. No ontological or theoretical commitment is intended. The notion of a restricted semantic type is meant to provide an intuitive and pretheoretical means of referring to attitudes identified by obliquely occurring expressions in 'that'-clauses of ascriptions of those attitudes.[22]

So, belief tokens that differ only in truth value (for example, two tokens of the belief that women in the United States have the franchise, one in 1900 and the other in 1940) or in objects denoted (for example, two tokens of the belief that the U.S. president is a Democrat, one in 1942 and the other in 1946) may be of the same restricted semantic

[22] The idea of restricted semantic type used here can tolerate varying intuitions about and theoretical positions on Kripke's puzzle about belief and Putnam's example of H_2O on Earth and XYZ on Twin Earth. See Saul Kripke, "A Puzzle About Belief," in *Meaning and Use*, ed. Avishai Margalit (Dordrecht: D. Reidel, 1979), 239–283; and Hilary Putnam, "The Meaning of 'Meaning,'" in his *Mind, Language and Reality: Philosophical Papers*, vol. 2 (Cambridge: Cambridge University Press, 1975), 215–271.

types. Beliefs not typically identified by restricted semantic type include *de re* beliefs, indexical beliefs, beliefs in singular propositions, and perhaps beliefs expressed by proper names. Examples of beliefs that differ in restricted semantic type are the general beliefs that snow is white and that grass is green.

The notion of restricted semantic type is intended only to capture a certain aspect of the intuitive identification of belief and other attitudes in terms of content. Since I make no theoretical use of the notion, it can be adjusted for various semantical views. In particular, my use of 're-stricted semantic type' leaves open whether or not differences in restricted semantic type amount to any more than differences in truth condition (as opposed to truth value), as we shall see in Chapter Three.

A theory that appeals to belief to explain behavior must be able to distinguish, for p and q that are obviously nonequivalent, tokens of a belief that p from tokens of a belief that q, where all the terms in the 'that'-clauses occur obliquely. To put the point in terms of the notion of restricted semantic type: A psychological theory that appeals to beliefs to explain behavior must have the resources to distinguish beliefs of different restricted semantic types. Such a theory must be able to distinguish, for example, tokens of a belief that snow is white from tokens of a belief that grass is green. If the condition is not met, as we shall see, putative explanations in terms of beliefs are incoherent.

Beliefs, hopes, intentions, suspicions, fears, inferences, preferences, and so on are characterized by semantic or conceptual content, which I have tried to clarify in terms of restricted semantic type. The importance of content is now apparent: Mental items that cannot be identified by 'that'-clauses at all have no claim to being beliefs or other propositional attitudes. One way, then, to put a central issue is this: To what extent can the pretheoretical notion of content be cast in physicalistically acceptable terms? How are attributions of intentional, semantic states (such as believing that p) related to attributions of nonintentional, nonsemantic states (such as being in brain state b or being caused by D) that may be postulated by physicalistic psychology?[23]

I said earlier that there are two important points to emphasize about the common-sense conception: (1) that what is at issue is the framework as a whole, not whether there is some discrepancy between uses of, say, 'desire' in ordinary language and in physicalistic psychology;

[23] Paul M. Churchland has argued that predicates like 'believes that p' are comparable to predicates like 'weighs n kilograms.' See his *Scientific Realism and the Plasticity of Mind* (Cambridge: Cambridge University Press, 1979), 105–106, and *Matter and Consciousness* (Cambridge, Mass.: MIT/Bradford, 1984), 63–66. Cf. his "Eliminative Materialism and Propositional Attitudes," *Journal of Philosophy* 78 (1981), 82–83.

and (2) that the mark of an element of the common-sense conception is content, understood as restricted semantic type. Since the common-sense conception is characterized by attributions of attitudes identified by content and by the intentional explanations in which they figure, the framework would be left more or less intact by physicalistic psychology if the ordinary concept of, say, belief were replaced by a concept of a state that was also identified by 'that'-clauses. Local defects pose no threat to the common-sense conception in the sense that interests us here.

Although I shall follow recent tradition by taking belief as the paradigmatic propositional attitude, let me emphasize that the points about belief apply to other attitudes (such as hopes, intentions, suspicions, fears, desires, wishes, conjectures, and so on) identified by restricted semantic type as well. It is not just arbitrary to take belief as the basic attitude. Belief, Donald Davidson has observed, "is central to all kinds of thought. If someone is glad that, or notices that, or remembers that, or knows that, the gun is loaded, then he must believe that the gun is loaded. Even to wonder whether the gun is loaded requires the belief, for example, that a gun is a weapon, that it is a more or less enduring object and so on."[24]

Since all propositional attitudes are identified by content, and since, as we shall see, the difficulty is with a physicalistically adequate construal of content, the same problems that arise with belief arise with all the propositional attitudes. So, I shall treat the concept of belief primarily as the test case: If, from the point of view of physicalistic theory, there is no difference between believing that p and believing that q, where 'p' and 'q' are obviously distinct, then, from the point of view of that theory, neither belief is available for explaining what the person does.

Let us turn to the first of the two central questions: Will physicalistic theory save belief? This question comes down to the issue of whether or not physicalistic psychology can accommodate a concept of content of attitudes that can play the appropriate role in the explanation of behavior.

[24] Donald Davidson, "Thought and Talk," in his *Inquiries into Truth and Interpretation* (Oxford: Clarendon Press, 1984), 156–157.

WILL COGNITIVE SCIENCE
SAVE BELIEF?

· 2 ·

BELIEF IN
COGNITIVE SCIENCE

Any scientific view of the mind must confront ordinary ascriptions of attitudes, such as believing, desiring, and intending, identified by content or meaning. Two obvious physicalistic approaches to the issue suggest themselves: either to press concepts like *belief* into the service of science by trying to line up beliefs with nonintentionally described states, or to deny that believing is a genuine phenomenon by relegating the concept of belief to the company of such conceptual castoffs as humors and phlogiston. We shall look at versions of each approach. Part I will focus on belief/desire psychology, which attempts to formulate scientific generalizations in the vocabulary of content. On this approach, scientific psychology not only tolerates attributions of propositional attitudes but fairly requires them.

Cognitive science stands out for the seriousness with which it regards traditional philosophical concerns. Fodor, for example, sees himself as heir to seventeenth- and eighteenth-century representational conceptions of the mind, embraced both by rationalists like Descartes and Leibniz and by empiricists like Locke and Hume. The task of cognitive science, on such a view, is to bring a version of that conception up to date by showing how attitudes identified by content may be scientifically respectable. The task, as we shall see, is by no means a simple one.

In this chapter, we shall explore the concept of content as constrained by 'methodological solipsism' (Fodor's term), a paradigmatically individualistic approach. In Chapter Three, we shall look in some detail at the use of the computer metaphor in physicalistic psychology; and then in Chapters Four and Five, we shall turn to nonindividualistic approaches. Each of these approaches to content will be found wanting. The reason for content's failure to be susceptible to incorporation into physicalistic psychology will be diagnosed in Chapter Five.

FORM AND CONTENT

Jerry Fodor has long been a champion of belief and other propositional attitudes.[1] As a leading advocate of intentional psychology, which ex-

[1] See, for example, Jerry A. Fodor, "Three Cheers for Propositional Attitudes," in his

plains behavior in terms of beliefs and other propositional attitudes attributed by 'that'-clauses or content clauses, Fodor has taken beliefs to be real states that causally interact with other states and with sensory input and behavioral output: "Mental states (including, especially, token havings of propositional attitudes) interact causally. Such interactions constitute the mental processes that eventuate (inter alia) in the behaviors of organisms."[2]

In support of an explanatory psychology that will allow beliefs and other propositional attitudes to play this role, Fodor takes psychological states to be relations to internal representations. The belief that Marvin is melancholy differs from the belief that Albert is fat (Fodor's examples) by virtue of being related to a different internal representation: *that* Marvin is melancholy, as opposed to *that* Albert is fat.

On Fodor's view, mental states that explain behavior include beliefs and other attitudes identified by content, or, as I shall say, by restricted semantic type.[3] Moreover, mental processes that explain behavior are "computational," where

> computational processes are both *symbolic* and *formal*. They are symbolic because they are defined over representations, and they are formal because they apply to representations, in virtue of (roughly) the *syntax* of the representations. It's the second of these conditions that makes the claim that mental processes are computational stronger than the representational theory of the mind.[4]

Fodor has taken cognitive science to be defined by two theses:

(1) *The content condition.* Mental states are relations to representations, and mental processes are operations on representations, which are identified "opaquely" by 'that'-clauses.

(2) *The formality condition.* Mental processes are "formal," in that

---

Representations: Philosophical Essays on the Foundations of Cognitive Science (Cambridge, Mass.: Bradford/MIT, 1981), 100–126. Also, see his "Propositional Attitudes," in ibid., 177–203; *The Language of Thought* (Cambridge, Mass.: Harvard University Press, 1979); and "Banish DisContent" (typescript, 1984).

[2] Fodor, "Propositional Attitudes," 182.

[3] Fodor calls such attitudes "opaque" or, sometimes, "*de dicto*." What I am calling 'restricted semantic type' is in line with at least some of Fodor's uses of 'content.' In "Propositional Attitudes," 183, Fodor takes the " 'content' of a propositional attitude, informally, to be whatever it is that the complement of the corresponding [propositional attitude]-ascribing sentence expresses." Fodor's "opaque" taxonomy of attributions of attitudes yields attitudes identified by restricted semantic type.

[4] Fodor, "Methodological Solipsism Considered as a Research Strategy in Cognitive Pychology," *Behavioral and Brain Sciences* 3 (1980), 64 (emphasis his). Hereafter the title of this article will be abbreviated by MS and page references will be given in the text.

they apply to representations by virtue of their nonsemantic (e.g., syntactic, computational, functional, physical) properties.

Although 'content condition' is my term, it is clear that the significance of the representational theory of the mind lies in its recourse to content. "[M]ental states are distinguished by the *content* of the associated representations, so we can allow for the difference between thinking that Marvin is melancholy and thinking that Sam is . . ." (MS, 63; emphases his).

Fodor's argument for the content condition is that attributions of beliefs and the like, via 'that'-clauses, are required for explaining action. He argues plausibly that nontransparent attributions explain behavior: "[I]n doing our psychology, we want to attribute mental states fully opaquely because it's the fully opaque reading which tells us what the agent has in mind, and it's what the agent has in mind that causes his behavior" (MS, 67). Or again, Fodor proposes the thesis that "when we articulate the generalizations in virtue of which behavior is contingent upon mental states, it is typically an opaque construal of the mental state attributions that does the work" (MS, 66). Finally: "[N]ontransparent taxonomies respect the way that the organism represents the object of its propositional attitudes *to itself*, and it is this representation which functions in the causation of behavior" (MS, 63).

In contrast to content, formal operations "are the ones that are specified without reference to such semantic properties of representations as, for example, truth, reference and meaning" (MS, 64). Although representations are said to have semantic properties, only the formal properties of representations—wholly dependent upon the "shapes" of the representations and independent of anything outside the subject—are relevant to mental operations. So mental operations "cannot apply in different ways to a pair of representations which differ only in their semantic properties" (MS, 104). Or again: Computational principles, which "apply in virtue of the form of entites in their domain,"[5] involve only formal properties. On the other hand, any (contingent) properties of representations that entail anything about the external environment in which the subject is situated or (contingent) properties that presuppose any actual relations between the subject and the environment are excluded by the formality condition as irrelevant to a scientific psychology.

Fodor's main argument for the formality condition is that it is "implicit in the computational model" of the mind (MS, 107), which he clearly regards as the only promising approach. The formality condi-

[5] Fodor, "Propositional Attitudes," 201.

tion, with its physicalistic import, is Fodor's vehicle for applying the computer metaphor to psychology (MS, 104). He takes the formality condition to be tantamount to *methodological solipsism*, which he advocates as a research strategy for cognitive psychology (MS, 65).

Methodological solipsism is the assumption that mental processes, or at least those that explain behavior, are wholly determined by properties of the individual whose processes they are. Developed from the plausible thought that whatever explains an individual's behavior must be "in the head" of the individual, methodological solipsism requires that mental processes that explain behavior must be considered in abstraction from the environment of the individual whose behavior is to be explained.[6]

Although the effect of the content condition is to allow beliefs with content to be explanatory, the effect of the formality condition is to bar certain properties of beliefs and other propositional attitudes—for example, semantic properties such as truth or reference to individuals, properties that specify relations between the subject and anything "outside the head"—from any explanatory role. This much accords with pretheoretical intuitions: A person may be motivated by beliefs that are not true and that are correctly ascribed by terms that fail to denote (recall Santa Claus).[7] But, as I shall try to show, the formality

[6] Putnam's Twin Earth case (Hilary Putnam, "The Meaning of 'Meaning,' " in his *Mind, Language and Reality: Philosophical Papers*, vol. 2 [Cambridge: Cambridge University Press, 1975], 215–271) may be pressed as an immediate counterexample to methodological solipsism. Since Fodor seeks to rebut such a use ("Cognitive Science and the Twin-Earth Problem," *Notre Dame Journal of Formal Logic* 23 [1982], 98–118), I shall give Fodor the benefit of the doubt here; successful defense against Putnam is irrelevant to my arguments, which raise different issues.

Fodor has another argument for methodological solipsism. He takes transparent and opaque taxonomies of attributions of attitudes to be associated with "naturalistic" and solipsistic psychologies, respectively. The only alternative that Fodor sees to solipsistic psychology is a naturalistic psychology that considers subjects as embedded in their environments. Fodor regards naturalistic psychology as unfeasible, since, he claims, it would have to wait upon the completion of all the other sciences to get canonical descriptions of environments, in the absence of which the project of explaining organism/environment relations is hopeless. Critics of this position include Gilbert Harman, "What Is Methodological Solipsism?" *Behavioral and Brain Sciences* 3 (1980), 81, and Stephen P. Stich, *From Folk Psychology to Cognitive Science: The Case Against Belief* (Cambridge, Mass.: Bradford/MIT, 1983), 162–63.

[7] There are other grounds, independent of the formality condition, for supposing that the truth and reference of an agent's beliefs are irrelevant to explaining behavior. See, for example, John Perry, "The Problem of the Essential Indexical," *Noûs* 13 (1979), 3–22; and William G. Lycan, "Toward a Homuncular Theory of Believing," *Cognition and Brain Theory* 4 (1981), 139–159.

condition has much stronger consequences than may be apparent initially. Indeed, it precludes belief/desire explanations altogether.

Unfortunately, the requirement of methodological solipsism has been formulated in several nonequivalent ways. In Hilary Putnam's original formulation, methodological solipsism is the assumption that "no psychological state, properly so called, presupposes the existence of any individual other than the subject to whom that state is ascribed."[8] Subsequent formulations—according to which, for example, narrow states are what molecular duplicates share—require that narrow states must be specifiable independently of any facts about the world outside the head. The subsequent formulation of methodological solipsism would be violated by presupposing that there exists anything other than the individual whose mental processes are being explained. Putnam's original formulation (read one way) would be violated only by presupposing the existence of a particular entity outside the head.

Formulating methodological solipsism as the requirement that mental states must be explained without presupposing the existence of anything outside the head is therefore ambiguous between the two readings. Although there may be states describable in terms of content without presupposing the existence of any particular entity other than the subject, my arguments will suggest that description of states in terms of content at all is incompatible with the presupposition that nothing exists other than the subject.[9]

Under the constraint of methodological solipsism, there are no psychological differences among molecularly identical individuals; relations between an organism and its environment can play no role in an explanatory psychology.[10] The basic difficulty is that classification of mental state tokens by individualistic computational features is incompatible with classification of mental state tokens by "content" or restricted semantic type. To put it another way, how an individual rep-

[8] Putnam, "The Meaning of 'Meaning,' " 220.

[9] For a discussion of difficulties and ambiguities regarding methodological solipsism from other angles, see John Heil, *Perception and Cognition* (Berkeley and Los Angeles: University of California Press, 1983), and Kent Bach, "*De Re* Belief and Methodological Solipsism," in *Thought and Object: Essays on Intentionality*, ed. Andrew Woodfield (Oxford: Clarendon Press, 1982), 121–152, esp. 123–129. Also, see H. W. Noonan, "Methodological Solipsism," *Philosophical Studies* 40 (1981), 269–274, and Katherine J. Morris, "In Defense of Methodological Solipsism: A Reply to Noonan," *Philosophical Studies* 45 (1984), 399–411.

[10] Stich's principle of autonomy is another, more precise formulation of a solipsistic restriction, according to which "any differences between organisms which do not manifest themselves as differences in their current, internal, physical states ought to be ignored by a psychological theory." *From Folk Psychology to Cognitive Science*, 164.

resents the environment cannot be understood in terms conforming to the formality condition.[11]

With the aid of a thought experiment, I shall try to exhibit the inability of any computational psychology that conforms to the formality condition to accommodate belief—even nonsingular, nonindexical, non–*de re* belief.[12] Although I shall discuss the thought experiment explicitly with regard to interpretations of Fodor's views, I believe that it has broad application. I shall begin with an interpretation of Fodor's view that is probably too weak to be plausible, but it is suggested by his own formulation at the beginning of his paper on methodological solipsism.[13] In any case, it will set the stage for a more enriched interpretation. Moreover, the counterexample to this interpretation shows that many varieties of type-type physicalism are false.

AN ANTI-CARTESIAN MEDITATION

The first thought experiment is aimed at refuting the view that classification of mental state tokens by their actual causal relations coincides with classification of mental state tokens by restricted semantic type. Invoking nonsingular, non–*de re*, nonindexical attitudes, considered apart from truth, the first thought experiment will tell against the following thesis:

[11] The consequence is that Fodor's program, in effect, collapses into Stich's. Stich adopts a "syntactic" view of the mind, according to which putative states—individuated by "content," such as believing that *p*—are not genuine psychological states. That is, they do not figure in explanations of behavior described "autonomously," where an autonomous behavioral description is one such that "if it applies to an organism in a given setting, then it would also apply to any replica of the organism in that setting." *From Folk Psychology to Cognitive Science*, 167.

[12] Attention will be exclusively on the opaque or nontransparent attributions that Fodor favors. Since arguments that behavior is not explained by indexical or *de re* beliefs are familiar, I shall not rehearse them here. See the Perry and Lycan articles cited in note 7. Also see Lynne Rudder Baker, "*De Re* Belief in Action," *Philosophical Review* 91 (1982), 363–387.

[13] MS, 64. There is no suggestion that dispositions are required to identify a token as being of a particular semantic type. Also see Daniel C. Dennett, "A Cure for the Common Code?" in his *Brainstorms: Philosophical Essays on Mind and Psychology* (Cambridge, Mass.: MIT/Bradford, 1978), 104, who raises questions about Fodor's apparent commitment to "the impossible view that . . . nothing can be believed, thought about or learned without being explicitly represented." Note, however, that my arguments strike at a different point: in the case envisaged, all the beliefs are explicitly represented. Also, I have no quarrel (unlike the Churchlands, for example) with the functionalists' contention that the objects of belief are (in some sense) linguistic entities. Rather, when assuming that beliefs are explicitly represented and dependent upon language, the difficulty lies in the solipsistic presuppositions about language.

(A) If two sequences of tokens cause two tokens of a single type of bodily movement, and if the tokens in the causal sequences are, pairwise, of the same physical types, then they are, pairwise, of the same restricted semantic types.

The thought experiments draw on several plausible assumptions. First, what a sentence says depends upon what language it is in. Second, people sometimes think in words. Third, which general belief a person expresses when sincerely and comprehendingly uttering a given sentence depends upon what language the person is speaking. Fourth, just as a single physical type of ink mark may have as tokens ink marks that have different meanings in different languages, so a single physical type of audible emission may have as tokens audible emissions that have different meanings in different languages. (If we were to add to the four assumptions a fifth—that what language one speaks is not determined solely by what is in one's head—we would be close to a valid argument for the conclusion that general beliefs, such as that life is too short, are not in the head. But rather than focus on such an abstract argument, it seems more illuminating to approach the issues more concretely through an example.)

Let me illustrate the fourth assumption. As Arthur Danto has pointed out, there could be two languages that are phonologically similar in this way: A token of one of the languages could be acoustically indistinguishable from a token of the second, yet the best translation of the first into English is "Motherhood is sacred," and the best translation of the second is "Beans are high in protein."[14] In each of two languages, then, there may be meaningful expressions that are phonologically, inscriptionally, and even syntactically identical (insofar as syntax is independent of semantics), but whose correct English translations differ. In such cases, native speakers of the first language and native speakers of the second language would typically express different beliefs when using the phonologically and syntactically identical sentences.

In the current context, questions of indeterminacy of translation do not arise; for it does not matter whether there is a unique correct translation, just that some translations would be clearly incorrect. We need

[14] Arthur Danto, "The Last Work of Art: Artworks and Real Things," in *Aesthetics: A Critical Anthology*, ed. George Dickie and R. J. Sclafani (New York: St. Martin's, 1977), 551–562. Umberto Eco has made a similar point: "Such is the magic of human languages, that by human accord often the same sounds mean different things." *The Name of the Rose* (New York: Harcourt Brace Jovanovich, 1983), 288. The story here extends this insight into the context of practical reasoning.

only imagine a case in which there are no plausible sets of analytical hypotheses relative to which the hypothetical sentence translated into English as "Motherhood is sacred," for example, could be translated into English as "Beans are high in protein." Nor do questions about the nontransitivity of translation bear upon anything I have to say.

Imagine a documentary movie that compares subjects in psychology experiments. Each subject is shown videotapes of violent episodes and is asked to classify the incidents. The subjects are encouraged to reason aloud. In the case of non–English-speaking subjects, what we hear is the narrator's translation of the subject's utterances.

In the first scene, a non–English-speaking subject, identified as Subject N, is speaking. We hear the voice-over: "Was the incident one of simple assault or of provoked assault? Provoked assault is serious, more serious than simple assault. Since a two-hundred-pound man is not endangered by a child's insults and the assault was particularly fierce, it was serious enough to be provoked assault. So, I'll check the box for provoked assault."

Later in the film, an English-speaking subject, identified as Subject E, has seen the same incident. We hear: "Was the incident one of simple assault or of aggravated assault? Aggravated assault is serious, more serious than simple assault. Since a two-hundred-pound man is not endangered by a child's insults and the assault was particularly fierce, it was serious enough to be aggravated assault. So, I'll check the box for aggravated assault."

We leave the film as the narrator explains that Subject N's society has no category of (mis)behavior corresponding to aggravated assault. In that society, where discipline and self-control are highly prized, what gets translated into English as 'provoked assault'—assault in response to being baited or goaded—is a more serious matter than simple assault. In the United States, aggravated assault is also a more serious matter than simple assault. But the English term 'aggravated assault' does not have the same extension as 'provoked assault.' For 'aggravated assault' applies to assaults that are particularly fierce or that result in serious bodily injury to the person assaulted;[15] it has nothing to do with provocation.

The beliefs that provide the materials for the experimental subjects' episodes of practical reasoning—that provoked assault is serious and that aggravated assault is serious—are clearly of distinct restricted semantic types. (As just noted, 'aggravated assault' and 'provoked as-

---

[15] *Webster's Ninth New Collegiate Dictionary* and Steven H. Gifis, *Law Dictionary* (Woodbury, N.Y.: Barron's, 1984), 30.

sault' apply to different kinds of behavior.) So, if their psychological states are determined by the restricted semantic types of their beliefs, then they are in different psychological states. Moreover, Subject E's deliberation concludes with checking the box for aggravated assault; Subject N's deliberation concludes with checking the box for provoked assault. Therefore, construed in terms of their opaque mental states, in terms of the content-clauses of ascriptions of attitudes, or in terms of attitudes identified by restricted semantic type, the intuitive psychological states of the two experimental subjects are dissimilar.

Suppose, however, that Subject N checks the box for provoked assault with a particular motion of her left hand and that Subject E labels the incident as aggravated assault with a particular motion of her left hand. In fact, suppose that Subject N and Subject E each flex the same muscles in the same way to the same degree. Considered as bodily movements, what each does is a token of the same physical type. And, considered physically, the proximate causes of their muscle-flexings may be supposed to be tokens of the same physical type.

Suppose further that the portion of Subject N's dialect relevant to the story is phonologically indistinguishable from English. In fact, certain well-formed expressions in her dialect are acoustically and syntactically similar to well-formed expressions in English (though, of course, some of them differ semantically). Considered nonsemantically, nothing about these expressions distinguishes them from English expressions. When Subject N utters aloud the sentence that is correctly translated into English as "Provoked assault is serious," her utterance sounds just like an utterance of the English sentence "Aggravated assault is serious."[16] There may be some play in what can be a correct translation from the non-English dialect to English, but one thing is certain: None of Subject N's current thoughts can correctly be translated into English as thoughts concerning aggravated assault.

Matters involving translation from one spoken language to another are notoriously tricky, so let me say a word more in defense of my description of the story. The key is that Subject N expresses her belief about provoked assault by uttering a sentence in her language that is syntactically and phonologically identical to the English sentence "Aggravated assault is serious." We may assume that books from Subject N's dialect have been translated into English and have met all the standards of adequacy met by translations from, say, Swahili into Eng-

[16] Indeed, a more contrived example would have the experimental subjects physically overlap in such a way that a single token expresses the two beliefs. This possibility indicates that the issue is how to characterize differences between the uses of a token. David F. Austin made this point to me, and I shall exploit it further in Chapter Six.

lish. In all these translations, every occurrence of what in English sounds like 'aggravated assault' gets translated as 'provoked assault.'

Since the bodily movements of the experimental subjects are of the same physical type, and the proximate causes of the movements are of the same type, and their languages have the odd relation just described, it is possible that, considered physically, the mental state tokens that constituted their episodes of practical reasoning are tokens of the same physical type.[17] For example, the physical operation that is Subject E's tokening of "Aggravated assault is serious" is of the same physical type as the operation that is Subject N's tokening that gets translated into English as "Provoked assault is serious." Of course, when Subject N uses her own dialect to express her belief, it *sounds* like Subject E's token of "Aggravated assault is serious." The vibrations of the air waves are of the same type.

Considered separately, there is nothing remarkable about either subject or her situation. Each is a competent speaker of her language who accepts responsibility to conform to the linguistic conventions of her community; neither makes any kind of mistake in reasoning. There are no complications concerning tacit beliefs. There is no appeal to any intuitions about translation, other than that it is possible. There is nothing extraordinary or untoward about the situation of either party. It is only comparison of their situations in light of a certain theoretical standpoint that suggests a peculiarity.

The story of the two subjects shows not only that two mental state tokens of the same kind (for example, belief, desire, or intention) may be of distinct restricted semantic types without differing physically, but also that two *sequences* of mental state tokens, pairwise of the same kind, may be pairwise of distinct restricted semantic types without differing physically. We can represent the practical reasoning of each sub-

---

[17] Tyler Burge's important articles make my description of the story all the more plausible. See Tyler Burge, "Individualism and the Mental," in *Studies in Metaphysics*, ed. P. A. French, T. E. Uehling, and H. K. Wettstein, Midwest Studies in Philosophy, 4 (Minneapolis: University of Minnesota Press, 1979), 73–122; "Other Bodies," in *Thought and Object: Essays on Intentionality*, ed. Andrew Woodfield (Oxford: Clarendon Press, 1982), 97–120. I hope that my examples forestall a criticism that I have heard repeatedly of Burge's 'arthritis' case, namely, that, for purposes of psychological explanation, the subject has the same beliefs in the actual and counterfactual cases. I suspect that one source of this criticism (other than the individualistic bias under attack) is that, as Burge presents his examples, he cannot express in English the attributions appropriate in the counterfactual cases; he claims only that they differ from the attributions appropriate in the actual cases. Although I am not impressed by the criticism, I hope that my more complicated example, in which all relevant attributions are stated in English and defended, avoids it altogether.

ject as an n-tuple of mental state tokens. Then we have two n-tuples of mental state tokens:

$$\langle m_{11}, m_{12}, \ldots, m_{1n} \rangle$$

and

$$\langle m_{21}, m_{22}, \ldots, m_{2n} \rangle,$$

such that, taken pairwise (for example, m_{11} and m_{21}, m_{12} and m_{22}, and so on), the members of each pair are of the same physical type but of different restricted semantic type.

An immediate consequence is that many varieties of type-type physicalism, even relativized to species, are false. For two subjects may be in the same type of physical state (for example, the brain state controlling emission of certain vocables, movement of one's hand in a certain way, and the like) without being in the same type of restricted semantic state (for example, believing that provoked assault is serious, as opposed to believing that aggravated assault is serious). Insofar as one takes such states, attributed by 'that'-clauses, to be typical psychological states, then psychological states are not wholly determined by physical states of the subject. Thus, the story of the experimental subjects, which shows that sequences of tokens of a single physical type need not be sequences of tokens of a single restricted semantic type, seems to refute type-type physicalism. At least, it seems to refute any type-type physicalism that holds that nonindexical, non–*de re* beliefs are psychological states and that for each distinct type of psychological state there is a distinct type of internal, physical state.[18]

What may be less apparent is that this thought experiment also refutes atomistic brands of Cartesian interactionism. If it were supposed that the relevant mental states were "occurrent" and dispositional states of immaterial souls rather than of brains, a similar conclusion would follow: Two individuals may be in the same type of soul state without being in the same type of restricted semantic state as long as soul states are individuated without presupposing that anything exists

[18] The story is applicable to numerous views. See, for example, D. M. Armstrong, *A Materialist Theory of the Mind* (New York: Humanities Press, 1968); Jaegwon Kim, "Physicalism and the Multiple Realizability of Mental States," in *Readings in the Philosophy of Psychology*, vol. 1, ed. Ned Block (Cambridge, Mass.: Harvard University Press, 1980), 234–236; David Lewis, "An Argument for the Identity Theory," in *Materialism and the Mind-Body Problem*, ed. David Rosenthal (Englewood Cliffs, N.J.: Prentice-Hall, 1971), 162–171; J.J.C. Smart, *Philosophy and Scientific Realism* (New York: Humanities Press, 1963). At times, Dennett also seems to assume that a robot that "models" a person's internal processes must have the same beliefs as the person. See Dennett, "A Cure for the Common Code?" 105.

other than the individual whose states they are. The issue of what makes Subject E's soul token a token of a particular restricted semantic state is just as problematic as the issue of what makes her brain token a token of a particular restricted semantic state. Which restricted semantic state Subject E is in, in the case imagined, is a matter of what language she speaks; but what language one speaks cannot be determined by an individual brain or soul, considered as if nothing else existed. To invoke putative soul states does not solve the difficulty I am raising, so I shall not assume here that there are immaterial souls.[19]

WHAT IF?

Even if the story of the experimental subjects tells against type-type physicalism and against some varieties of Cartesian interactionism, Fodor's functionalism seems to remain unscathed. Although the actual states of Subject E and Subject N are of the same physical types, we have no reason yet to think that any of their mental states play the same functional role—that is, have the same causal relations to sensory inputs, to other (nonintentionally described) mental states, and to behavioral outputs.[20] I must therefore try to show that beliefs of different restricted semantic types can play the same functional role.

Consider Subject N's belief that provoked assault is serious and Subject E's belief that aggravated assault is serious. These beliefs (call them the 'designated beliefs') are obviously of different restricted semantic types; they have the same functional role if and only if tokens of them are causally related to the same sensory inputs, other mental states (nonintentionally described), and behavioral outputs.

So let us enrich the thesis under attack as follows:

(B) If two sequences of tokens cause two tokens of a single type of bodily movement, and if there is a pair of tokens, one from each sequence (for example, m_{13}, m_{23}) *of a type that plays the same causal*

---

[19] These points emerged in conversation with Robert Hambourger. Although the thought experiment so far does not defeat holistic varieties of Cartesian interactionism, I believe that the example in Chapter Five does.

[20] If we assume that there is a "computational path" from every functional state to every other, then, if the experimental subjects have *any* functional state in common, they have *all* their functional states in common. Cf. Ned Block and Jerry A. Fodor, "What Psychological States Are Not," in *Readings in the Philosophy of Psychology*, vol. 1, ed. Ned Block (Cambridge, Mass.: Harvard University Press, 1980), 246. In that case, on a functionalist account of belief, unhappily, it would be unlikely that any two individuals (say, you and I) share any beliefs.

role in the two individuals, then members of that pair are of the same restricted semantic type.

Before I try to show that (B) is false, let me emphasize what is (and is not) at stake here. First, throughout this chapter, the concern is with methodological solipsism; hence, mental states are to be identified without regard to environmental causes, and behavior is to be identified without regard to environmental effects. (Chapters Four and Five will broaden the range of the discussion.) Second, future dispositions that Subject E and Subject N may come to have are irrelevant. Only their *current* dispositions matter: given the same type of stimulation now, they both produce or both fail to produce tokens of their designated beliefs.

To refute (B), I must make it plausible that the mental token that is Subject N's belief that provoked assault is serious is of a type that has the same causes and effects (nonintentionally and individualistically described) as the mental token that is Subject E's belief that aggravated assault is serious. Assume that each came to her degree of mastery of the relevant term by hearing other experimental subjects describe videotaped incidents, all of which, as it happened, could plausibly be interpreted as being particularly fierce, as inflicting serious bodily injury, and as involving some sort of provocation. Since their languages are phonologically similar in the way described, they could have come to their beliefs simply by having had the same aural stimulation. In that case, the subjects acquired the designated beliefs in the same (nonintentionally and individualistically described) circumstances.

Likewise, the circumstances that would cause Subject E to produce a token of her belief that aggravated assault is serious are the same ones that would cause Subject N to produce a token of her belief that provoked assault is serious. For example, if asked, "Which is more serious, aggravated assault or provoked assault?" Subject E would produce a token of "Aggravated assault is serious, but I have never heard of provoked assault." And if asked a phonologically (but, of course, not semantically) equivalent question, Subject N would give a phonologically (but not semantically) equivalent reply.

In addition, the designated beliefs have the same behavioral consequences (nonintentionally and individualistically described). Given the same stimulation and the same other mental states, a token of Subject N's belief that provoked assault is serious causally contributes to a particular (nonintentionally and individualistically described) type of behavior if and only if a token of Subject E's belief that aggravated assault is serious causally contributes to the same type of behavior. For example, in any circumstances in which Subject E's belief that aggravated assault is serious would causally contribute to E's leaving a rough tavern, Subject N's belief that provoked assault is serious would causally contribute to N's leaving a rough tavern.

Finally, the designated beliefs have the same causal connections to other mental states as well. For example, suppose that in Subject N mental state tokens of functional type F are of the restricted semantic type "Some people convicted of simple assault should have been convicted of a more serious crime." Suppose that every time Subject N produces a mental token of functional type F, it also occurs to her that provoked assault is serious; then every time Subject E produces a mental token of functional type F, it also occurs to her that aggravated assault is serious.

The thought experiments suggest that, as long as the designated belief tokens are characterized nonsemantically (in accordance with the formality condition), then the only difference between them is that they occur in different people; mere differences in restricted semantic type elude anyone adhering to the formality condition.[21]

It may be objected that we should speak of functional states only *within an individual*, and hence that examples considering states in different individuals are not to the point. The objection is not to the point. First, we could just as well generate the problem by considering a single individual at two times (or in two possible worlds). Second, the objection denies that we can make sense of the notion of functional equivalence across individuals; but if functionalism failed to allow that two individuals are in the same functional state, then it would lack the gen-

[21] Dennett makes a similar point. See his "Three Kinds of Intentional Psychology" in *Reduction, Time and Reality*, ed. Richard Healey (Cambridge: Cambridge University Press, 1981), 37–61, esp. 56; and "Beyond Belief," in *Thought and Object: Essays on Intentionality*, ed. Andrew Woodfied (Oxford: Clarendon Press, 1982), 1–95. The arguments just given apply to at least some versions of "conceptual role" semantics. For example, in "Social Content and Psychological Content," in *Contents of Thought: Proceedings of the 1985 Oberlin Colloquium in Philosophy*, ed. Robert H. Grimm and Daniel D. Merrill (Tucson: University of Arizona Press, 1988), Brian Loar says that "the conceptual roles of one's thoughts determine *how* one *conceives* things . . ." (12, emphasis his). He also assumes that conceptual roles determine narrow psychological contents, which molecular replicas share. Insofar as he takes conceptual roles to be how one conceives of things, he should say that the beliefs of the experimental subjects differ in conceptual role, since to conceive of something as aggravated assault is different from conceiving of it as provoked assault; but insofar as he takes conceptual roles to be narrow contents, then he should say that the beliefs of the experimental subjects do not differ in conceptual role, since the differences between them are social and linguistic and not "in the head." One of the morals of this chapter is that how one conceives of things is not adequately construed solipsistically.

erality required of a science. Third, the example concerns sequences of physically similar *tokens* that have causally similar relations; the notion of function would make no sense if it did not follow that such sequences may be functionally equivalent.

Now let us see in greater detail how the augmented thought experiment applies to Fodor's conjunction of the content condition and the formality condition in his paper on methodological solipsism. My key claim, supported by the augmented thought experiment, is that tokens cannot be classified by restricted semantic type without violating the formality condition. Fodor does not consider this possibility, because he supposes the content condition and the formality condition to be mutually supportive. Fodor holds—and I take this to be a central theoretical claim—that "mental states are distinct in content only if they are relations to formally distinct mental representations; in effect, that aspects of content can be reconstructed as aspects of form, at least insofar as appeals to content figure in accounts of the mental causation of behavior" (MS, 68). Fodor qualifies this somewhat by saying, "That taxonomy in respect of content *is* compatible with the formality condition, plus or minus a bit, is perhaps *the* basic idea of modern cognitive theory" (MS, 68). I do not believe that the "plus or minus a bit" affects my argument; nor do I see a better way to try to reconcile the content condition and the formality condition than the way I suggest here.

Since the term 'content' has many uses, and since Fodor avails himself of more than one, let me reformulate Fodor's theoretical claim— that aspects of content can be reconstructed as aspects of form—like this:

(T) Two mental state tokens of the same kind (belief, desire, and the like) are of distinct psychological types only if their representations differ formally.

Recall the story of the experimental subjects E and N. The only differences in their representations are restricted semantic differences, which are not mirrored by any formal differences: Subject E's representation concerns aggravated assault; Subject N's, provoked assault. So we have:

(T′) Two mental state tokens of the same kind (belief, desire, and the like) may be of distinct restricted semantic types even if their representations fail to differ formally.

From (T) and (T′), it follows that:

(T″) Two mental state tokens of the same kind (belief, desire, and the like) may be of distinct restricted semantic types without being of distinct psychological types.

That is, the formality condition allows no distinction between Subject E's belief token that aggravated assault is serious and Subject N's belief token that provoked assault is serious. So, if (T) is true, then such tokens are not of distinct psychological types. Subject E's belief that aggravated assault is serious is thus counted as being of the same psychological type as Subject N's belief that provoked assault is serious.

This result seems to undermine *any* belief/desire psychology that conforms to the formality condition. In particular, it refutes Fodor's conception of propositional attitudes and, with it, his view of cognitive science: "That is, one might think of cognitive theories as filling in explanation schema of, roughly, the form: *having the attitude R to proposition P is contingently identical to being in computational relation C to the formula (or sequence of formulae) F.*"[22] If to have an attitude were to be in a certain computational state, then having the belief that provoked assault is serious would be at least "contingently identical" to having the belief that aggravated assault is serious. Although it is unclear what contingent identity comes to in this context, there is surely no possible world in which those are the same beliefs. Although this alone does not force abandonment of (T), retention of (T) (and of the formality condition) becomes quite costly. In order to save the formality condition, what must be given up is the view that individuation by sentence believed coincides with individuation by psychological type.[23]

In the case of abstract beliefs, such as that aggravated assault is serious, it is difficult to see how beliefs could be individuated in any way that failed to coincide with individuation by sentence believed. Thus, the price of the formality condition is that beliefs are precluded from explaining behavior, and a psychology that adheres to the formality condition must be blind to any differences in belief between Subject E and Subject N. This consequence alone seems decisive reason to reject the formality condition; for there seems to be a clear psychological difference between believing that provoked assault is serious and believing that aggravated assault is serious, and any theory that fails to countenance that difference is inadequate as a psychological theory.

[22] Jerry A. Fodor, *The Language of Thought* (Cambridge, Mass.: Harvard University Press, 1979), 77 (emphasis his).

[23] The argument here presupposes no particular semantic theory, nor can it be avoided by appeal to a semantic theory. Cf. Chapter Three.

Others may take a harder line, however, and remind us that the price of a good theory is often to give up certain intuitions. So suppose that, for the sake of the theory, we take the experimental subjects to be in the same psychological state. In that case, it is unclear that there remains any purpose in attributing beliefs (or desires or intentions) at all; such attributions would certainly be unsuitable candidates for explaining anything.

Let me sharpen the point by imagining an alternative to the original story. Suppose that just before the episodes of practical reasoning occurred, the experimental subjects were exchanged; so, in this alternative, unknown to either of them, their respective environments are not what they believe them to be. Since each is unaware of the switch, she reasons as before, in her own language. But in the alternative version, Subject E checks the same box that Subject N checked in the original. So, believing that she is checking the box for aggravated assault, Subject E actually checks the box for provoked assault. What is disconcerting is that psychological explanations cannot distinguish Subject N's (deliberately) checking the box for provoked assault in the first version from Subject E's (unwittingly) checking the box for provoked assault in the alternative version without violating the formality condition.

Before I show why, let me emphasize that there is no incoherence at the level of intuitive intentional explanation. From the alternative version of the story, we have this information: Subject E does not believe that she is checking the box for provoked assault; she is in the same physical state as Subject N, who (in the first version) *does* believe that she is checking the box for provoked assault. Both, in fact, check the box for provoked assault. Intuitively, without regard for the formality condition, it is fairly clear how to give a belief/desire explanation of each of the actions; the explanation of Subject E's (unwittingly) checking the box for provoked assault would have two parts—an "intentional" part, including such attributions as that she believed that she was checking the box for aggravated assault; and a "factual" part, including such information (unavailable to Subject E) as that what she took to be the box for aggravated assault was, in her altered environment, the box for provoked assault.[24] So, there is nothing particularly

---

[24] In "*De Re* Belief in Action," I proposed such a two-stage approach to explaining intentional action; the result of the argument of the current chapter is that even the first stage, in terms of the agent's point of view, is not available to the methodological solipsist. In "Why Computers Can't Act" (*American Philosophical Quarterly* 18 [1981], 157–163), I alluded to the fact that the first-person perspective is not logically private.

puzzling about the stories as told. Now, let us subject the story to the theory that includes the formality condition.

Suppose that Fodor explained Subject N's pressing the button as satisfying this schema:

x believes that the incident was either simple assault or provoked assault.
x believes provoked assault is serious, more serious than simple assault.
x believes that the incident was serious enough to be provoked assault.
Therefore, x checks the box for provoked assault.

Within the strictures of methodological solipsism, there is no way to rule out explanation of Subject E's (unwittingly) checking the box for provoked assault by the very same schema. Since differences in psychological state, considered solipsistically, require formal differences, and since there are no such formal differences between Subject N's belief that she is checking the box for provoked assault and Subject E's belief that she is checking the box for aggravated assault, we attribute to Subject E a single psychological state regardless of whether we characterize it as a belief that she is checking the box for provoked assault or as a belief that she is checking the box for aggravated assault.[25] But if these are attributions of a single psychological state, one attribution is correct if and only if the other is.

This result is doubly unfortunate. First, *ex hypothesi*, Subject E did not believe that she was checking the box for provoked assault (she had never heard of provoked assault); therefore, such a belief cannot help explain her checking that box. And since the formality condition does not permit a distinction between attributing to Subject E the belief that she was checking the box for provoked assault and attributing to her the belief that she was checking the box for aggravated assault, the latter belief can be no more explanatory than the former. Thus, it is doubtful that beliefs, desires, or intentions can ever be explanatory if psychological explanations conform to the formality condition.

Second, an action performed deliberately should not receive the same psychological explanation as the same type of action (under the same

[25] I think that this consideration also tells against Brian Loar's argument that psychological contents of beliefs attributed in common-sense explanations are not individuated by 'that'-clauses; his ground is that 'that'-clauses depend upon "social facts" but that (narrow) psychological contents do not. If Loar were correct to claim that common-sense explanations are "narrow," then the actions of the experimental subjects should receive the same *common-sense* explanations. But although the experimental subjects do not differ in their relevant internal states, they are subject to very different common-sense explanations.

description, for example, 'checking the box for provoked assault,' in the same external circumstances) performed unwittingly. This suggests that the psychological explanations that do conform to the formality condition are defective; for without attributions of belief, such explanations must be blind to psychological differences between doing something deliberately and doing it unwittingly. From another angle: as long as the formality condition is honored, two *incompatible* intentional explanations are equally justified.[26] Thus, it appears that the formality condition and the requirement of methodological solipsism preclude belief/desire explanations of action, in which case the formality condition renders practical reasoning irrelevant to what one does.

To sum up the argument against the merger of methodological solipsism and belief/desire psychology: If we take psychological states in accordance with the formality condition, we cannot coherently ascribe content to them, in which case beliefs, desires, and intentions do not count as psychological states and do not figure in psychological explanations. On the other hand, if we take psychological states in accordance with the content condition, we can attribute beliefs, desires, and intentions, but only by violating the formality condition.[27]

More generally, the story shows that even very abstract beliefs, such as that aggravated assault is serious, fail to conform to the strictures of methodological solipsism. The identity of such beliefs depends in part upon the language-using community of the believer; so even considered apart from semantic properties of truth and reference, such beliefs are not wholly "in the head." Therefore, if behavior is to be explained only by what is in the head, it is not to be explained by belief.

Fodor remarks, "I shall simply take it for granted that you cannot save the cognitive science program by going syntactic. Either mental

---

[26] In addition, Fodor's account does not seem to meet his own conditions. In "Propositional Attitudes," 177, Fodor proposes a set of conditions of adequacy on views of propositional attitudes. Of the five "a priori conditions, which, on [Fodor's] view, a theory of propositional attitudes (PA's) ought to meet," I believe that the theory that Fodor actually proposes in "Methodological Solipsism Considered as a Research Strategy in Cognitive Psychology" fails to meet at least three. The only condition clearly fulfilled by the conjunction of the content condition and the formality condition is that propositional attitudes are analyzed as relations.

[27] David F. Austin has pointed out that my stories may be seen as an extension of inverted-spectrum objections to belief states, the states that are thought most susceptible to a functionalist account. Vis-à-vis Block's examples against functionalism, David Sanford noted that my stories are analogous to comparing China's pain to India's tickle. Cf. Shoemaker's remark that the inverted-spectrum problem for functionalism is one of a class of 'qualia inversion' problems for that view. Sydney Shoemaker, "Inverted Spectrum," *Journal of Philosophy* 79 (1982), 368 n. 10.

representations are going to honest-to-God represent, or we are going to have to find an alternative to [the representational theory of the mind]."[28] But as we have seen, given the formality condition, they cannot represent. If psychological states are construed as computational states, then beliefs, desires, intentions, and other states identified by content fail to qualify as psychological states.

[28] Fodor, "Cognitive Science and the Twin-Earth Problem," 102.

· 3 ·

MIND AND
THE MACHINE ANALOGY

The computer metaphor has spawned one of the most promising approaches to a science of the mind: functionalism. In recent years, functionalism has been the dominant expression of the hope that beliefs, intentions, and desires, identified by content, can be accommodated by a scientific theory of mental processes. I shall regard as functionalist those views that define behavior-explaining psychological states by means of causal relations among sensory inputs, internal states, and behavioral outputs, all ultimately nonintentionally describable in terms applied to automata. More informally, Richard Rorty has remarked, "Functionalism comes down to saying that anything you want to say about persons will have an analogue in something you can say about computers. . . ."[1]

Considerations similar to those adduced in Chapter Two, however, will show functionalist optimism to be misplaced. As we saw in Chapter Two, two formally indistinguishable individuals may differ in their beliefs identified by restricted semantic type; thus the formality condition precludes coherent attribution of attitudes identified by content. And since computers are paradigms of formal systems, it may be obvious that the line of thought pursued in the story of the experimental subjects in Chapter Two tells against the computer analogy, at least as long as that analogy is taken to underwrite attributions of attitudes identified by content. But in light of the pervasiveness and tenacity of physicalists' allegiance to the computer metaphor of mind, I should like to expose the difficulty in some detail, especially since in this chapter I shall not rely on a thought experiment but on a valid deductive argument.

THE MACHINE ANALOGY

The root idea of the machine analogy is that human beings and machines are both species of information-processing systems; however different their embodiments, they have mental operations fully explainable by the theory of automata. According to John Haugeland, the

[1] Richard Rorty, "Contemporary Philosophy of Mind," *Synthese* 53 (1982), 335.

guiding inspiration of cognitive science is that, "at a suitable level of abstraction, a theory of 'natural' intelligence should have the same basic form as the theories that explain sophisticated computer systems. It is this idea which makes *artificial* intelligence seem not only possible, but also a central and pure form of *psychological* research."[2]

One rather picturesque way to see the general idea is to think of a person as a kind of corporate entity, made up of various departments performing complex mental functions.[3] Each department, in turn, is organized into subunits, each of which performs slightly less complicated tasks; members of the subunits are themselves teams, performing even less complicated tasks. The teams have subteams as members, and so on. The activity of each sub- . . . team is explained by its constituent sub-sub- . . . teams, which have less talented members performing simpler and more specialized tasks, until finally at the bottom level, the tasks are purely mechanical—on the order of flipping switches—requiring no talent or intelligence at all. Individuals organized in terms of such functional hierarchies are describable by means of flow charts.

What minds and computers seem to have in common, broadly speaking, is that they can be seen as sequences of logical states, understood abstractly, apart from their physical embodiments in organic or in inorganic matter. The leading way to construe the metaphor is to say that mental states are identified by their functional roles in the operation of the whole system. But just as each token (or instance) of a logical, or functional, state of a computer is nothing other than a token of a particular physical configuration, so each token of a mental state is seen as nothing other than a token of some physical configuration of the brain. So, functionalist theories may well fill the physicalistic bill for science.

On the machine analogy, mental processes are to be understood as computations. One way that this claim has been understood is to say that mental processes are taken to be reducible to Turing machine operations. This construal of the machine analogy is spelled out in the form of universal Turing machine functionalism in Hilary Putnam's "Minds and Machines."[4] A Turing machine is any machine completely described by a machine table, which specifies, for various inputs, the possible states of the machine; and a machine table is an abstraction. A

[2] John Haugeland, "Semantic Engines: An Introduction to Mind Design," in *Mind Design: Philosophy, Psychology, Artificial Intelligence*, ed. John Haugeland (Cambridge, Mass.: MIT/Bradford, 1981), 2 (emphasis his).

[3] See William G. Lycan, "Form, Function, and Feel," *Journal of Philosophy* 78 (1981), 24–50.

[4] Hilary Putnam, "Minds and Machines," in his *Mind, Language and Reality: Philosophical Papers*, vol. 2 (Cambridge: Cambridge University Press, 1975), 362–385.

given Turing machine, then, may be realized by different types of physical devices.[5]

The machine analogy, however, is not dependent upon the Turing machine model. It may be construed more broadly, as Fodor takes it, as a claim that mental processes are to be understood as "formal operations on symbols."[6] Although the idea of formality must remain, as Fodor says, "intuitive and metaphoric,"[7] to say that an operation is formal is to say that it depends only on the "shape" or structure of the symbol it operates upon and that it does not depend on semantic properties, such as truth or reference. Computers manipulate sentences, as Stich agrees, by virtue of their form.[8] Therefore, 'symbol' should be understood as something semantically interpretable or subject to interpretation.[9] Exactly what interpretation a symbol is given is irrelevant to its identity as a symbol and to its formally characterized role in the functioning of the system.

The point of the computer metaphor in psychology, as Fodor notes, is not that psychological theories can "be run on computers." (Church's Thesis, if true, guarantees that a Turing machine can compute *any* "effective" procedure.)[10] Rather, Fodor virtually equates the computer metaphor with the idea of formality: "Where the [computer] metaphor cuts some ice is in the suggestion that the *mental operations* that (some) psychological theories postulate are like computations: that they apply to mental representations in virtue of their nonsemantic properties" (MS, 104; emphasis his).

[5] More recently, Putnam has argued that "psychological states are not machine states nor are they disjunctions of machine states." Hilary Putnam, "Reduction and the Nature of Psychology," in *Mind Design*, 216.

[6] Fodor, "Introduction: Something on the State of the Art," in his *Representations: Philosophical Essays on the Foundations of Cognitive Science* (Cambridge, Mass.: MIT/ Bradford, 1981), 23–24. Another good discussion of the machine analogy is Ned Block's "What Is Functionalism?" in *Readings in the Philosophy of Psychology*, vol. 1, ed. Ned Block (Cambridge, Mass.: Harvard University Press, 1980), 171–184.

[7] Jerry A. Fodor, "Methodological Solipsism Considered as a Research Strategy in Cognitive Psychology," *Behavioral and Brain Sciences* 3 (1980), 64. Hereafter the title of this article will be abbreviated as MS, and page references will be given in the text.

[8] Stephen P. Stich, *From Folk Psychology to Cognitive Science: The Case Against Belief* (Cambridge, Mass.: MIT/Bradford, 1983), 40.

[9] Cf. Robert Cummins, *The Nature of Psychological Explanation* (Cambridge, Mass.: MIT/Bradford, 1983), 34. Also see Patrick Hayes, "The Logic of Frames," in *Readings in Artificial Intelligence*, ed. Bonnie Lynn Webber and Nils J. Nilsson (Palo Alto, Calif.: Tioga Publishing Co., 1981), 451.

[10] An effective procedure is one that can be completed by mechanical application of instructions (generated, for example, by a series of yes/no questions) in a finite number of steps.

The machine analogy may be cast in either a metaphysical or a scientific light. It may be interpreted metaphysically by supposing that it reveals the nature of the mind: minds and machines are ultimately two species of information-processing systems. Alternatively, the analogy may be interpreted scientifically by supposing that it offers a research strategy for psychology: mental processes are composed of computations on "representations." (I put 'representations' in scare quotes because the term is used in crucially different ways by leading proponents of the computer model: for example, Fodor uses it to designate sentences-in-the-head, physical tokens that are classified by restricted semantic type; Dennett uses it as a general purpose term that need not designate anything in the head.)[11] The scientific or methodological interpretation of the analogy, when it is joined with the assumption of physicalism, collapses into the metaphysical interpretation.

The machine analogy is attractive for several reasons. First, it promises to solve the venerable problem of intentionality, the problem of how one thing can be about or represent another. Successful application of the machine analogy by physicalists would seem to demonstrate a sense in which the intentional is "reducible" to the nonintentional (that is, to the physical); for a computer is a wholly material object, all of whose operations can be completely described and explained without attributing to it states with content. So, if a computer can have beliefs and other "contentful" attitudes in the same sense that humans do, then the question of how a material object can exhibit intentionality seems solved at a stroke. In that case, the machine analogy suggests how a theory of mentality can be properly scientific and non–question-begging. Dennett, for example, takes the task of a theory of the mind to be to explain intelligence without (circularly) presupposing intelligence; the machine analogy seems appropriate for that purpose in that it implies that intentionality does not go "all the way down." It thus seems to relieve the mind of any lingering mysteries.

In addition, the machine analogy seems to offer an alternative to behaviorism as a basis for a science of the mind. Unlike behaviorist models, computer models freely employ the teleological terminology of means and ends, as well as general mentalistic terms such as 'meaning,' 'search,' and 'belief.'[12] For example, Marvin Minsky has characterized

[11] See, for example, Fodor, "Propositional Attitudes," in *Representations*, 177–203; and Daniel C. Dennett, "Styles of Mental Representation," *Proceedings of the Aristotelian Society* 83 (1982/1983), 213–226.

[12] John McCarthy and Patrick Hayes, "Some Philosophical Problems from the Standpoint of Artificial Intelligence," 431, Patrick Hayes, "The Logic of Frames," 451, and

this alternative to behaviorism as one of "finding useful mechanistic interpretations of those mentalistic notions that have real value."[13] It should be noted that, for Minsky, not all mentalistic notions turn out to have real value. Indeed, "traditional, everyday, precomputational concepts like believing and understanding are neither powerful nor robust enough for developing or discussing" the study of the mind.[14] But the fact that the machine analogy does not jeopardize mentalistic or teleological vocabulary per se has heightened its appeal.

Nowhere does the machine analogy seem more promising than in its application to theoretical and practical reasoning, the mental processes that come closest to calculation and computation.[15] Moreover, it is legitimate to expect a scientific psychology, whether based on the machine analogy or not, to pronounce on practical reasoning; for prima facie at least, practical reasoning is a cognitive capacity and thus is within the purview of a scientific psychology that aims to explain cognitive capacities.[16]

Someone may object: (1) an account of practical reasoning would have to countenance beliefs or states of believing, desires or states of desiring, and other states identified by content; and (2) prescientific concepts, such as those of belief and desire, may or may not be regimentable for purposes of science; therefore, (3) it cannot be assumed at the outset that a scientific psychology will have anything at all to say about practical reasoning or about beliefs, desires, and intentions. Such an argument may be elicited from remarks by Minsky:

> [T]hough prescientific idea germs like 'believe,' 'know' and 'mean' are useful in daily life, they seem technically too coarse to support powerful theories; we need to supplant rather than to support and explicate them. Real as 'self' or 'understand' may seem to us to-

Robert Moore, "Reasoning about Knowledge and Action," 473, all in *Readings in Artificial Intelligence.*

[13] Marvin Minsky, "Introduction," in *Semantic Information Processing*, ed. Marvin Minsky (Cambridge, Mass.: MIT Press, 1968), 2.

[14] Marvin Minsky, "Decentralized Minds," *Behavioral and Brain Sciences* 3 (1980), 439 (commentary on John Searle's "Minds, Brains and Programs").

[15] Herbert A. Simon has proposed some of the most influential models of practical reasoning. See, for example, his classic "A Behavioral Model of Rational Choice" (1955), reprinted in his *Models of Thought* (New Haven: Yale University Press, 1979), 7–19.

[16] See, for example, Alan Newell, "On the Analysis of Human Problem Solving Protocols," 46–61, Terry Winograd, "Formalisms for Knowledge," 62–71, and Marvin Minsky, "Frame-System Theory," 355–376, all in *Thinking: Readings in Cognitive Science*, ed. P. N. Johnson-Laird and P. C. Wason (Cambridge: Cambridge University Press, 1977). Also see Saul Amarel, "On Representations of Problems of Reasoning about Actions," in *Readings in Artificial Intelligence*, 2–22.

day, they are not (like milk and sugar) objective things our theories must accept and explain; they are only first steps toward better concepts.[17]

Of course, I do not want simply to assume that a scientific psychology will explain practical reasoning; indeed, I consider in detail a "syntactic" view of the mind (Stich's), in terms of which practical reasoning defies description. But even on such a view, the question arises: If, as our working assumption has it, scientific psychology gives the truth about the mind, and if such psychology has *nothing* to say about beliefs and believing and hence nothing to say about practical reasoning, how is it that we are inclined to say that we *seem* to deliberate, and how is it that we say that what we do *seems* to be related to what we (seem to) decide to do? In what do our errors consist? A true theory of the mind should at least explain how we have gone wrong.

Because Part II will be concerned with the consequences of rejecting attitudes identified by content, here I shall set aside views like Minsky's, which deny that "precomputational" concepts like belief are even relevant to a study of the mind.[18] In this chapter, the focus will be on functionalists, again like Fodor, who invoke the computer metaphor with the hope of developing a computational psychology that allows certain beliefs and other attitudes to be explanatory.

Finally, it is worth drawing attention to two related, but erroneous, assumptions that sometimes infect discussions of computer models of anything. The first is that a computer model is the criterion of understanding, that a person does not understand, in the fullest sense, anything that is not susceptible to being rendered as a program. Such an assumption lies behind Marvin Minsky's remark that the lack of programs for producing art and music exposes no special difficulties in programming such activities; the fault lies in the lack of semantic models that could be the basis for programs: "That these [semantic models] are not available is not so much a reflection on the state of heuristic programs as on the traditionally disgraceful state of analytic criticism in the arts—a cultural consequence of the fact that most esthetic analysts wax indignant when it is suggested that it *might be possible to understand what they are trying to understand*."[19] This suggests that

---

[17] Minsky, "Decentralized Minds," 439.

[18] Ibid.

[19] Minsky, "Introduction," 12 (emphasis mine). Cf. Daniel C. Dennett, "Why the Law of Effect Won't Go Away," in his *Brainstorms: Philosophical Essays on Mind and Psychology* (Montgomery, Vt.: Bradford, 1978), 82–83.

Minsky thinks of 'understanding' simply as limited to what can be programmed.

Minsky is free to define terms for his own persuasive purposes; but then we should still have to ask: What does "understanding," so defined, have to do with ordinary understanding? Why should we care about ' "understanding" ' as a code word for 'programmable'? What interest would such a stipulative definition have, a definition whose purpose appears to be purely rhetorical? In any case, serious discussion of understanding is short-circuited by such a stipulative definition at the outset. Conversely, the fact that programs or data structures are given names like 'UNDERSTAND' does not entitle us to infer that there is any understanding. Drew McDermott, an AI researcher, has characterized such "wishful mnemonics" as a "major source of simple-mindedness in AI."[20]

The second erroneous assumption is the equation of determinateness, or completeness, or absence of vagueness with computability. It is assumed that any view that is noncomputational is thereby imprecise. For example, Patrick Henry Winston and Mike Brady introduce a series on AI with the comment:

> Of course psychology, philosophy, linguistics, and related disciplines offer various perspectives and methodologies for studying intelligence. For the most part, however, the theories proposed in these fields are too incomplete and too vaguely stated to be realized in computational terms.[21]

This is to say that philosophical views have not been susceptible to computational modeling.

We must first distinguish two uses of the term 'computational,' and then look at the connections, if any, between computational models and vague or incomplete theories. The term 'computation' in 'computational model' can describe either the model (as in 'wooden model') or what is being modeled (as in 'cash-flow model').[22] If mental processes are in fact computational, as they are taken to be on the machine analogy, then in principle they may be modeled by computational models (in the second sense). Such models are paradigms of precision. If, however, mental processes are not in fact computational, if they are not ad-

[20] Drew McDermott, "Artificial Intelligence Meets Natural Stupidity," in *Mind Design*, 144.

[21] *Artificial Intelligence: An MIT Perspective*, vol. 1, ed. Patrick Henry Winston and Richard Henry Brown (Cambridge, Mass.: MIT Press, 1979), series forward.

[22] This distinction was pointed out by John Haugeland at the MIT/Sloan Foundation Conference on Philosophy and Cognitive Science, at MIT, May 16–20, 1984.

equately represented in the form of a flow chart, then computational models (in the second sense) will to one degree or another misdescribe them; in that case, the precision of the models is positively misleading. In the latter case, maximally precise views of the mind, if they are correct, will fail to be computational (in either sense).

Thus, it does not follow—and it is surely false—that views that cannot be realized in computational terms are incomplete or vague; nor does it follow that views that can be realized in computational terms are complete or precise. On the one hand, to characterize, say, Aristotle's views on virtue as incomplete or vague is to impose a standard of completeness or precision inappropriate to the subject matter, a standard that it would be impossible for any view on that subject matter to meet, and then to criticize the best views for not meeting it. The effect of such methodological imperialism is simply to stipulate that certain areas of deep human interest are intellectually suspect.

On the other hand, even explicitly numerical representation does not guarantee useful precision. Consider fortunetelling based upon precise calculations of time of birth, positions of planets, and so on. In the case of astrology, there is an obvious gap between the numbers crunched and what they are alleged to be crunching; in other cases, the issues are more subtle. For example, claims about relations between being in a certain functional state, say, and believing such-and-such call for serious conceptual, and hence philosophical, reflection—reflection on issues whose resolutions are presupposed (and, therefore, are not reached) by use of flow charts.

Since discussion of computers arouses passion in enthusiasts and detractors alike, let me mention several things that I am not doing. I am not making predictions about whether or not we ever will be justified in attributing beliefs and other attitudes to artifacts in the same way that we attribute them to each other. If we do, it will be because we interact with artifacts—share forms of life with them—as we do with each other, and such interaction would blur the putative distinction between the narrowly internal and the external environment on which so much current thinking in cognitive science and philosophy of mind rests.

Nor am I challenging the usefulness of the field known as 'Artificial Intelligence,' under the rubric of which falls the development of so-called expert systems and robotics. The existence of a discipline called 'Artificial Intelligence' no more implies that machines are intelligent than the existence of a discipline called 'Political Science' implies that politics is a science; still, I am as enthusiastic as the next person about the potential of the field of Artificial Intelligence.

The issue at hand is whether or not the computer analogy, via functionalism, can reveal attributions of attitudes identified by content to be physicalistically respectable. This issue, as we saw in the discussion of the formality condition, turns on the concept of narrowness. The variability of the use of that concept has masked an ineliminable equivocation, which vitiates attempts to equate beliefs and so on with classical functional states.[23]

ON BEING NARROW: A DILEMMA

Classical functionalism fails because it is caught in an unrecognized dilemma, a dilemma concerning the individuation of psychological states that explain behavior. Beliefs are individuated by most functionalists in terms of 'that'-clauses; classical functional states are individuated "narrowly" (that is, they are specifiable without presupposing the existence of anything other than the individual whose states they are). If beliefs are to be functional states, individuation in terms of 'that'-clauses (on some construal) must coincide with genuinely "narrow" individuation. Items that cannot be identified in terms of 'that'-clauses do not qualify as beliefs; items that cannot be identified narrowly do not qualify as functional states. But, as we shall see, individuation in terms of 'that'-clauses leads to the following dilemma: Either the classical functionalist is committed to an inconsistent triad, or no states identified by 'that'-clauses are sufficiently narrow to allow beliefs to be functional states. Before we turn to the inconsistent triad, let us first consider the notion(s) of narrowness.

Functionalists claim that the beliefs that play a role in the etiology of (brute) behavior must be understood as functional states. They recognize that many beliefs—indexical beliefs, *de re* beliefs—are not plausibly construed as functional states and hence fall outside the purview of the functionalist claim. Since the functionalist concern is with beliefs and other psychological states that explain behavior, the issue of identifying beliefs becomes one of construing 'that'-clauses ("contents") in

[23] Although the classical versions of functionalism construe functional states narrowly, there have recently been moves toward a "wide" functionalism, which individuates functional roles by reference to objects in the environment. See, for example, Patricia Kitcher, "Narrow Taxonomy and Wide Functionalism," *Philosophy of Science* 52 (1985), 78–97. See also Robert van Gulick, "Mental Representation—A Functionalist View," *Pacific Philosophical Quarterly* 63 (1982), 3–20. The arguments in Chapter Five will bear on these views. For criticisms different from my own, see Joseph Owens, "Functionalism and Propositional Attitudes," *Noûs* 17 (1983), 529–550; and Jay L. Garfield, "Propositional Attitudes and the Ontology of the Mental," *Cognition and Brain Theory* 6 (1983), 319–331.

such a way that behavior-explaining beliefs can be understood as functional states.

If beliefs are to be understood as classical functional states, they must be construed as *narrow states*. As the idea of narrowness was introduced by Putnam, psychological states in the narrow sense were to be those permitted by methodological solipsism, that is, by the "assumption that no psychological state, properly so-called, presupposes the existence of any individual other than the subject to whom that state is ascribed."[24] Fodor brought the idea of *narrow content* to prominence as the constraint that mental states that explain behavior should be individuated by content without regard to truth or reference to individuals, or as the constraint (which may not be the same thing) that for purposes of explaining behavior, attitudes should be attributed "opaquely" rather than "transparently" (MS, 66–67). (Notice that Fodor's use of 'narrow content' coincides with my use of 'restricted semantic type.' I prefer the latter because of the multiple uses of 'narrow' and of 'content.') Yet another characterization of narrowness that has currency is that narrow states are those shared by molecule-for-molecule duplicates.

It may be thought that the descriptions 'state common to molecular replicas,' 'state specifiable without regard to truth or reference,' 'state specifiable without presupposing the existence of any individual other than the subject to whom that state is ascribed,' and 'state "opaquely" attributed' are co-extensive. Such an assumption is abetted both by an equivocal use of the term 'narrow content' and by the widespread view that there is an interesting sense of 'behavior' that requires explanation solely in terms of what is "in the head" of the subject. Although all the criteria for narrowness *aim* to isolate psychological states that are "in the head," it does not follow that they in fact isolate the same things; indeed, I have argued in Chapter Two that they do not. However, no matter how narrow states are characterized, every criterion rules out as "wide" any beliefs individuated in part by particular objects in the believer's environment.

The history of artificial intelligence has increased the plausibility of taking psychological states to be independent of the subject's actual environment. For example, SHRDLU is a famous program in which a computer manipulates a "block" world and answers questions about what it is doing.[25] For instance, in response to "Pick up a big red block," it

[24] Hilary Putnam, "The Meaning of 'Meaning,' " in *Mind, Language and Reality*, vol. 2, 220.

[25] See Terry Winograd, *Understanding Natural Language* (New York: Academic Press, 1972).

prints out "OK" and removes the green block on top of the red one in order to obey the command. In response to "What does the box contain?" it prints out "The blue pyramid and the blue block." And so on.

What is significant for our purposes is that the block world need not actually exist; what was needed were not blocks and boxes but merely representations of blocks, pyramids, and boxes and apparent "memories" of the commands that the computer has executed. The actual environment was regarded as irrelevant to the claims made on behalf of SHRDLU. Since there were no actual objects to be perceived or manipulated, all the computer's "beliefs" were false. The device, as Fodor has remarked, "is in precisely the situation that Descartes dreads; it's a mere computer which dreams that it's a robot" (MS, 65).

The irrelevance of the actual environment to the descriptions offered for SHRDLU strongly suggests that, if psychological explanation is to be based on the machine analogy, the actual environment may be irrelevant to psychological explanation. The cognitive processes that figure in the etiology of behavior must be construed independently of the actual environment; all that matters is how the individual represents the environment. The construal of classical functional states as narrow is to ensure this independence of the subject from the environment.

Let us say: A state is *narrow* if and only if whether or not x is in that state is determined solely by properties of x, without presupposing that anything other than x exists. Classical functional states are narrow in the specified sense; and if functionalism is correct, beliefs that explain (brute) behavior may be individuated without presupposing that anything other than the believer exists.

Since the term 'content' is employed in multifarious ways, I shall again use the locution 'restricted semantic type' to indicate beliefs individuated by 'that'-clauses in the following sense: Beliefs are individuated by *restricted semantic type* if they are identified by means of the obliquely occurring expressions in the 'that'-clauses of their ascriptions, where obliquely occurring expressions are those that freely permit neither existential generalization nor substitution of co-extensive terms.[26]

---

[26] Call this criterion for belief identified by restricted semantic type, 'Criterion (I).' Criterion (I), which individuates beliefs by obliquely occurring expressions in content clauses, suggests another formulation, Criterion (II): Belief that p is a different belief from belief that q if and only if there are semantic differences between p and q other than differences in truth value or reference to specific individuals. Although (I) and (II) are nonequivalent, I shall assume for purposes here that beliefs that are different on (I) are also different on (II), and that beliefs individuated by either (I) or (II) are individuated by restricted semantic type. To see the nonequivalence, consider the theory according to

As noted in Chapter One, my use of 'restricted semantic type' leaves open whether or not differences in restricted semantic type amount to any more than differences in truth condition (as opposed to truth value). The argument leading to the second horn of the dilemma, for example, rests on the claim that, while beliefs may be individuated (as wide states) by truth condition or (as genuinely narrow states) by functional role, there is no place for restricted semantic type as a *tertium quid*; all differences in restricted semantic type can be handled as differences in truth conditions. Whatever the merit of this position, as we shall see, it cannot save the functionalist construal of beliefs as functional states.

Here, then, is the key question: Does individuation by restricted semantic type coincide with individuation by functional state? An affirmative answer leads to the inconsistent triad (the first horn); a negative answer leads to a denial that beliefs, individuated by obliquely occurring expressions in 'that'-clauses (that is, by restricted semantic type), are functional states (the second horn).

The inconsistent triad is this:

(a) Beliefs individuated by restricted semantic type are psychological states.
(b) Psychological states are classical functional states.
(c) Two tokens of a single classical functional type may differ in restricted semantic type.

The reasoning leading to commitment to (a)–(c) (the first horn of the dilemma) is found in Fodor's "Methodological Solipsism Considered as a Research Strategy in Cognitive Science." The only way that I know for a classical functionalist to avoid the contradiction leads straight to the second horn of the dilemma. The argument out of the inconsistent triad consists of maintaining that individuation by restricted semantic type requires recourse to truth conditions and hence that individuation by restricted semantic type does not individuate beliefs narrowly enough to coincide with individuation by functional state. I shall give

---

which names are rigid designators with no semantic role other than to pick out objects. On that theory, either (1) the opacity of '*S* believes that Cicero was an orator' and '*S* believes that Tully was an orator' must be denied altogether, or (2) beliefs that are different on (I) fail to be different on (II). For a discussion of the first alternative, see Lynne Rudder Baker, "Underprivileged Access," *Noûs* 16 (1982), 227–242. To preserve both opacity and the claim that beliefs different on (I) are also different on (II), we can modify (I) by replacing the expression 'co-extensive terms' by 'co-extensive nonrigid designators.' Since the points that I want to make do not depend on any particular semantic theory, I would accept the alternative formulation, noting only that to restrict (I) in this way is to undercut the motivation for (I) in the first place. These points are due to Alan Berger.

an example of this approach, suggested in several articles by William G. Lycan,[27] and then point out that the consequence is a denial that beliefs are functional states.

First, consider (a). The term 'restricted semantic type,' is intended to accommodate an intuitive sense in which beliefs are said to have content. As we saw in Chapter Two, on Fodor's view, to think that Marvin is melancholy is to be in a particular relation to a "representation the content of which is *that* Marvin is melancholy." And the belief that Marvin is melancholy is distinguished from the belief that it sometimes snows in Cincinnati by the contents of the associated representations. Fodor's initial assumption is that "the *content* of representations is a (type) individuating feature of mental states" (MS, 63, 64; emphasis his).

Fodor argues that (at least some) psychological states that explain behavior are to be understood in terms of "opaque" attribution of attitudes:

> Thesis: when we articulate the generalizations in virtue of which behavior is contingent upon mental states, it is typically an opaque construal of the mental state attributions that does the work; for example, it's a construal under which believing that *a is F* is logically independent from believing that *b is F*, even in the case where a = b. It will be convenient to speak not only of opaque construals of propositional attitude ascriptions, but also of *opaque taxonomies* of mental state types. . . . So, the claim is that mental states are typically opaquely taxonomized for the purpose of psychological theory. (MS, 66; emphases his)

This is a clear statement of the view that beliefs individuated by restricted semantic type are the psychological states that explain behavior. Thus, (a) is one of Fodor's central claims.[28]

Statement (b) is the backbone of functionalism. To say that psychological states are functional states is to say that, for purposes of psychological classification, mental tokens are typed nonsemantically by their

---

[27] William G. Lycan, "Semantics and Methodological Solipsism," read at the Davidson Conference at Rutgers University, 1984. A different version of these points may be found in Lycan's *Logical Form in Natural Language* (Cambridge, Mass.: MIT/Bradford, 1984). See also his "Toward a Homuncular Theory of Believing," *Cognition and Brain Theory* 4 (1981), 139–159.

[28] See also Jerry A. Fodor, "Cognitive Science and the Twin-Earth Problem," *Notre Dame Journal of Formal Logic* 23 (1982), 98–118.

(typical) causes and effects. Since *content* is a "semantic notion par excellence" (MS, 64), there may seem to be a conflict between (a), according to which certain mental tokens are classified by restricted semantic type, and (b), according to which those mental tokens are classified by their nonsemantic properties. But Fodor takes it as a *desideratum* of a theory of the mind that it reconcile semantic and nonsemantic properties of mental tokens:

> By thus exploiting the notions of content and computation *together*, a cognitive theory seeks to connect the *intensional* properties of mental states with their *causal* properties vis-à-vis behavior. Which is, of course, exactly what a theory of the mind ought to do. (MS, 68)

Such congruence is supported by the claim (or conjecture) "that mental states are distinct in content only if they are relations to formally distinct mental representations; in effect, that aspects of content can be reconstructed as aspects of form, at least insofar as appeals to content figure in accounts of the mental causation of behavior" (MS, 68). The argument for this claim is that it provides an explanation of "how beliefs of different content *can* have different behavioral effects."

> The form of explanation goes: it's because different content implies formally distinct internal representations (via the formality condition) and formally distinct internal representations can be functionally different; can differ in their causal role. Whereas, to put it mildly, it's hard to see how internal representations could differ in causal role *unless* they differed in form. (MS, 68)

Thus, Fodor is unlikely to take exception to (b). In any case, although (b) is stated as a specifically functionalist thesis, other ways of typing mental tokens nonsemantically (in conformity with the formality condition) can play the same role in generating the contradiction below.

Now, consider (c). Statement (c) also seems acknowledged by Fodor, who explicitly considers computer programs that simulate, on the one hand, the Six-Day War and on the other hand, a chess game: "It's a possible (though, of course, unlikely) accident that these programs should be *indistinguishable when compiled*; viz., that the [machine language] counterparts of these programs should be identical, so that the internal career of a machine running one program would be identical, step by step, to that of a machine running the other." In addition: "machines typically don't know (or care) what the programs that they run are about; all they know (or care about) is how to run their programs. This may sound cryptical or even mystical. It's not. It's merely banal."[29]

I believe that Fodor here underestimates the significance of his own observation. As Georges Rey has remarked even more pointedly:

> [O]n Wednesday [a computer] deals with the intricacies of the SALT negotiations, on Thursday it plays chess with Bobby Fischer. Now it is perfectly possible in principle for the machine to pass through type identical computational and physical states on both days. All that would normally be needed is that on both occasions the input decks be themselves type identical, and that would occur should the two problem domains be construed, as it were, iso-morphically. It's just that on Wednesday the punches in the cards are interpreted (say, by Carter) to refer to Brezhnev, Vienna and 100-megaton bombs; and on Thursday the very same punches are interpreted (say, by Spassky) to refer to moves and pieces in chess.[30]

So although a belief that cruise missiles can repel an invasion from the East is of a different restricted semantic type from a belief that pawns can ward off an attack on the Queen's side, insofar as a computer may be said to have beliefs at all, both beliefs may be equally "subserved" by a single type of computational and physical state. Then the computer, in exactly the same sequence of functional states, could equally well be interpreted as reasoning about negotiating an arms agreement or about winning a chess game. Thus, tokens of a given functional type may be of different restricted semantic types. Indeed, the fact that a token of a particular functional type is of one retricted semantic type does not preclude its also being of another (nonequivalent) restricted semantic type. So, I take it both that (c) is true and that Fodor is committed to it.

The three theses together lead to a contradiction. In case the contradiction is not apparent, let me provide a simple proof. '∃' will stand for the existential quantifier, and universal quantifiers will be omitted. Read '∼' as 'it is not the case that,' and read '→' as 'if-then.' Let x,y range over restricted semantic states.[31]

---

[29] Jerry A. Fodor, "Tom Swift and His Procedural Grandmother," in *Representations*, 207. Although Fodor uses the illustration to criticize procedural semantics, the point is independent of any particular semantic theory.

[30] Georges Rey, "The Formal and the Opaque," *Behavioral and Brain Sciences* 3 (1980), 90–92 (commentary on Fodor's "Methodological Solipsism").

[31] This formulation of the proof was suggested by both Alan Berger and Michele LaRusch.

Px: *x* is psychological state no. 34.
Fx: *x* is functional state no. 7.
a, b are restricted semantic state constants.

Suppose that a person is in a restricted semantic state S_i if and only if the person has a belief individuated by restricted semantic type T_i. Then, according to (a), together with the biconditional, distinct restricted semantic states are distinct psychological states, in which case if one restricted semantic state is psychological state no. 34, then a different restricted semantic state is not psychological state no. 34.

1. $(x \neq y) \rightarrow (Px \rightarrow \sim Py)$.

According to (b), distinct psychological states are distinct functional states, in which case if a semantic state's being psychological state no. 34 precludes a second semantic state's also being psychological state no. 34, then the first semantic state's being functional state no. 7 precludes the second semantic state's being functional state no. 7.

2. $(Px \rightarrow \sim Py) \rightarrow (Fx \rightarrow \sim Fy)$.

According to (c), together with the biconditional, tokens of distinct restricted semantic states may be tokens of a single functional state. To simplify the argument, assume that there is an instantiation of this possibility.

3. $(\exists x,y)(x \neq y \ \& \ Fx \ \& \ Fy)$.

Instantiate 3:

4. $a \neq b \ \& \ Fa \ \& \ Fb$.

Instantiate 1 and 2 and apply the rule for hypothetical syllogism:

5. $(a \neq b) \rightarrow (Fa \rightarrow \sim Fb)$.

From 4 and 5, via modus ponens derive:

6. $Fa \rightarrow \sim Fb$.

After applying the modus ponens rule to 6 and 4, conjoin the consequent of 6 with the last conjunct of 4:

7. $Fb \ \& \sim Fb$.

The last line is an explicit contradiction. Notice that it is no help to make explicit the relativity of restricted semantic type to an overall scheme of interpretation. If restricted semantic types were relativized to interpretations and new variables (I_1 and so on) were introduced to range over interpretations, evidently the argument would still go through. Moreover, although states of a machine may be given any consistent interpretation that serves the purposes of the user or programmer, there is no such license in attributing attitudes to people. Moral considerations aside, it would be an outright error to attribute to Carter beliefs concerning moves in chess when he was negotiating with Brezhnev, regardless of his internal states.

The significance of the first horn of the dilemma is this: As long as functional state tokens can have more than one semantic interpretation—and I take it to be a central feature of the dominant interpretation of the computer analogy that they can—mental states like beliefs cannot be understood as functional states. So unless Fodor and other functionalists are willing to abandon the view that beliefs are functional states (the second horn), I do not see how they can avoid the contradiction, which stems from the very machine analogy that has given functionalism its impetus.

How is it that an easily derivable contradiction has been overlooked? I would conjecture that the answer lies in the apparent fruitfulness of the machine analogy itself. Like any analogy, the machine analogy has two moments, as it were. It must draw both on features of computers and on features of mental states. None of the features relevant to the contradiction has gone unremarked by functionalists; nor, as we have seen, have the consequences of holding (a) and (b) together been overlooked. What no one has thought to do is to conjoin the "mind side" of the analogy (as represented by (a) and (b)) with the "machine side" of the analogy (as represented by (c)). It is only here that the contradiction emerges.

On the one hand, if psychological states are functional states, it seems almost evident that there can be no semantic difference between psychological states without a functional difference between them. On the other hand, implicit in the computer model, as currently conceived, is the idea that any functional state may be given more than one interpretation; and since interpretation is, as Fodor says, "a semantic notion par excellence" (MS, 64), there can be differences in restricted semantic type without functional differences. So the possibility even of molecular duplicates with different beliefs individuated by restricted semantic type is implicit in the computer analogy itself. Thus, it seems that two aspects of the computer analogy are in conflict, as long as the analogy is taken to apply to mental states, such as beliefs, desires, and intentions, that are identified in part by restricted semantic type.[32]

[32] The points in this paragraph emerged from a conversation with Jonathan Malino.

SECOND HORN: BELIEFS ARE NOT
FUNCTIONAL STATES

Perhaps a functionalist could escape the contradiction as follows: Beliefs individuated by restricted semantic type must go the way of the indexical beliefs and *de re* beliefs already excluded from consideration; none is narrow enough to be a functional state. To put it another way, a functionalist may try to accommodate the fact that individuation by restricted semantic type (that is, individuation by obliquely occurring expressions in 'that'-clauses) may fail to coincide with individuation by genuinely narrow state (that is, individuation without presupposing the existence of anything other than the subject).

The argument may proceed from truth-conditional semantics. The claim would be that states individuated by restricted semantic type are not narrow states, on the grounds that states individuated by restricted semantic type presuppose the existence of things other than the subject to whom they are ascribed. Individuation by restricted semantic type, according to this view, is no narrower than individuation by truth condition. But differences in truth condition are not narrow differences; they are not "in the head" but rather are differences "in the world." Familiar arguments conclude that individuation by truth condition does not coincide with individuation by functional role.[33]

Therefore, the argument goes, since differences in restricted semantic type are exhausted by differences in truth condition, it is no surprise that there can be differences in restricted semantic type without differences in functional states; again, this is so, it may be claimed, because functional states are narrow, whereas states individuated by restricted semantic type are not. Thus, the truth-conditional semanticist may cheerfully deny that he ever intended to identify functional states with restricted semantic states.

Without taking issue with this line of reasoning, let me just point out its implications for classical functionalism. In a word, if the functionalist claims that even beliefs individuated by restricted semantic type are too "wide" to be functional states, there seem to be no beliefs left to be candidates for functional states. What is left over "in the head" cannot be coherently characterized as belief that such-and-such. This is so because what is in the head does not suffice to distinguish between belief that p and belief that q, where 'p' and 'q' are obviously nonequivalent and all the terms in both occur obliquely. Beliefs are taken to be attributable by 'that'-clauses; but if, as the truth-conditional semanticist urges, items individuated by the least wide construal of 'that'-

---

[33] See Lycan, "Toward a Homuncular Theory of Believing."

clauses (that is, by restricted semantic type) are still too wide to be functional states, then no beliefs are functional states.[34]

I need not claim (or deny) that there is a *tertium quid*—a difference in restricted semantic type that outruns sameness of physical constitution but is not merely a difference in truth-conditional semantics. But a *tertium quid* seems to be the solipsist's best shot if he wants a belief/desire psychology; for without it, classification by 'that'-clauses obviously violates the formality condition.

Therefore, individuation by 'that'-clauses fails to coincide with individuation by functional role. So if, as functionalists hold, it is functional states that explain behavior (under the preferred descriptions), then beliefs and other states classified by 'that'-clauses do not. In that case, the entire practice of belief/desire explanation is jeopardized.

The conflict between individuation in terms of functional role and individuation in terms of 'that'-clauses seems insuperable.[35] The discussion here has shown that the notion of functional state and the notion of belief state (classified by restricted semantic type) come apart. Thus, on the second horn, no belief that p is ever genuinely narrow, and hence no belief that p can be an explanatory psychological state in the sense required by functionalism. Since on functionalism, (brute) behavior is to be explained in part by tokens of beliefs, to take this line is to abandon functionalism.

To sum up the main line of argument: On the first horn of the dilemma, the functionalist is committed to an inconsistent triad. On the second horn of the dilemma, the functionalist argues that differences in restricted semantic type are really differences in truth condition and, hence, that belief states are not genuinely narrow states in the relevant sense. The latter approach has the immediate consequence that, since

[34] This argument from individuation is an argument against classical functionalism in principle. Some philosophers, such as Stephen P. Stich (*From Folk Psychology to Cognitive Science*, 228ff.) and Paul M. Churchland (*Scientific Realism and the Plasticity of Mind* [Cambridge: Cambridge University Press, 1979], 113ff., and *Matter and Consciousness* [Cambridge, Mass.: MIT/Bradford, 1984], 43ff.), have been dubious of functionalism on empirical grounds; they have entertained the possibility that concepts of the best scientific psychology will not "match up" with intuitive concepts of belief. My arguments may be taken to show that if the best scientific psychology construes explanatory psychological states as classical functional states, then there is a reason in principle for failure of one-to-one correspondence between the taxonomies.

[35] In "Observation Reconsidered" (*Philosophy of Science* 51 [1984], 23–43), Fodor proposes a return to the observation/inference distinction. It may seem possible to use such a distinction to argue that there are beliefs based directly on observation that may be individuated in a way that would qualify them to be classical functional states. I shall argue against such an eventuality in Chapter Four. In any case, few of the beliefs attributed in intentional explanations are based directly on observation.

two tokens of a single functional state may be different beliefs, beliefs are not functional states. Therefore, either beliefs are not psychological states, or psychological states fail to be functional states. In neither case is the functionalist's optimism borne out.

So the machine analogy, as it has been developed by classical functionalists, fails to have room for attributions of attitudes identified by content (construed as restricted semantic type). Far from pointing the way to understanding attitudes identified by content in nonintentional terms, physicalistic deployment of the machine analogy has the opposite effect: To the extent that the machine metaphor of the mind is apt, attribution of attitudes identified by content is not.[36]

---

[36] John Searle has been a persistent critic both of what he calls 'strong AI' and of cognitive science generally. I share some of his views (for example, that mental processes are not purely formal), but not others (for example, that the brain has intrinsically intentional states). See his "Minds, Brains and Programs," with commentary, in *Behavioral and Brain Sciences* 3 (1980), 417–457; *Intentionality: An Essay in the Philosophy of Mind* (Cambridge: Cambridge University Press, 1983); and *Minds, Brains and Science* (Cambridge, Mass.: Harvard University Press, 1984). For other penetrating criticisms of the machine analogy, see Hubert Dreyfus, *What Computers Can't Do*, rev. ed. (New York: Harper Colophon Books, 1979). For an early criticism of mine, see "Why Computers Can't Act," *American Philosophical Quarterly* 18 (1981), 157–163.

· 4 ·

UNSPEAKABLE THOUGHTS

The search for a concept of content suitable for cognitive science so far has proved fruitless. Until now, we have taken the relevant concept of content to be the one appropriate for ordinary general beliefs. This construal has been in line with Fodor's characterization of the psychology that he envisages: "in canonical psychological explanations of the sort that [the representational theory of the mind] contemplates, the required specifications of propositional attitudes are characteristically *de dicto* rather than *de re*," where a *de dicto* specification of a propositional attitude is "approximately one in which substitution of coreferring expressions does not, in general, preserve truth unless the expressions are synonymous."[1]

We have been referring to attitudes that are *de dicto* in this sense as attitudes specified by restricted semantic type, where content is determined by restricted semantic type. However, since two individuals may be physically similar while differing in their attitudes identified by restricted semantic type, we have found that restricted semantic type is still not narrow enough to secure content in the required sense. So let us turn to another attempt to formulate an adequate concept of content that will ensure that molecular duplicates have their narrow contents in common.

Let us suppose that belief is determined by two independent components: some kind of narrow content and a context of evaluation. Molecular duplicates are to share narrow content, but the narrow content by itself does not determine the truth conditions of a belief. What is to be semantically evaluated is not narrow content at all, but rather wide content—that is, narrow content together with a context.

PHENOMENOLOGICAL ACCESSIBILITY

The proposal to be examined in this chapter is that narrow content is expressible in a vocabulary that denotes phenomenologically accessible properties of distal objects, where phenomenologically accessible prop-

---

[1] Jerry A. Fodor, "Cognitive Science and the Twin-Earth Problem," *Notre Dame Journal of Formal Logic* 23 (1982), 101.

erties of distal objects are discernible by casual observation.[2] For example, *being green*, construed as a property not of sense data but of lawns and trees, is the appropriate kind of property to determine narrow contents. (Hence, the present proposal is nonindividualistic in Burge's sense.) Then the truth conditions of beliefs that explain behavior are a product of narrow content together with a context.

The approach may be illustrated by showing how it applies, seemingly in the right way, to Twin Earth cases. The cases are familiar enough: An Earthian and her counterpart on Twin Earth, where what is called 'water' is not H_2O but XYZ, both think (or say) "water is wet" and behave similarly toward the stuff; yet their utterances and beliefs have different truth conditions. How do we give a unified account of their similarities and differences? On Fodor's view, what they share is narrow content, expressed in a vocabulary denoting phenomenologically accessible properties of distal objects. The narrow content of both beliefs (Earthian's and Twin Earthian's) may be expressed like this: The local stuff that is transparent, drinkable, swimmable in, and so on is wet. On Earth, this belief gets evaluated with respect to H_2O; on Twin Earth, it is evaluated with respect to XYZ. (There is no way to say "water is wet" in the vocabulary accessible to narrow content.)[3] So, as we may have hoped, the beliefs that both Earthian and Twin Earthian would express by saying "water is wet" differ in truth conditions; yet the Earthian and Twin Earthian both seem to entertain the same narrow contents. A tidy resolution of Twin Earth cases is significant motivation for a view of propositional attitudes.

Although semantic arguments like the one just given motivate his approach, Fodor needs to give some reason to think that there is a principled distinction between properties that are phenomenologically accessible and those that are not. For this, he turns to arguments that provide a psychological basis for theory-neutral observation, arguments grounded in a sharp distinction between observation and theory, or rather in its psychological counterpart, a distinction between perception and cognition. Whether a given property is observable for an

---

[2] Jerry A. Fodor, "Narrow Content and Meaning Holism" (unpublished). Narrow concepts may be expressed by Ramsey formulas as well as by constants denoting phenomenologically accessible properties of distal objects. Distal objects/events are contrasted with ("proximal") surface irritations of, say, skin or retina.

[3] Fodor, "Narrow Content and Meaning Holism," 22. Although this explicit exposition of narrow content in terms of phenomenologically accessible properties remains unpublished, the view may be pieced together from Fodor's "Cognitive Science and the Twin-Earth Problem" and from his "Observation Reconsidered," *Philosophy of Science* 51 (1984), 23–43, bolstered by *The Modularity of Mind* (Cambridge, Mass.: MIT/Bradford, 1983) and *Psychosemantics* (Cambridge, Mass.: MIT/Bradford, 1987), ch. 2.

organism is largely independent of what the organism believes, since the distinction between perception and cognition is grounded in architectural features of an organism's psychology.[4] Fodor develops the distinction between perception and cognition in *The Modularity of Mind*. There he distinguishes three kinds of cognitive mechanisms: transducers, which have as output representations denoting "proximal" events at sensory surfaces; input systems, which take as input representations of proximal stimulus configurations resulting from transduction and, via "inference-like transformations," deliver as output "representations of the character and distribution of distal objects";[5] and finally, the central processes, the characteristic activity of which is problem solving.

The key to the perception/cognition and observation/nonobservation distinctions is input analysis, performed by the second of Fodor's cognitive mechanisms. Input systems are modular; that is, they are both inferential and "informationally encapsulated" in that their access to information available to the organism is severely restricted. Fodor postulates such mechanisms for each of the senses and for language. The output of these mechanisms may be expressed in a vocabulary denoting phenomenologically accessible properties—properties of objects in the world, not of sensory surfaces, properties "as revealed to casual observation." Since phenomenological accessibility is supposed to be "supervenient" on brain states, narrow content in terms of representations denoting phenomenologically accessible properties is supposed to be shared by molecular duplicates.[6]

Moreover, the language input systems yield "shallow" representations, which seem to provide a basis for a concept of the narrow content of linguistic beliefs. Linguistic input systems, like perceptual ones, are informationally encapsulated, and their output is confined to what can be inferred from premises like these: "Whatever information about the acoustics of the token the mechanisms of sensory transduction provide, whatever information about the linguistic types in L the internally represented grammar provides, *and nothing else*."[7] So, the linguistic input system is at bottom a mechanism for computing linguistic token-to-type relations. In Fodor's words, "Understanding a token sentence presumably involves assigning it a structural description, this being part and parcel of computing a token-to-type relation; and that is pre-

---

[4] Fodor, "Narrow Content and Meaning Holism," 19.
[5] Fodor, "Observation Reconsidered," 42.
[6] Fodor, "Narrow Content and Meaning Holism," 20.
[7] Fodor, "Observation Reconsidered," 37 (emphasis his).

cisely the sort of function we would expect an input system to per-form."[8]

If this psychological picture is broadly correct—and for present pur-poses I shall assume that it is[9]—then it may seem at first glance to pro-vide a basis for distinguishing properties of distal objects that are phe-nomenologically accessible from those that are not, a distinction required for the account of narrow content. The first glance here is mis-leading, however. For the observation/nonobservation (or the percep-tion/cognition) distinction yielded by the modularity of input systems is in fact not the distinction required to secure the account of narrow content. The account of narrow content must be simply insensitive to the line drawn between input systems and central processing.

One way to see this is to ask: Is narrow content fixed by input anal-ysis? It may be supposed so, since the products of the input systems are expressed in just the vocabulary needed for narrow content—that is, in symbols that denote phenomenologically accessible properties of distal objects. Narrow content is to play a semantic role, however; it is to contribute to the truth conditions of attitudes that explain behavior. As Fodor suggests,

(S) (Narrow content + context) → Truth conditions of beliefs.

But if it is to be useful in schema (S), where the truth conditions are those for beliefs that explain behavior, then narrow content—even the narrow content of perceptual beliefs—cannot be fixed by input sys-tems.

This becomes clear if we consider Fodor's distinction between the re-sults of input analysis ("observation") and perceptual belief. He argues that we must "distinguish between *observation* and *the perceptual fix-ation of belief*. It is only for the former that claims for theory neutrality have any plausibility." That is, what is theory-neutral is how things look, how they seem, "the fixation of appearances—what I'm calling observation." So, "to a first approximation, the activity of the modules determines what you would believe if you were going on the appear-ances alone."[10]

The distinction between observation (how things appear to an or-ganism) and belief (what the organism takes to be true) may be illus-trated by the Müller-Lyer illusion: Even after one confirms that the two lines are of equal length, they still look to be unequal. One's visual

---

[8] Fodor, *The Modularity of Mind*, 44.

[9] For discussion of related issues, see Fodor's "Precis of *The Modularity of Mind*," with peer commentary, in *Behavioral and Brain Sciences* 8 (1985), 1–42.

[10] Fodor, "Observation Reconsidered," 40; cf. *The Modularity of Mind*, 102.

processing seems to be isolated from one's belief that they are equal in length. Input systems seem to have no access to the background information at one's disposal. As Fodor puts it, "modules offer hypotheses about the instantiation of observable properties of things, and the fixation of *perceptual belief* is the evaluation of such hypotheses in light of the totality of background theory. According to this usage, what you observe is related to what you believe in, something like the way that what you want is related to what you want on balance."[11] But the individual's contribution to her beliefs—and certainly to those that explain her behavior—are to be determined by "what's in the head" *all things considered*, not simply by "what's in the head" as a result of informationally encapsulated input analysis. Otherwise, the wrong things would be subject to semantic evaluation.

For example, if the truth conditions of your belief about the Müller-Lyer illusion were determined by the results of input analysis (the lines appear to be unequal) together with context (in fact, they are equal), then your belief would be false. But you actually have the true belief that the Müller-Lyer lines are the same length, even though they appear to be of unequal lengths. If Fodor is right, then beliefs (even perceptual beliefs) are results of global cognitive processes, the mechanisms for which seem to be *unencapsulated*. It is such beliefs that we want semantically evaluated, not the intermediate output of perceptual systems.

Therefore, the psychological considerations about modularity of input systems seem idle, at least as far as specifying a concept of narrow content is concerned. On the one hand, if we take narrow content to be the product of input analysis, then the wrong things get semantically evaluated, and narrow content fails to make the right contribution to the truth conditions of the individual's beliefs. On the other hand, if we take narrow content to be the product of higher-level processing, then we remove the psychological warrant for construing narrow content in terms of symbols denoting phenomenologically accessible properties. In that case, the fact (if it is a fact) that input systems are modular is irrelevant to narrow content, which is determined by global processes that fix belief. Thus, the semantic proposals construing narrow content in terms of phenomenological accessibility must stand on their own, with no support from the psychological proposals concerning modularity. Nevertheless, even without independent argument, if narrow content construed in terms of phenomenological accessibility had the

___

[11] Fodor, "Observation Reconsidered," 41.

consequence that narrow contents are necessarily shared by molecular duplicates, we should not argue with success.

COMPLICATIONS

Before I show that narrow content construed in terms of phenomenologically accessible properties of distal objects does *not* have the consequence that narrow contents are necessarily shared by molecular duplicates, let me put aside three other difficulties, not because I find them negligible, but because, even if they are resolved, the deeper issue remains. The first is the difficulty of drawing a nonarbitrary distinction between those properties that are phenomenologically accessible and those that are not, or between observation terms and nonobservation terms. Even if we were to restrict phenomenologically accessible properties to those representable in the output of encapsulated input systems, the difficulties are not removed. To give a sample: Is being a piece of furniture a phenomenologically accessible property? Being a chair? Being a wingchair? Being a Queen Anne chair? Is fuchsia phenomenologically accessible? Is Middle C?

The second difficulty concerns observable properties of utterances. Linguistic input systems, like perceptual ones, are "informationally encapsulated," and their output is confined to what can be inferred from premises like these: "Whatever information about the acoustics of the token the mechanisms of sensory transduction provide, whatever information about the linguistic types in L the internally represented grammar provides, *and nothing else.*"[12]

The linguistic input system is basically a mechanism for computing token-to-type relations. Fodor claims that such computation is isolated from background information, and he tries to explain away evidence that seems to indicate otherwise. But it would seem that the hearer could not compute token-to-type relations without background information concerning which language is being spoken. For example, a perfectly bilingual speaker could not compute the type of a token of 'aggravated assault is serious' on the basis of nothing more than acoustical information. Since the semantic type of such a token depends upon which language it is in, information outside the parser that computes sentence type would be required in order to determine type from token.[13]

---

[12] Ibid., 37 (emphasis his).

[13] Jerry Samet has pointed out that a multilingual speaker may have a different linguistic input system for each language that she speaks and that a higher-level mechanism

Another indication of at least the lack of clarity of the notion of the observable properties of utterances comes from a comment by Fodor. Properties of utterances that are not to be counted as observable include "being uttered with the intention of deceiving John; being ill-advised in the context, containing a word that is frequently used in restaurants where they sell hamburgers. . . ." By contrast, observable properties "ought to include things like: being an utterance of a sentence, being an utterance of a sentence that contains the word 'the,' being an utterance of a sentence that contains a word that refers to trees."[14]

If "being an utterance of a sentence that contains a word that refers to trees" is an observable property of utterances of sentences, then being an utterance of a sentence that contains a word that refers to water should likewise be an observable property. But it is precisely the fact that the latter is not an observable property that forces Fodor to make the observation/nonobservation distinction in the first place. The point of the distinction is to isolate a class of properties detectable without background information. In that case, being an utterance of a sentence that contains a word that refers to water is not an observable property of tokens.

Consider an utterance of 'water is wet.' In some contexts, the utterance has the property of containing a word that refers to water and would be taken to have that property; in other contexts, the utterance does not have the property of containing a word that refers to water and would not be taken to have that property by the same hearers. Whether or not a particular utterance has that property cannot be detected apart from background information.

To see this, suppose that, in developing Star Wars technology, the United States discovers Twin Earth and scientists observe it for some time without attempting to communicate with its inhabitants. By watching Twin Earth scientists, our scientists discover that what Twin Earthians call "water" is really XYZ. At some point, our scientists decide to make their presence known, and among the first communications received from Twin Earth is a piece of information: "Water is wet." Given standard intuitions concerning Twin Earth, our scientists would not take this token to have the property, observable or not, of containing a word that refers to water. Twin Earth has no water, and, in the example, our scientists know it. But in other contexts—at home,

could trigger the appropriate encapsulated system. Even if this is the case, however, the computation of token-to-type relations still seems not as isolated as Fodor suggests.

[14] Fodor, "Observation Reconsidered," 39.

CHAPTER FOUR

say—those same scientists would take such a token to have the property of containing a word that refers to water. Whether the token has the property in question, and whether the token is taken to have the property, are determined by context. Hence, the property of containing a word that refers to water (or to trees or to anything else) is not an observable property of tokens.

Suppose that Fodor is merely mistaken in the example and that properties like the one of being an utterance of a sentence that contains a word that refers to trees are not observable properties. In that case, it is difficult to see how any mechanism can compute what has been said on the basis of observable properties alone.

On the one hand, as Twin Earth cases show, a property such as that of being an utterance of a sentence that contains a word that refers to trees is not a property of any utterance taken in isolation; therefore, such properties are not observable properties of linguistic utterances. On the other hand, ruling out such semantic properties of utterances as observable seems at most to leave only acoustical and syntactic properties as observable, in which case input analysis does not suffice for narrow content in terms of phenomenological accessibility. The problem cases concerning phenomenological accessibility, especially regarding utterances, could be multiplied; but these are enough to illustrate the complex matters that must be resolved.

The final difficulty to be set aside concerns the completeness of specification of narrow contents. The complication may be illustrated by asking: Are narrow contents purely qualitative, or do they have indexicals as constituents? Suppose that they have indexicals as constituents. Then consider the consequences. Narrow contents are to contribute to the truth conditions of beliefs that explain behavior. Such beliefs, as Fodor emphasizes,[15] are specified *de dicto*. But as Fodor remarks in passing, "since indexicals always occur *transparently* in descriptions of propositional attitudes, no such formula [containing indexicals] can, even in principle, specify a belief *de dicto*."[16] Thus, if narrow contents are constituents of the *de dicto* beliefs that are to explain behavior, and if *de dicto* beliefs must be specified by formulas free of indexicals, then narrow contents cannot admit indexicals, at least not without qualification.

But could narrow contents be purely qualitative? Suppose that we tried to express the narrow content of the belief that water is wet in

[15] For example, see Fodor's "Cognitive Science and the Twin-Earth Problem" and "Methodological Solipsism Considered as a Research Strategy in Cognitive Psychology," *Behavioral and Brain Sciences* 3 (1980), 63–109.
[16] Fodor, "Cognitive Science and the Twin-Earth Problem," 117.

some language like this: The local stuff that is drinkable, transparent, sailable on . . . is wet. No matter how we fill in the ellipses, we have no guarantee of adequate specification of an individual's concept of water. This is so because we generally lack fully individuating qualitative descriptions of the things about which we have beliefs.[17] The absence of wholly qualitative identifying descriptions suggests that even the narrow content will have some indexical element—for example, 'the liquid that I brush my teeth with,' 'the stuff in that lake over there.'

Although unwelcome, the appearance of an indexical element need not be fatal to the project of formulating a concept of narrow content.[18] (It does suggest, however, that the beliefs that explain behavior are not *de dicto* in Fodor's sense.) We still may supply a semantics for indexical terms, according to which molecular duplicates could have the same narrow contents expressed indexically. One may approach the task by way of the kind of self-ascription theory of belief suggested by Roderick Chisholm and David Lewis:[19] The content of the belief is not a proposition or sentence but a property that the believer ascribes to himself. In our case, the narrow content of the belief that water is wet may be given by the self-ascribed property expressed by the following sentence:

[17] See Tyler Burge, "Belief *De Re*," *Journal of Philosophy* 74 (1977), 338–362. Also see Saul A. Kripke, "A Puzzle about Belief," in *Meaning and Use*, ed. Avishai Margalit (Dordrecht: D. Reidel, 1979), 239–283.

[18] It may seem that the indexical elements could be avoided by adding to the narrow content of each a reference to language: 'referred to as "water." ' Besides the unhappy consequence that the narrow content of beliefs about water would turn out to be beliefs about language, this addition does not eliminate the indexical element anyway. Since a third speech community may use what sounds like the English word 'water' to refer to cyanide, the addition of 'referred to as "water" ' is still insufficient to identify the narrow content. What is needed is a further specification: 'referred to as "water" in my speech community.' (Fodor has expressed doubts about individuating speech communities.) So the indexical is not avoided. Moreover, the objections raised by Burge ("Other Bodies," in *Thought and Object: Essays on Intentionality*, ed. Andrew Woodfield [Oxford: Clarendon Press, 1982], 97–120) to treating natural-kinds terms as indexical apply here, for the move under consideration would seem to make every term in every language an indexical.

[19] Peter van Inwagen has suggested combining appeal to phenomenological properties with self-ascription theory as a response to what he calls "Putnam's Intuition" about natural kinds. See his review of volume one of David Lewis's *Philosophical Papers* in *Mind* 95 (1986), 246–256. Also, David F. Austin has argued that self-ascription theories are just notational variants of Stephen Schiffer's propositional theory of belief; see Austin's *What's the Meaning of 'This'?* (Ithaca, N.Y.: Cornell University Press, forthcoming). The possibility of an alternative to a qualitative approach to narrow content will be considered in the next section.

x is such that (the local stuff[20] that is drinkable, sailable on, that *x* brushes *x*'s teeth with . . .) is wet.

Now, one may suppose that the above expresses the common narrow content of the Earthian's and the Twin Earthian's belief that each would express by uttering (what sounds like) "water is wet." This suggestion has several drawbacks, however. First, as our consideration of 'red' in the next section will imply, the same problem that arises with 'water' extends to more observational predicates like 'drinkable,' 'brushes,' or any other qualitative term. Second, there is no principled way to determine what to include in the parentheses, still less an indication of how to complete the specification. Finally, standard readings like that just given are faulty. Suppose that an Earthian transported to Twin Earth went walking in the Twin woods and uttered, "There's water in that stream over there." Since the local stuff on Twin Earth that is drinkable and so on *is* in that stream, the belief that our Earthian expressed would be evaluated as true. But since there is no water on Twin Earth, in that stream or elsewhere, his belief is false.[21]

Thus, it is just as unclear that narrow contents can be adequately specified without fully individuating representations as it is that a nonarbitrary distinction exists between phenomenologically accessible properties and others. But even if these difficulties—the absence of a principled observation/nonobservation distinction and the apparent incompleteness of the conceptual content of most of our beliefs—were overcome, we should still lack a concept of narrow content in terms of representations of phenomenologically accessible properties that would ensure that molecular duplicates share their narrow contents.

OBSERVATION TERMS IN MENTALESE

Recall that Fodor emphasizes—with good reason, in my opinion—that the properties denoted by representations are not just phenomenal properties (such as would be exemplified by sense data) but are properties of physical objects in the environment. Fodor's answer to the question "By virtue of what does a representation denote what it does?" is broadly causal. In a critical discussion of causal accounts of

---

[20] Fodor treats 'local stuff' as indicating what stuff (for example, H_2O or XYZ) is relevant to evaluating the belief in question. "If I had to make a stab at it, I would guess that relevant localness is fundamentally an etiological notion so that what the Principle of Reasonableness is telling us to do, in this case, is to evaluate beliefs about phi-stuff with respect to the kind of phi-stuff that gave rise to them." "Cognitive Science and the Twin-Earth Problem," 113.

[21] The example comes from Burge's "Other Bodies."

representation, he remarks, "The point of all of this, I emphasize, is *not* to argue against causal accounts of representation. I think, in fact, that something along the causal line is the best hope we have for saving intentionalist theorizing, both in psychology and in semantics."[22]

Fodor, who takes mental symbols in a language of thought to be the primary bearers of semantic properties, has argued at length that "the internal language [Mentalese] must be rich enough to express the extension of any natural language predicate that can be learned."[23] So Mentalese in general is not restricted to denoting phenomenologically accessible properties. Nevertheless, it may be that Mentalese can aid the proponent of narrow content. Perhaps Mentalese, unlike natural language, represents phenomenologically accessible properties in such a way that:

(R) For any type of Mentalese representation, R, such that R denotes a phenomenologically accessible property, if S_1 and S_2 are molecular duplicates, then S_1 has a token of R if and only if S_2 has a token of R.

For the moment, suppose that (R) is true. Then it may seem that we have at hand a concept of narrow content that ensures that molecular duplicates have all the same contents. The proposal would be that narrow contents should be construed as Mentalese representations of phenomenologically accessible properties of distal objects to which they are causally connected. Then, by (R), molecule-for-molecule duplicates would have the same narrow content.

Unfortunately, (R), together with two other components of Fodor's view and the assumption that *being red* is a phenomenologically accessible property, leads to a contradiction. For it will emerge that the following set of statements is inconsistent:

[22] Jerry A. Fodor, "Semantics, Wisconsin Style," *Synthese* 59 (1984), 234. The idea of causal connection is quite loose and may be filled in in various ways. For example, the appropriate causal connection could be restricted to normally functioning individuals. In "Psychosemantics," Fodor outlines a broadly teleological account of wide representation, which assumes that cognitive mechanisms have certain normal functions. My discussion does not abrogate his teleological assumptions, which in any case, I suspect, threaten his physicalism. There seems no bar to supposing that there could be molecular duplicates, one of whose cognitive mechanisms function normally and the other's not; then, to the extent to which the semantic properties of their mental representations are determined by normal functioning, the molecular duplicates differ in their semantic properties. Representation in this sense is thus too wide to underwrite narrow content.

[23] Jerry A. Fodor, *The Language of Thought* (Cambridge, Mass.: Harvard University Press, 1979), 82.

(1) Representations denote properties of distal objects to which they are causally connected.

(2) If two tokens of representations denote different properties, then they are tokens of different types.

(3) (= R) For any type of Mentalese representation, R, such that R denotes a phenomenologically accessible property, if S_1 and S_2 are molecular duplicates, then S_1 has a token of R if and only if S_2 has a token of R.

To bring out the contradiction, I shall resort to a (regrettably exotic) thought experiment.

Consider another possible world, Mars. Suppose that central to the Martians' religion (whose origins are lost in prehistory) is the wearing of special glasses. Imagine the elaborate "emplacement" ceremony practiced on infants shortly after birth. The glasses are attached in such a way that they cannot be removed, except when exchanged for larger pairs as the youth matures. The actual exchanges, considered quite dangerous, are also attended by ritual, during which the young person is unconscious. Since all other attempts to remove the glasses are taboo, no one has ever been known to remove the glasses.

Further suppose that there are no red objects on Mars; nothing on Mars reflects the appropriate wavelengths for red. Nevertheless, Martians do enjoy a full range of experiences because their ritual glasses (little computers, actually) transform certain ambient energies that would be perceived as gray in the absence of the glasses; when stimulated by light reflected from certain gray objects, the Martians' transducers are affected in exactly the same way that ours are when we see red.

Now suppose that there is an Earthly religion, practiced similarly. The only difference is that the glasses used by the Earthians are clear. Now consider an Earthian and a Martian who are molecularly identical. The only differences between them are environmental: no red distal objects on Mars, but compensating red glasses; red distal objects on Earth, but clear glasses. Neither an individual's transducers nor her visual input systems can detect whether the individual is in an Earthian or a Martian environment.

Earthian and Martian are the same in their computational, functional, neurophysiological, and other "internal" states. The relevant difference between the Earthian and her Martian counterpart is this: Most of the beliefs that the Earthian would express by uttering 'red' are about red things, but none of the beliefs that the Martian would express by uttering the acoustically identical sound are about red things; most are about gray things.

Now, suppose that the English-speaking Earthian tokens the Mentalese representation that some round things are red, which in part causes her to utter in English, "Some round things are red." At the same time, the Martian produces a Mentalese representation molecularly identical to the Earthian's. This representation in part causes the Martian to utter, in what sounds like English but is not, "Some round things are red."[24]

By (1), the Earthian's and Martian's Mentalese representations denote properties of distal objects to which they are causally connected. The Earthian's relevant representations are caused in the most straightforward way by red things. The causal chain is traced from red objects that reflect light of a certain wavelength to stimulation of visual transducers by light of that wavelength, through the input systems, perhaps through some central processing. The output of these computations is a Mentalese representation, R_e, which denotes the phenomenologically accessible property of *being red*.

But if it is by virtue of its causal connection to red things that the Earthian's Mentalese representation, R_e, denotes the property of being red, then the Martian's Mentalese representation, R_m, does not denote the property of being red. For no Mentalese representation of any Martian is causally connected in any way to any red thing; there are no red things on Mars. Indeed, the cause of the Martian's representation is traceable to gray things, which reflect light of a certain wavelength, which is transformed by the glasses into light of the wavelength reflected by red things, which then impinges on her visual transducers in exactly the same way that the Earthian's transducers are stimulated. Moreover, this causal chain is not idiosyncratic; all over Mars, there is a systematic connection between gray things and Mentalese representations of the same type as R_m.[25]

Here, then, is the contradiction: By (1) and (2), R_e and R_m are differ-

[24] The Martians do not speak English because what sounds like 'red' in Martian is a different word from the English 'red.' Unlike 'I,' 'here,' and 'now,' 'red' is not an indexical, which gets evaluated differently in different contexts. See note 18.

[25] This thought experiment is a kind of converse of standard inverted-spectrum cases, according to which the same type of external source of stimulation is associated with differences in qualitative character: The same fire engine that looks red to one person looks to a second the way that grass looks to the first (although the second is *functionally* equivalent to the first and both call the color 'red'). In my case, different types of external sources of stimulation are associated with the same types of qualitative character: Gray things look to the Martian the way that red things look to the (*molecularly* identical) Earthian.

ent types of representation, but by (3), R_e and R_m are the same type. This contradiction vitiates the proposal that narrow content be construed in terms of Mentalese representations of phenomenologically accessible properties of distal objects.

Let me dispose quickly of two objections: (i) Someone may object: Suppose that a child says, "Some animals are unicorns." We should say that she has a false belief about unicorns, even though there are no unicorns to have caused her representation of unicorns. Perhaps we should say likewise that the Martian has beliefs about red things, in which case Earthian and Martian may share narrow contents after all. But this objection is closed to someone who is trying to isolate an observation language (which is to exclude natural-kind terms). Even with the lack of clarity about what are to count as phenomenologically accessible properties, *being a unicorn* is not a likely candidate for such a property; if it were, the point of isolating such properties would be lost. But if representations of unicorns are not plausibly supposed to satisfy (R) in the first place, they are not appropriate counterexamples to the argument against (R). The advocate of an austere observation language would not give the same account of the semantics of terms like 'unicorn' (or 'tiger') and terms like 'red' in any case. Since 'unicorn' will not be an observation term anyway, beliefs about unicorns, like beliefs about water, will have causal histories different from those of beliefs about red things. So, the fact that one may have beliefs about unicorns (in an intuitive sense of 'about') even if there are no unicorns to cause those beliefs is no grounds for supposing that one may have beliefs about red things even if there are no red things to cause those beliefs.

(ii) Perhaps we should say that *if* the Martian's representations had had a typical or standard causal history, they would have been caused by red things. To this, I reply that we may assume that the Martian's case is atypical only in relation to a population that provides some norm of what is to count as typical. Different kinds of causal chains are typical or standard in different possible worlds. Since there is no sense to an idea of typical or standard causal chains across possible worlds, the typicality of the history of the Martian's representations can be determined only relative to her possible world, where she is undoubtedly typical.[26] Since representations like the Martian's are typically (indeed, uniformly) caused by interaction with gray things that affect all Mar-

[26] See David Lewis, "Mad Pain and Martian Pain," in *Readings in the Philosophy of Psychology*, vol. 1, ed. Ned Block (Cambridge, Mass.: Harvard University Press, 1980), 216–222, for a population-relative version of functionalism.

tians' transducers in the way that red things affect ours, it would seem question-begging to deny that the Martians are in normal circumstances. They are in circumstances normal on Mars.[27]

The only way that I see to avoid the conclusion that Earthian and Martian differ in narrow contents, and hence that (R) is false or at least inconsistent with other elements of Fodor's view, is to resort to phenomenalism, a desperate move that Fodor is understandably unwilling to make. But even that move would be to no avail unless it could be shown that narrow contents in terms of properties of sense data could make the required contribution to truth conditions of beliefs. In any case, what has gone wrong, I think, is that in order to avoid phenomenalism, Fodor invokes phenomenologically accessible properties of distal objects, that is, properties of objects in the environment. But if narrow contents represent properties of objects in the environment, then there is no guarantee that molecular duplicates share narrow contents.

In summary, the account of narrow content in terms of phenomenologically accessible properties of distal objects was recommended for the way that it accommodates the Twin Earth thought experiment. But it turns out that this account is heir to difficulties analogous to those raised by the Twin Earth stories. The same difficulties that arise for natural-kind terms like 'water,' in English or in Mentalese, also arise for observation terms like 'red,' in English or in Mentalese.[28] So it seems that narrow content, understood as expressible in an observation language denoting phenomenologically accessible properties, fails to provide the needed concept of content.

More on Mentalese

Many critics have found fault with Mentalese as a nonconventional language of thought.[29] I should like simply to pose a challenge to anyone invoking Mentalese as a vehicle for narrow content. The challenge arises from considering relations between Mentalese and natural lan-

---

[27] If one suspects that wearing glasses per se abrogates normal conditions (a suspicion confined, I imagine, to those who do not wear glasses), we could modify the example so that the normal atmosphere on Mars has the same effect as the glasses.

[28] Kripke suggests certain similarities between natural-kinds terms and terms like 'yellow.' *Naming and Necessity* (Cambridge Mass.: Harvard University Press, 1980), 128n.

[29] For example, see Patricia Churchland, "A Perspective on Mind-Brain Research," *Journal of Philosophy* 78 (1980), 185–207, esp. 189. Also see Daniel C. Dennett, "A Cure for the Common Code?" in his *Brainstorms: Philosophical Essays on Mind and Psychology* (Montgomery Vt.: Bradford, 1978), 90–108; and Gilbert Harman, "Language Learning" in *Readings in the Philosophy of Psychology*, vol. 2, ed. Ned Block (Cambridge, Mass.: Harvard University Press, 1981), 38–44.

guage—relations about which Fodor gives little, if any, guidance—and is brought out by a question: In principle, is it possible to specify in English a particular narrow content? Before considering the possibility that narrow content is not specifiable in English, let us take a look at four construals of narrow content: (A) [(a) and (b)] and (B) [(a) and (b)].

(A) For now, we shall disregard the difficulties we have seen in specifying generally narrow contents nonindexically and assume that narrow contents are wholly qualitative. Returning to the Earthian and Martian, we ask: What are the narrow contents of the belief expressed by the Earthian when she sincerely said in English, "Some round things are red," and of the belief expressed by the Martian when she emitted an acoustic twin?

(Aa) Consider the view that representations are typed by their (narrow) conceptual roles. Perhaps conceptual roles will yield shared narrow contents expressible in English. Since the Martian's representations caused by gray things have the same inferential connections as the Earthian's representations caused by red things, then, on the proposal to type representations by conceptual role, the Martian's representation R_m is of the same type as Earthian's representation R_e. On the proposal that conceptual role is to yield narrow contents, how can we express in English the narrow content of the beliefs expressed by (what sounds like) 'Some round things are red?'

If narrow contents are to be shared by Earthian and Martian, they cannot be expressed by a term like 'red.' Since nothing is red on Mars, what makes R_m the type (individuated by conceptual role) of representation that it is has nothing to do with the property of being red. On a nonphenomenalist view, then, whether wholly qualitative representations are typed by narrow conceptual role or by distal objects that cause them, 'red' cannot help to express narrow contents that the Earthian and Martian (putatively) have in common.

Or, from the other direction, the extension of 'red' in English is the set of red things; the extension of 'red' in Martian is the set of gray things.[30] So 'red' in English and 'red' in Martian differ in extension.

---

[30] This seems in accord with Kripke's views as expressed in *Naming and Necessity*, 128n and 140n. Kripke points out that "if we had different neural structures, if atmospheric conditions had been different, if we had been blind, and so on, then yellow objects would have done no such thing [as tending to produce certain characteristic sensations]." In that case, I take it, the extension of 'yellow,' whose reference is rigidly fixed by "the external physical property that tends to produce in normal conditions such-and-such sensations," would have been different. Since different external physical properties satisfy

Since the Martian word differs in extension from 'red,' we cannot translate it into English as 'red' but would have to invent a term, for example, 'fred.' But "for every predicate in the natural language it must be possible to express a coextensive predicate in the internal code."[31] So 'red' in English and 'red' in Martian must have different Mentalese representations, in which case Earthian and Martian do not have the same narrow contents.

(Ab) Consider the alternative of typing wholly qualitative representations by their phenomenal qualities. In that case it may seem that, in light of the neurophysiological similarity between Earthian and Martian, they may have representations with the same phenomenal qualities and hence the same narrow content. On this proposal, can the narrow content of the belief expressed by (what sounds like) 'Some round things are red' be expressed in English? Since the English term 'red' has no application in the Martian environment, whatever Earthian and Martian share cannot be expressed in English by means of the English term 'red.' Perhaps someone would suggest that their shared narrow content could be expressed as, "Some things that produce roundlike sensations produce redlike sensations."

Besides being (understandably) unpalatable to cognitive scientists like Fodor, this suggestion has further difficulties. In particular, 'redlike' in English seems close to synonymous to 'resembles red things,' in which case the meaning of the term 'redlike' is dependent on the meaning of the term 'red' in English. But unless we can identify things as being redlike without comparing them to red objects, which do not exist on Mars, then Earthian and Martian do not share redlike sensations, any more than they share representations of red things.[32]

Here is another stab: Suppose that the English term 'redlike' is rigidly fixed by whatever is qualitatively similar to the sensations actually produced in Earthians by red objects. Then, even though there are no red things on Mars, we English speakers can attribute to the Martians redlike sensations by attributing to them sensations qualitatively similar to certain of our sensations that happen to be produced by red things. But which of their sensations are those? There must be some standard of similarity of sensations without reference to external red objects; otherwise, the proposal is empty. (The problem here is not the vagueness of the notion of similarity but rather what would make a Martian

the reference-fixing descriptions on Earth and on Mars, English 'red' and Martian 'red' have different extensions.

[31] Fodor, *The Language of Thought*, 85.

[32] Phenomenalism has been widely criticized. See, for example, Roderick Chisholm, *Perceiving* (Ithaca, N.Y.: Cornell University Press, 1957).

sensation a paradigm case of one phenomenally similar to an Earthian's sensation of red.)

One suggestion that does not refer to external red objects is the neurophysiological similarity of the Earthian and Martian. The Martian enjoys redlike sensations when he is in the same neurophysiological states that are (or that produce) redlike sensations in Earthians. If, however, we were to take redlike sensations to be individuated by certain neurophysiological states (a practically impossible suggestion), then we would no longer be typing representations by their phenomenal qualities. In addition to assuming that all redlike sensations are subserved by a single type of neurophysiological state, to *type* representations in terms of neurophysiological states would seem to abandon the project of showing how states *identified by content* can be physicalistically adequate altogether.

(B) Now suppose that narrow contents are not wholly qualitative.

(Ba) The thought experiment also defeats at least some versions of what Stephen White has called the "indexical description theory of meaning," according to which the meaning of 'water,' for example,

> would be characterized by descriptive terms, for example, 'whatever is wet, fills the lakes, comes out of faucets, etc.,' which would pick out water in the actual world and which, together with the explicit indexical 'here,' would insure that 'water' as used by us functions rigidly to denote, in every possible world, H_2O. 'Water' as used on twin earth will have a different meaning, at least in the sense that it will denote XYZ in any possible world.[33]

Since 'red' is a paradigm of a qualitative or descriptive predicate, the same kind of argument that showed that molecular duplicates may fail to express the same meaning when they both utter (what sounds like) 'red' can show that molecular duplicates may fail to express the same concepts when they both utter (what sounds like) 'wet,' or 'fills the lakes,' or 'comes out of faucets.'

(Bb) Perhaps a different approach to narrow contents as nonqualitative would permit specification of particular narrow contents in English. Consider, for example, Stephen White's proposal. On analogy with David Kaplan's treatment of indexicals in terms of content and character, suppose that each word or concept in a speaker's vocabulary has two components: an indexical component and an "autonomous"

---

[33] Stephen L. White, "Partial Character and the Language of Thought," *Pacific Philosophical Quarterly* 63 (1982), 354. I did not see White's argument against the indexical description theory until I had formulated mine.

component that does "not depend on environmental facts which could vary from one physical duplicate to another."[34] (Kaplan's circumstances of evaluation are termed by White 'contexts of evaluation,' and Kaplan's contents—that is, functions from circumstances of evaluation to truth values—White calls 'intensions.') The lesson of Twin Earth is that the character (that is, function from contexts of utterance to intensions) of ostensibly nonindexical predicates (like 'water' or 'red') varies with the context of acquisition of the word.

Thus, White introduces another function—partial character—from possible contexts of acquisition of a word W to characters of W. (A possible context of acquisition is an ordered pair of a possible world and a functional state token that exists in that world.) Once acquired, an ostensibly nonindexical word like 'red' has a constant character; that is, every context of utterance is mapped into the same intension (the same function from context of evaluation to denotation). Now, Earthian and Martian seem to share partial characters: Given the same contexts of acquisition, Earthian's and Martian's words would have had the same character. Partial character, then, is to supply the sense in which functional duplicates share beliefs.

Despite its elegance, this proposal seems to result in bizarre semantic categorizing. Let us use 'semantic counterparts' to denote members of a set of words whose characters are the values of a given partial character function. Then 'red' and 'fred' in the story of the Earthian and Martian are semantic counterparts. But other of their semantic counterparts would include words that denote no visible property. For example, consider Venus, where a functional duplicate of the Earthian acquires a word that sounds like 'red' in situations in which certain invisible objects emit ultrasonic sound waves that are transformed by the atmosphere into energy that produces tokens of the type produced on Earth by red things.[35] Thus, words used to denote red things, gray things, and even no visible things are all semantic counterparts.

The oddness of taking partial character as semantic classification becomes more apparent with terms whose application is farther removed from observation. Return to the story of Subject E, who believes that aggravated assault is serious, and Subject N, who believes that provoked assault is serious. They acquired the relevant words in similar contexts of acquisition, defined by the ordered pair consisting of the same possible world and tokens of the same functional type that exist

[34] Ibid., 354. If my argument is correct, then there are no autonomous predicates.

[35] Cf. White, "Partial Character," 355, where White criticizes the indexical description theory.

in that world. There is no functional difference between them with respect to the use of the words in question; they may even be (as the two girls described in Chapter Five clearly are) functional duplicates. If they are, then they have the same partial characters; and thus, on the partial character view, their words are semantic counterparts. For example, 'aggravated assault' for Subject E and (what sounds like) 'aggravated assault' for Subject N are taken to be semantic counterparts. But as the story was told, the relation between 'aggravated assault' in the mouth of Subject E and (what sounds like) 'aggravated assault' in the mouth of Subject N is just an acoustical coincidence, with no semantic significance. In general, there seems to be no natural semantic grouping of words whose characters are the values of a particular function; it is only an accident that a single partial character function has among its values both the character of 'aggravated assault' and 'provoked assault.'

A related worry about the proposal that partial character captures semantic similarities among duplicates is that there seems to be no principled way to determine whether or not any particular character is in the range of a given partial character function. Who would have thought that the characters of 'aggravated assault' and 'provoked assault' would both be values of a single partial character function? How are we to determine what other values it may have? There seem to be no systematic or predictable semantic similarities between functional duplicates. Thus, it is unclear that particular partial character functions are specifiable anyway. To the extent that they are not, they are of little help in showing how the presumably semantic similarities of functional duplicates can be specified in English.[36]

The difficulties of specifying narrow contents, wholly qualitative or not, that are expressible in English pale beside the consequences of taking narrow contents to be *inexpressible* in English. For, if narrow contents are inexpressible, it would seem that the concept of narrow content could not have the required role in belief/desire psychology. First, inexpressible narrow contents would undermine the whole project of pressing belief into the service of physicalistic psychology, a project Fodor has described as follows:

> [W]e need the notion of the content of a mental representation to reconstruct the notion of the content of a *de dicto* propositional

---

[36] Moreover, the proposal concerning partial character seems to leave out the believer's point of view altogether, and it assumes the adequacy of a strongly reductive form (devoid of any intentional or semantic notions) of the causal theory of reference, which I shall call into question in Chapter Five.

attitude; and we need the notion of a *de dicto* propositional attitude in order to reconstruct the notion of the intentionality of behavior; and we need the notion of the intentionality of behavior in order to state a variety of psychological generalizations which appear to be (more or less) counterfactual supporting and true, and which subsume behavior in virtue of its satisfaction of intentional descriptions.[37]

If narrow contents are inexpressible in English, then it is difficult to see how the notion of the content of a mental representation could aid in reconstructing the notion of the content of a *de dicto* propositional attitude; we could never say how narrow content is related to the content of a *de dicto* propositional attitude. But since it is the latter that Fodor invokes to explain behavior, we could never say or know how narrow content bears on explanation of behavior. Such a concept of narrow content would hardly bolster belief/desire psychology: What is the point of a belief/desire psychology whose fundamental concept can be applied to nothing?[38]

Moreover, if we could never specify the narrow content of an individual's belief, we could never say how that narrow content contributed to truth conditions of behavior-explaining beliefs; in that case, narrow contents would seem unable to serve their purported semantic function. Fodor says that "questions about the (narrow or other) content of propositional attitudes are reduced to questions about the logico-semantic properties of mental symbols."[39] But if narrow contents in Mentalese are untranslatable into English, these logico-semantic properties turn out to be private in such a strong sense that we cannot say what they are. It is difficult to see how a science can be erected on such

[37] Fodor, "Cognitive Science and the Twin-Earth Problem," 101.

[38] In "Social Content and Psychological Content" (in *Contents of Thought: Proceedings of the 1985 Oberlin Colloquium in Philosophy*, ed. Robert H. Grimm and Daniel D. Merrill [Tucson: University of Arizona Press, 1988]), Brian Loar says: "If we then lack specifications of narrow content, in the sense in which we have specifications of wide, social content, that must mean that psychological explanation does not require such specifications." But since explanations must be statable, if psychological explanation does not require specification of narrow contents, narrow contents are not explanatory. In that case, the project of distinguishing (wide) social content from (narrow) psychological content seems to lose its point. Loar's attempt to establish the independence of psychological content from "social factors" is unsuccessful, I think, because his attributions of psychological content presuppose social facts, such as the fact that the subject is speaking a public language. Moreover, Loar's examples do not require the interpretation that he gives them. Thus, I think that his claim that psychological contents of beliefs attributed in ordinary explanations are not individuated by 'that'-clauses is unjustified.

[39] Fodor, "Narrow Content and Meaning Holism," 17.

private properties. Far from providing a basis for semantics of natural language, recourse to narrow content in terms of untranslatable Mentalese would simply make natural language a mystery.

Finally, the proposal of inexpressible Mentalese bristles with counterintuitive consequences. If Mentalese is the medium of thought, and if Mentalese expressions are inexpressible in English, then no one has ever had a thought in English, in which case no one has ever had the slightest idea what she was thinking. Let me mention just a few consequences of such a proposal. All our practical reasoning and deliberation—concerning, say, whether to accept a particular offer of a job—would go on behind our backs, so to speak. (Then we should be surprised when we find ourselves accepting one offer and declining another.) Or sincerity, ordinarily conceived as saying what one really believes, would be impossible. For if one's propositional attitudes are in Mentalese, and if Mentalese is inexpressible in English, then one can never say what one believes. Generally, inexpressible Mentalese would make a mystery of the connections between what we think and what we say.

The only way to ensure that molecular duplicates have all their "narrow contents" in common is to rob the concept of narrow content of the semantic significance that it has for beliefs and other attitudes. For if narrow contents are expressible in English, then they are not necessarily shared by molecular duplicates; but if they are not expressible in English, then their connection to natural language is severed and we have no grounds for assigning them any semantic (or any other) properties at all. It would seem that we could know no more about such "content" than we could about Kant's noumenal world. A concept of narrow content with no specifiable semantic properties is called 'content' only by courtesy.[40]

---

[40] I wish to thank Jerry A. Fodor for permission to cite his unpublished "Psychosemantics, or Where Do Truth Conditions Come From?" and "Narrow Content and Meaning Holism."

· 5 ·

THE ELUSIVENESS
OF CONTENT

Vast philosophical energies are being expended in order to provide a physicalistic account of mind. Such an account either would countenance mental states identified by content or it would not. In Part I we have been seeking a concept of content that is conducive to the physicalistic project of providing nonintentional and nonsemantic conditions for mental states. In Part II we shall consider the possibility that, common sense to the contrary, our mental states are not "contentful."

Focusing largely on Fodor's developing conception of cognitive science, we have examined, and found wanting, several approaches to a concept of content that satisfies the physicalistic constraint. In this chapter I want to suggest the reason for the failure to formulate an adequate concept of content—a reason that suggests that no physicalistic psychology can employ a concept of content.

The requisite concept of content is called upon to do two things: it must allow content to play a semantic role in the determination of truth conditions of an individual's beliefs,[1] and it must allow "contentful" states to figure in the etiology of an individual's behavior in a way that permits generalizations about content. As we have seen, truth conditions are too "wide" to individuate behavior-explaining states. For example, the belief that an English speaker expresses by saying "water is wet" has the same truth conditions as a belief expressed by "H_2O is wet." But for purposes of explaining behavior, we should not count them both as expressing a single belief.[2] To play its explanatory role, then, content must be understood more "narrowly" than identification by truth conditions permits, and the quest becomes one for "narrow content."

So, what is wanted is a concept of content with semantic properties

[1] In "Thought Without Content," presented at the Sloan Conference at MIT in May 1984, Hartry Field voiced suspicion that in the best psychological theory there will be no role for a concept of truth-theoretic content. Such a possibility is not directly relevant here, where the question is: Will cognitive science save belief identified by 'that'-clauses? On the common-sense conception, beliefs identified by 'that'-clauses are evaluated as to their truth or falsity.

[2] This point is discussed in Chapter One. Also see my "Underprivileged Access," *Noûs* 16 (1982), 227–242.

that molecular duplicates necessarily have in common. More precisely, if the concept of content is both to play its semantic role in the determination of truth conditions of attitudes and to be adequate for incorporation into a physicalistic theory that explains behavior, it must satisfy two constraints, one semantic and the other physical:

(S) (Narrow content + context) → Truth conditions of beliefs

and

(P) If C is a given narrow content, and if S has a belief with narrow content C and S' is a molecule-for-molecule duplicate of S, then S' has a belief with narrow content C.

Informal motivation for these constraints is easy to find.[3] The general physicalistic constraint is that any science of the mind, whether it invokes content or not, must provide a level of psychological description at which molecularly identical individuals necessarily receive the same description. That is,

(C) Molecular duplicates necessarily make the same contribution to their psychological states: For some level of description in the vocabulary of the physicalistic psychology, if S is in a state of that description, and if S' is a molecule-for-molecule duplicate of S, then S' is in a state of that description.

As a special case of (C), the general physicalistic constraint on a science of the mind, (P) may be thought of as a condition on any candidate for narrow content. Although molecular identity is not necessary for sameness of narrow content, it must be sufficient; otherwise, a taxonomy of states identified by narrow content would be useless for the kind of science of behavior under consideration. As we have seen in Chapters Two through Four, what has been needed, and what has eluded friends of content, is a concept of content that ensures that (at least) molecule-for-molecule duplicates have the same narrow contents. A condition of adequacy on the concept of narrow content, (P) guarantees that the molecular replicas have the same narrow contents.

Condition (S) likewise seems natural. A major obstacle to the formulation of an appropriate concept of content, brought out vividly in Twin Earth cases, is that truth conditions of beliefs (and satisfaction

---

[3] Fodor discusses such motivation throughout his writings, including the unpublished "Narrow Content and Meaning Holism." See, for example, "Cognitive Science and the Twin-Earth Problem," *Notre Dame Journal of Formal Logic* 23 (1982), 98–118. Also see "Individualism and Supervenience," in Fodor's *Psychosemantics* (Cambridge, Mass.: MIT/Bradford, 1987).

conditions of desires, and the like) seem to be determined in part by the believer's environment. This suggests a "two-factor" semantic theory of psychological states: one factor, narrow content, is to be determined solely by nonrelational properties of the subject; the other factor, the truth condition, is to be determined in part by the subject's environment. What makes a concept of narrow content a semantic concept is that narrow contents are to contribute to the meanings, or at least to the truth conditions, of psychological states. The joint semantic contribution of the subject and the environment to psychological states is indicated by (S).[4]

The picture now at issue is this: The truth conditions of a belief result from two vectors, the "internal" states of the believer and the "external" environment. On this assumption, the individual's contribution to her intentional states is separable from and identifiable independently of the contribution due to her environment. An adequate concept of narrow content would capture the contribution of the individual's internal states to her overall states of believing, and so on. On this picture, the truth conditions of an individual's beliefs are the product of an "inner" component (narrow content) and an "outer" component (context). Condition (S) captures this requirement.

In addition, (P) and (S) seem to work together to show how an intentional psychology may satisfy the general physicalistic constraint (C). Any concept of narrow content that jointly satisfied both (S) and (P) would have this consequence: If molecular replicas were in the same contexts, their beliefs would have the same truth conditions. (On the physicalistic conception of science, contexts must be specified nonintentionally and nonsemantically in order to avoid circularity. See the section "Strategies and Assessments," below.) The reductive strategy is to confine the intentional component of beliefs and other attitudes to narrow content; scientific respectability of intentional psychology is to be secured by the requirement that narrow content, whatever it turns out to be, must satisfy (P). A candidate for narrow content that fails to satisfy (P) is a nonstarter; a candidate for narrow content that fails to satisfy (S) is not a concept of content at all.

As promising and as unavoidable as the combination of (S) and (P) may seem, I believe it unlikely that any concept satisfies both conditions; and that fact explains the failure of the several approaches to

---

[4] The formulation of (S) should not suggest that beliefs with the same truth conditions have the same narrow content. It is compatible with (S) that a belief that water is wet have the same truth conditions as a belief that H_2O is wet, even though the beliefs differ in narrow content. What (S) precludes is any *difference* in truth conditions without some difference either in narrow content or in context.

content that we have considered. Considerations in the following two sections suggest that nothing that satisfies (P) can make the requisite contribution to truth conditions of attitudes. Hence, no concept that satisfies (P) is a genuinely semantic notion.

Although joint satisfaction of (S) and (P) would be one way to vindicate a physicalistic concept of content, it would not be the only way. Other approaches to content—for example, those based on the idea of belief as reliable indication—do not distinguish between narrow and wide contents and, hence, do not endorse (S) and (P). Nevertheless, in later sections I shall try to show how the argument that I develop specifically against (S) and (P) also casts doubt on other approaches to physicalistic content that aim to satisfy (C) as well.

Speaking One's Mind

As we saw in Chapter Four, narrow content understood as mental representation of phenomenologically accessible properties fails to satisfy (P). In this chapter I shall suggest that no genuinely semantic concept (such as would satisfy (S)) will satisfy (P). Doubts about physicalistic content arise from considering molecule-for-molecule duplicates with the same histories and in the same contexts, described nonintentionally and nonsemantically. It appears that, contrary to any version of physicalism, their beliefs may differ in truth conditions. In that case, if (S) is satisfied, then the duplicates' beliefs differ in narrow content and (P) is violated; and if (P) is satisfied, then the duplicates' beliefs have the same narrow content and (S) is violated. A thought experiment will illustrate this possibility.

Suppose that two teen-aged girls, both far from their respective homes, are invited to their first embassy party. Although their societies developed independently of each other, they are so similar in geography, climate, and so on that the girls are molecular duplicates. One girl is from a country where standard American English is spoken; the other is from a country where a language similar to English, with a single exception, is spoken. The exception is this: In English the word 'vodka' designates vodka and in the mythical country the word 'vodka' designates gin. Assume that translators have established that the foreign word that sounds like the English word 'vodka' should be consistently translated as 'gin,' because it occurs in contexts that are unproblematically translated into English as 'x is what British officers in India drank with tonic in order to ward off malaria,' 'Hogarth depicted the tragic effects of excessive consumption of x in eighteenth-century England,' and 'Russia does not export x.' Just as the Spanish word 'burro' means 'donkey' and the Italian word 'burro' means 'butter,' so the English word 'vodka' means 'vodka' and the mythical language word 'vodka' means 'gin.' In all other respects, translation between the mythical language and English is homophonic.

At the embassy party, one of the most popular refreshments is a clear liquid served in shot glasses. Each girl gestures toward trays of drinks and utters what sounds like the English sentence, "Vodka is good to drink." In so uttering, one girl indicates in the mythical language that gin is good to drink, and the other girl indicates in English that vodka is good to drink. By producing the same "output," described nonsemantically, they say different things. There is no question about what each says.

Suppose not only that the girls are in the same current physical environment but also that they have acquired their beliefs in the same environments, described nonintentionally. In particular, the episodes in which each acquired her beliefs merit the same nonintentional descriptions. Suppose that the English speaker's beliefs about vodka have their origin in a training session for children of diplomats in which she was presented with an artist's lifelike rendering of a glass filled with a clear liquid and told that it was vodka and good to drink at receptions. Likewise, the non-English speaker's beliefs about gin have their origin in a training session in which she was presented with an artist's lifelike rendering of a glass filled with a clear liquid and told that it was gin and good to drink at receptions. The pictorial episodes by which each girl acquired her attitudes satisfy the same nonintentional descriptions; the pictures of the glass filled with a clear liquid are indistinguishable. Both teachers pointed to the pictures and emitted the same sequence of sounds.

Thus, I think it plausible to conclude that at the embassy party the two girls are similar in all relevant nonintentional respects. They acquired their beliefs in the same nonintentionally described contexts; they display the same linguistic and nonlinguistic behavior (nonintentionally described); they are in the same current physical environment; they are in the same internal states; their relevant internal states are caused by the same physical environmental condition. Indeed, they are molecular duplicates in the same nonintentionally specified contexts.

We have seen that the girls' utterances, each in her own language, of what sounds like the English sentence, "Vodka is good to drink," have different truth conditions. Since each speaks sincerely and is a competent speaker of her native language, each expresses her belief—the English speaker that vodka is good to drink and the non-English speaker that gin is good to drink. These beliefs clearly have different truth conditions.

Since the girls are in the same context, nonintentionally specified, and since their beliefs have different truth conditions, then by (S) they differ in their narrow contents. But since they are molecular duplicates, then by (P) they do not differ in their narrow contents. Therefore, (S) and (P) cannot both be satisfied.

The argument is perfectly general. Nothing hinges on whether or not the girls' beliefs are *de re* or *de dicto*. The point is independent of any particular specification of narrow content; I do not claim, for example, that 'vodka is good to drink' expresses narrow content. The example suggests that (S) and (P) are not jointly satisfiable because they impose different identity conditions on narrow content—no matter how narrow content is specified. The semantic and the nonsemantic (whether construed as physical, causal, functional, computational, syntactic, or as any other states shared by molecular duplicates) just do not seem to pull in the same direction.

STRATEGIES AND ASSESSMENTS

The example just given should be seen as a challenge to the physicalist who hopes to accommodate belief, for the suggestion is that the intentional and semantic, in principle, may be irreducible to the nonintentional and the nonsemantic.[5] Nevertheless, the physicalist has available several strategies for saving belief. In this section, I shall consider two such strategies and indicate how difficult it would be to defuse this kind of example.

The first physicalistic strategy is to object that the girls really are not in the same relevant contexts after all and that the difference in the truth conditions of their beliefs is attributable to the difference in context. (Differences in context that are irrelevant to differences in the truth conditions of the beliefs cannot meet the challenge raised by the example.) The second physicalistic strategy is to object that the girls

[5] Stephen Stich, Patricia Churchland, and Paul Churchland have also discussed the possibility that the intentional is irreducible to the nonintentional, but my arguments (as well as my general philosophical orientation) are significantly different from theirs. For example, see Stephen Stich, *From Folk Psychology to Cognitive Science: The Case Against Belief* (Cambridge, Mass.: MIT/Bradford, 1983); Paul M. Churchland, "Eliminative Materialism and Propositional Attitudes," *Journal of Philosophy* 78 (1981), 67–90; and Patricia S. Churchland, "A Perspective on Mind-Brain Research," *Journal of Philosophy* 77 (1980), 185–207.

really lack the beliefs ascribed to them and that there is no difference between their beliefs correctly ascribed.[6]

First Strategy:
Find Relevant Difference in Contexts

The first physicalistic strategy is to claim that, although in many respects the girls are in the same context, in fact there is a difference in their contexts, which is responsible for the difference in the truth conditions of their beliefs. On this line, the physicalist's goal is to show how the contexts differ. To achieve that goal, a physicalist must specify the girls' contexts nonintentionally and nonsemantically in a way that reveals a relevant difference between them.

Why, one may ask, must the relevant difference in the girls' contexts be specified nonintentionally and nonsemantically? A physicalist may suppose that a context could be intentionally specified without jeopardizing the physicalistic project; in that case, such intentionally specified contexts might reveal the relevant difference that the physicalist needs between the two girls' contexts. Let me digress for a moment to show why, for physicalistic purposes, the needed difference between the two girls' contexts must be specified nonintentionally and nonsemantically.

Physicalists who disagree on other issues nonetheless construe their project to be one of showing how semantic and intentional facts are wholly determined by ("supervene on") nonsemantic and nonintentional facts. The strategy of those who endorse (S) is to confine intentional elements to narrow content, which is to be guaranteed by (P) to supervene on the physical. If intentional or semantic elements slipped into context, then the physicalist would come up short of his goal of showing that the intentional supervenes on the nonintentional. For there would be no gain in making narrow content physicalistically respectable via (P) if intentional elements were allowed in elsewhere.

"But," a physicalist may reply, "we could allow context to be specified partly intentionally if we could assume that intentional elements that determine a context themselves could be cashed out in terms of

---

[6] A third physicalist strategy would be to concede that the girls differ in belief but to argue that differences of *that* sort cannot be expected to be incorporated into physicalistic psychology. This strategy concedes the point that (S) and (P) are not jointly satisfiable and suggests a version of physicalism that rejects (S). Versions of physicalism that reject (S) include eliminativism and instrumentalism (discussed in detail in Part II) and at least some "reliable indicator" accounts of belief, which, as discussed in the next section, are also challenged by the gin/vodka case.

narrow content, the physicalistic credentials of which are secured by (P). For example, perhaps the context of the English speaker in the gin/vodka case could be specified in part by citing the physical impingements on her at the time she acquired the belief together with an intention to maintain the referent of the term conveyed by those physical impingements. Then, that intention itself may be part of the context."

This line does not work, however. Either the intention would be construed narrowly—that is, in conformity with an analogue of (P) for intentions—or it would not be construed narrowly. Suppose that the relevant intention could be construed narrowly (a supposition whose truth I doubt). Construed narrowly, no attitude can furnish the relevant difference between molecular duplicates; for (P) and its analogues for other attitudes guarantee that molecular duplicates, such as the girls, have all the same attitudes construed narrowly.

So suppose that the intention is not construed narrowly. Then its satisfaction conditions would in some way depend upon context. But to invoke a context-dependent attitude in the determination of context would be to risk circularity or regress. Here is the reason: The physicalist's point here is to decompose belief and other attitudes into two components, "internal" and "external." If (non-narrow) attitudes were included in the "external" component (that is, in context), then they in turn should be decomposable into two components, internal and external; in that case, the task of decomposing attitudes into two components would simply be reintroduced.

It may seem that the dilemma could be avoided by claiming that there is an indexical component to any intention to refer to what others in one's speech community refer, a component that indexes place, time, individual persons, or whatever else goes into picking out *that* group of people. In this case, it may seem that the girls can be in the same narrow state by virtue of their molecular identity but in different wide states by virtue of the differences in the values of the relevant indices.[7]

I have two replies to this proposal. First, differences in the girls' intentions to refer are semantically described differences. Unless such semantically described differences can be cashed out nonsemantically (and I shall consider the prospects for this shortly), the proposal is no help to a physicalist, who would not be satisfied with showing how the intentional depends upon the physical-cum-irreducibly-semantic.

Second, the risk of circularity or regress is not avoided anyway. On the "two-factor" view, the narrow content of the intention must be either part of the narrow content of the belief (that vodka is good to

[7] Joseph Levine has suggested this approach.

drink, say) or part of the context. If it is part of the narrow content of the belief (a prima facie implausible suggestion), then how is the narrow content of any particular attitude ever to be disentangled from the narrow contents of other attitudes? But if the narrow content of the intention is part of the context, then the context itself divides into two parts—one internal and the other external—with no obvious place for the ramification to stop.

Thus, to show (noncircularly) that the girls differ in context, a physicalist would seem to be required to specify contexts nonintentionally and nonsemantically. Physicalists generally grant that they aim to specify contexts nonintentionally and nonsemantically.[8]

I cannot produce an a priori argument to show that no nonintentional and nonsemantic specification of the relevant difference can be given. But I can indicate how enormous the task is—and, perhaps surprisingly, how slight would be the payoff if it were accomplished in any given case.

There is no obvious relevant difference, specifiable nonintentionally and nonsemantically, between the girls as the story was told. Clearly, the difference cannot be specified by saying, "The relevant difference is that people in the English speaker's country use 'vodka' to refer to vodka and 'gin' to refer to gin," for that is a semantic specification. And as the story was told, the girls are similarly located when they make their statements; they have similar causal histories (nonintentionally described); gin and vodka are both plentiful in their environments, past and present. It is even possible that the instructors themselves were molecular duplicates who acquired their beliefs about gin and vodka, respectively, from other molecular duplicates. . . .

Of course, there are relevant differences between the contexts of the two girls, and it is no feat to state them in intentional or in semantic terms. Since one such difference is that 'vodka' denotes one drink in one language and another drink in a second language, it may be thought that the problem shifts to the semanticist, who attempts to explain semantic relationships like reference in nonsemantic terms.[9] Suppose, for example, that one had a semantic theory according to which an expression refers to or denotes an object or kind by virtue of a causal chain that links current uses of the expression to a first use that causally links the expression to the object or kind. Then, one might think, the relevant semantic difference could be specified in nonsemantic, causal terms.

---

[8] For example, see Jerry A. Fodor, "Psychosemantics, or Where Do Truth Conditions Come From?" (unpublished).

[9] For example, see Michael Devitt, *Designation* (New York: Columbia University Press, 1981), 28.

I have several responses that indicate how far from convincing such a proposal is at the present stage of development. First, to be useful for the physicalist who wants to show that differences in belief in molecular duplicates are attributable to nonintentional and nonsemantic differences in context, the causal theory would have to be comprehensive. It must apply not only to expressions for objects or kinds, but to expressions generally. For differences in belief may be generated by differences in usage of (almost?) any term. The point, made here in the example of the two girls, does not depend upon any special features of 'gin' or 'vodka.' Yet no semantic theory of sufficient scope or detail is in the offing.

Second, the most widely accepted causal account, Saul Kripke's picture of names,[10] cannot be pressed into service for the physicalist here because it explicitly employs intentional characterizations in a central way. The way that a word is passed along from one member of the community to the next, at least on this picture, is that the learner *intends* to use it with the same extension as the teacher. Nor are the initial dubbings characterized nonintentionally. As I understand him, it is not part of Kripke's project to give nonintentional sufficient conditions for semantic phenomena like reference.

Third, even from the point of view of a causal picture, it cannot be assumed that the causal chains from English speakers' and non-English speakers' uses of (what sounds like) 'vodka' are traceable to vodka in the first case and to gin in the second. A further fantasy suggests that the English use of 'vodka' for vodka could have had its origin in the same nonintentionally and nonsemantically specified circumstances as the non-English use of (what sounds like) 'vodka' for gin.

Suppose that hundreds of years before the girls were born each of their countries, in which alcoholic beverages had been unknown before, sent out molecularly identical explorers who stumbled upon a single group of natives at the same time. The natives were fond of vodka, which they called 'vodka' and which they introduced to the explorers as 'vodka.' On returning to her home country, each explorer, confident in the keenness of her sense of taste, decided to reconstruct vodka and introduce it to her society. After much trial and error, the English-speaking explorer did manufacture vodka and pronounced herself successful. The non-English speaker, likewise bent on reconstructing vodka, was not so lucky; when she hit upon gin, she pronounced herself successful. Simultaneously, just before each explorer had a fatal heart attack, she sent the only copies of her recipe to her central government.

[10] Saul A. Kripke, *Naming and Necessity* (Cambridge, Mass.: Harvard University Press, 1980), 96–97.

Somehow, the recipes got in the international mail, and each ended up in the hands of the other's government. Thereafter, the non-English speaker's fellows drank vodka, passed laws controlling it, and so on; of course, they called it 'vodka.' The English speaker's fellows drank gin, passed laws controlling it, and so on; of course, they called it (what sounded like) 'vodka.'

As time went on, both countries passed prohibition laws, which were so successful that gin and vodka were, for a time, totally absent. So avid were the prohibitionists that they destroyed all distilleries and recipes. After several generations of prohibition, during which all that was left of gin and vodka in the respective countries was the lore, molecularly identical explorers again went out and, without realizing it, happened upon the same group of natives as before. Again, the natives shared their vodka; and when the natives said, 'Vodka,' each explorer exclaimed (what sounded like), "Vodka! I've heard of that and I've always wanted to try it!" Again, each explorer returned to her country without a recipe, determined to reconstruct vodka and reintroduce it to her society. This time the English-speaking explorer was not so lucky; she made gin and called it 'vodka.' But the non–English-speaking explorer hit upon vodka and called it 'vodka.' However, the ensuing mix-up in the mail resulted in the English-speaking country's drinking vodka and the non–English speaking country's drinking gin.

Again, as time went on, both countries passed prohibition laws, which were so successful that gin and vodka were, for a time, totally absent. And so the cycle began again. This time, the English-speaking explorer made vodka and called it 'vodka,' but the non–English-speaking explorer made gin and called it 'vodka.' And on and on. The cycle could be repeated indefinitely, so that the causal histories of the countries' uses of (what sounds like) 'vodka' are both traceable to the same substance originally, vodka; the causal chains cross each other over and over and pass through both gin and vodka over and over.

So, assuming that reference is determined by current community usage, it is entirely unclear how to distinguish the causal chains nonintentionally and nonsemantically. A causal theorist cannot simply suppose that the difference in the current references or denotations of two terms lies in a nonintentionally and nonsemantically specifiable difference in the two causal chains.[11] In sum, no one has come close to showing how nonintentional and nonsemantic specifications could be ade-

[11] This story is a complicated extension of Gareth Evans's "Madagascar" case of reference change. See Kripke's remarks in "Second General Discussion Session," in the proceedings of the Conference on Language, Intentionality and Translation Theory at the University of Connecticut at Storrs, March 1973, in *Synthese* 27 (1974), 510–511.

quate to describe the appropriate chains leading to the girls. Of the countless causal chains leading to the girls' utterances, there is no obvious way, to say the least, to specify the relevant ones nonsemantically and nonintentionally.

Let me make a final point about the notion of context. Even if the physicalist were to find a relevant nonintentional and nonsemantic difference between the two explorers or the two girls, it is not clear how much would have been achieved. The reason is that the notion of context in (S) seems ill suited to play a theoretically significant role. For it is far from obvious that there is any principled way to rule out in advance any event as relevant to determining a context. But if the notion of context were allowed to expand in such a way, then contexts may not be identified in terms of values of antecedently specifiable sets of parameters. Such a notion of context would seem unable to serve the purposes of an explanatory science.

Recall that the motivation for introducing notions of narrow content and context in the first place was to secure a concept suitable for physicalistic psychology. But for a concept of context to be useful for science, it must be determinate. For example, whereas it is useful and important to postulate that simultaneity is relative to inertial frame, it would not be useful or important to postulate that simultaneity is relative to whatever is relevant to determining that two events are simultaneous. Similarly, there is no theoretical gain in taking context to be whatever, given an individual's internal states, is relevant to determining the truth conditions of her beliefs. Although it is not a specifically philosophical task to say which parameters fix a context, theorists must ultimately specify sets of parameters that (according to the particular theory) determine a context if the notion of context is to have any theoretical import. So, on the face of it, the gin/vodka case calls into question the scientific usefulness of a notion of context to which narrow content could be relativized.

In light of these difficulties, both about specifying a relevant nonintentional and nonsemantic difference between the contexts in the case of the two girls and about the scientific usefulness of any resulting concept of context, the objection to the story that the girls relevantly differ in context has not been sustained.

Second Strategy: Deny Ascribed Beliefs

The second physicalistic strategy against the thought experiment concerning the two girls may be elaborated like this. Not only do the girls fail to distinguish between gin and vodka, but neither is aware that there is a second liquid similar to the one about which she was told. Since the girls have exactly the same (nonintentionally and nonsemantically specified) behavioral dispositions toward *both* gin and vodka, one may reasonably ask: Do the girls have enough information about the drinks to be said to have the concept of one drink but not the other? If not, then, on one intuitive sense of 'about,' they do not have beliefs about gin or beliefs about vodka. In that case, the example fails to show two molecularly similar individuals in the same circumstances nonintentionally described but in different narrow intentional states.[12]

But since we typically acquire beliefs in the fashion described and we typically lack omniscience, I see no credible way of denying that the girls have the beliefs ascribed. As the story was told, if either of the girls has the belief ascribed to her, the other has the belief ascribed to her. And since the story may be filled in in indefinite detail, any principle that denied both beliefs would seem to be too strong; it would seem to make the following a necessary condition of S's believing that F is G: For any kind of thing that is H and not F, there are circumstances in which S, without acquiring new information, can distinguish things that are F from things that are H. (The murkiness of 'new information' does not affect the present point.)

Clearly, no such principle governs belief. If it did, most of us would lack the belief that gold pieces are costly (since most of us are unable to distinguish gold from "fool's gold" without acquisition of new information), and most of us would lack the belief that U.S. hundred-dollar bills are green (since most of us are unable to distinguish them from counterfeits). Nor would adoption of such a principle seem desirable or even feasible; not only would it impoverish our store of beliefs, but it also would render miraculous our ability systematically to utter truths about, say, gold or hundred-dollar bills.

Thus, I think it unlikely that there is an adequate, principled way to deny that the girls have the beliefs ascribed. The English speaker believes that vodka is good to drink, and the non-English speaker believes that gin is good to drink. Each girl is simply unaware that there is a drink similar to the kind that she has beliefs about. But there is no reason that this lack of further information should threaten the information that each has.

A physicalist may want to separate the analysis of belief from the semantics of belief attribution and hold that what beliefs should be attributed depends on how finely we require that the subjects discriminate among relevant alternatives. (For example, if our interest is in

---

[12] Fred Feldman made a similar suggestion in conversation.

finding a bartender, we may not need to attribute to the girls different beliefs.) What we should be concerned with, he may contend, is not belief attribution, with its well-known context-dependence, but rather the girls' beliefs themselves.

Throughout this book, however, the context of attribution does not shift. The question is always: What is the relevant belief to be attributed for purposes of psychological explanation? Suppose that a physicalist insisted that, for purposes of psychological explanation, the girls have the same belief: they have the same nonintentionally described dispositions; they make the same discriminations between gin and vodka on the one hand and other drinks on the other hand.

I think that such an approach to explanation loses plausibility when we consider linguistic behavior. The girls sincerely and competently *said* different things: one said in English that vodka is good to drink, and the other said in the mythical language that gin is good to drink.[13] (If their dispositions are described semantically, they do differ in their dispositions regarding gin and vodka.) Here the concern is with physicalists who want to explain what each girl said in terms of her beliefs.[14] If such physicalists also hold that the girls had the same beliefs, then, since their utterances had different truth conditions, it must be concluded that the girls failed to express their (putatively shared) beliefs.

Of course, from time to time one fails to express one's belief in sincere utterance. For example, you might say, "The book on the table is well worth reading," if you believe that the book is Milan Kundera's latest. If Kundera's book has been replaced with one of Stephen King's, which you would not recommend, then you failed to express your belief. Or you might make a linguistic mistake. Wrongly thinking that 'pusillanimous' means 'stingy,' you might fail to express your belief if you said, "Scrooge is the most pusillanimous character in all of literature."[15] In both kinds of cases, the speaker makes a mistake, and his

[13] A certain kind of physicalist may hold that truth conditions of utterances are determined by truth conditions of internal representational states and that, since the girls' beliefs have the same truth conditions, their utterances also have the same truth conditions. But this is no argument that the girls' beliefs (or utterances) have the same truth conditions, only an insistence that they do. Of course, the same kind of physicalist may hold that public languages are idealized constructions out of idiolects without taking that claim to be relevant to this case.

[14] A physicalist who wants to confine the *explananda* of psychological explanation to behavior described nonintentionally and nonsemantically need not appeal to belief or other attitudes identified by content at all. In any case, for many of us, the psychological interest is in why someone said that p, not just why someone emitted certain sounds. (This theme will be picked up in the next section and elaborated in Part II.)

[15] 'Pusillanimous' was a favorite source of examples for the late Herbert Heidelberger.

failure to express his belief depends upon his having made that mistake. In the typical case, however, sincere and competent speakers succeed in expressing their beliefs.

If one tries to save narrow content by protesting that the girls really have the same belief but fail to express it in their utterances, then one should give some indication, as I just did in the examples above, of what prevents the girls from expressing their beliefs. Otherwise, the objector is just whistling in the dark.

Well, what would prevent them from expressing their beliefs? Nothing. Neither has made a mistake, linguistic or nonlinguistic. There is no further information on the basis of which either would be willing to admit that what she said was not really what she believed. Each is in excellent circumstances to say what she believed. I suppose, however, that a friend of narrow content may insist that such sincere and competent speakers of their language—whom no addition of new information, linguistic or nonlinguistic, would convince that they had "misspoken" themselves or failed correctly to express what they actually believed— still did not express their beliefs.

The arbitrariness of such a "bite the bullet" strategy may be brought out by imagining a variation on the story. Suppose that there is no such country where the word that sounds like 'vodka' denotes gin but that the course of the English speaker's life proceeds as before. Then there are absolutely no grounds for denying that the English speaker expresses the belief that vodka is good to drink when she sincerely and competently says, "Vodka is good to drink." To insist in this case, with the non-English speaker out of the picture, that the English speaker fails to express the ascribed belief would be to impose an impossible standard on belief expression. Any principle that precluded belief expression in the case of the English speaker considered alone would make it enormously difficult for us routinely to express our beliefs. Indeed, we may rightly wonder, if people fail to express their beliefs under the circumstances described, whether we are ever justified in supposing that anyone ever expresses her belief. There is no other belief that the English speaker would agree that she mistakenly expressed when she said, "Vodka is good to drink." Thus if any other belief helped to cause her utterance, it is one unknown to and unknowable by the English speaker, and incommunicable to anyone else. It is an unspeakable belief. Recourse to such "beliefs" has the desperate ring of the ad hoc.

If belief/desire psychology is to be saved, it is a Pyrrhic victory at best to rely on unknowable and incommunicable beliefs. It is difficult to see how such beliefs could have explanatory efficacy. Indeed, it is difficult to see what would entitle such to be called 'beliefs' at all. Thus, I think that to insist that the girls actually had the same belief, which they failed to express, is not a promising line of objection.

Therefore, we may conclude, at least provisionally, that (S) and (P) are not jointly satisfied by any concept of narrow content. It does not matter whether the language of thought is a conventional language or not; nor does it matter whether narrow content is expressed in a restricted observation language or not. Here is one final way to put the dilemma: If an individual's narrow contents depend in any way on the individual's environment, then (P) is violated, as we saw in Chapter Four when we considered observation terms in Mentalese. But on the other hand, if an individual's "narrow contents" are completely independent of the environment and (P) is not violated, then, as we saw in considering the gin/vodka case, "narrow contents" (understood now as what is shared by molecular replicas) do not make the requisite contribution to the truth conditions of the individual's beliefs. So a concept of "narrow content" that honors (P) is no concept of *content* at all.

APPLICATION: BELIEF AS RELIABLE INDICATION

The thought experiment about the embassy party has broad implications for any physicalistic program that aims to explain the intentional and semantic in terms of the nonintentional and nonsemantic. Before I catalogue some of the implications (in the next section), I want to show specifically how the thought experiment applies to construals of belief as "reliable indication." This approach deserves special attention because it does not depend upon isolating a wholly internal component of belief, such as narrow content, but rather may seek to satisfy the general physicalistic constraint (C) in another way.[16] Moreover, consideration of belief as reliable indication provides an opportunity to formulate a *minimal* constraint on physicalistic belief and to show that the case of the embassy party militates against any concept of content satisfying it.

A prominent alternative to the appeal to narrow content is to hold that a belief has the content it has by virtue of its being a reliable indicator of some state of the environment.[17] The general idea is that to be-

[16] Although belief as reliable indication need not advert to narrow content, the notion of reliable indication may be used as a basis of a semantics for mental representations.

[17] There are several ways to work out this general idea. See, for example, Dennis W. Stampe, "Toward a Causal Theory of Linguistic Representation," in *Contemporary Perspectives in the Philosophy of Language*, ed. Peter A. French, Midwest Studies in Philosophy, 4 (Minneapolis: University of Minnesota Press, 1979), 81–102; Fred I. Dretske,

lieve that p is to be in a state that, under normal (or optimal or "fidelity") conditions, one would be in only if p. What links the belief to the relevant state of affairs is that, under normal conditions, the relevant state of affairs causally contributes to one's having the belief in question. For example, suppose that Smith believes that there is an apple in front of her. Then Smith is in a state that, under normal conditions, she would be in only if there was an apple in front of her; and under normal conditions an apple's being in front of her would causally contribute to her being in that state.

This account thus requires specification of the subject's relevant states, of causal laws between states of the environment and states of the individual, and of normality conditions. Normality conditions are to preclude not only such external conditions as poor lighting and trick mirrors but also such internal conditions as abnormal functioning of the perceptual system. (One immediate difficulty is that, aside from these intuitive examples, there has been no provision of clear normality conditions. In the past, attempts to work out normality conditions have been either circular or unsuccessful.)[18]

Nevertheless, if the relevant states, laws, and normality conditions could all be specified nonintentionally, then we would have a physicalistically acceptable concept of content without appeal to narrow content. Although philosophers who take this line do not need (S) and (P), they still need a concept of content that satisfies a minimal condition of physicalism, (P'):

(P')   There are no differences in content between molecular duplicates who have been in the same types of contexts, described nonintentionally and nonsemantically, throughout their existences.

Any physicalistic concept of content must satisfy at least (P'); otherwise, it is not physicalistic.

I believe, however, that the argument regarding the story of the girls at the embassy party challenges any program committed to (P'). Let us see, for example, how the argument may be applied to the idea of belief

---

Knowledge and the Flow of Information (Cambridge, Mass.: MIT/Bradford, 1981); Dretske, "Machines and the Mental," in *Proceedings and Addresses of the American Philosophical Association* 59 (1985), 23–33; Robert C. Stalnaker, *Inquiry* (Cambridge, Mass.: MIT/Bradford, 1984); Jerry A. Fodor, "Psychosemantics, or Where Do Truth Conditions Come From?"

[18] See, for example, Jerry A. Fodor, "Semantics, Wisconsin Style," *Synthese* 59 (1984), 231–250. Insofar as abnormality is a teleological (as opposed to a merely statistical) idea, these views require a naturalistic account of teleology that does not presuppose intentionality if they are to avoid circularity. An evaluation of such accounts of teleology must await another occasion.

as reliable indication. It certainly seems as though the English speaker is in a state that, under normal conditions, she would be in only if vodka is good to drink; and the non-English speaker is in a state that, under normal conditions, she would be in only if gin is good to drink. Any doubts about this, I think, would concern normality conditions.

Absence of specification of normality conditions makes it difficult to know exactly how the theory of belief as reliable indication would treat the case of the two girls. In obvious ways, however, neither girl is in any abnormal condition: both are awake, alert; their auditory apparatus is in good shape; they are competent speakers of their languages, which are also spoken by their respective teachers; they make no mistake about the training they are undergoing or about what they are being told.

Suppose that someone objected that, in the circumstances described, the girls would be in the same states even if vodka and gin were poisonous and, hence, that, in those circumstances, it is not a necessary condition of their being in the those states that vodka and gin, respectively, be good to drink. Notice that, on the view of belief as reliable indication, this possibility emerges with regard to any belief that one acquires by being told something. In general, what you say need not be true for me to believe it, even in the best of (nonintentionally described) conditions. So anyone pressing this as an objection to the description of the girls at the embassy party must either show why, in the present case, the girls failed to acquire the beliefs ascribed or deny that one ever acquires beliefs by being told things.[19] I take it as obvious that it is untenable to deny that one ever acquires beliefs by being told things. (Otherwise, we should all stop giving directions to lost people, lecturing to students, bringing up children as we do, and so on.) Thus, the objector must argue that the girls failed to acquire the beliefs ascribed—a claim that the last section gave us reason to view with skepticism.

Nevertheless, someone might press like this: Although the girls are not reliable indicators that gin and vodka, respectively, are good to

---

[19] I think that the reliable-indication view has a general difficulty handling beliefs that one acquires by being told something. For example, in "Psychosemantics," Fodor explains an entry condition for a mental representation, M, as a state of affairs such that a normally functioning cognitive system, in epistemically appropriate circumstances, puts M into its belief-box if and only if the state of affairs obtains. Then he identifies entry conditions with truth conditions. To put it briefly, the state of affairs that makes the relevant causal contribution to the English speaker's acquisition of the belief that vodka is good to drink seems to be the girl's having been so told by her protocol teacher; but this state of affairs does not give the truth conditions of the belief acquired. Moreover, I think that there are difficulties with the account of false belief on the reliable-indication view, but these are beyond the scope of the present project.

drink, they are both reliable indicators that a clear, alcoholic beverage is good to drink, and that fact yields the belief that they share. Notice that such a proposal is not available (at least without further argument) to anyone who hopes to isolate narrow content or a component of belief wholly in the head of the believer. For, as we saw in Chapter Four, appeal to observation terms does not yield a satisfactory sort of narrow content. A reliable-indicator theorist who is committed not to narrow content but only to (P') may still press the current proposal that the girls have in common a belief that a clear, alcoholic beverage is good to drink.

But I need not deny that the girls have that belief, or many other beliefs, in common. What (P') requires is that they have *no* beliefs that differ in content. So anyone pressing the current proposal must hold not only that the girls share a belief about a clear, alcoholic beverage but also that they lack beliefs about gin and vodka, respectively. Although, for reasons given in the last section, I think that this latter claim is plainly implausible, a physicalist may remind us that our concern here is with psychological explanation; and for that purpose the shared belief that a clear, alcoholic beverage is good to drink may be thought to suffice. He may claim that we need not appeal to beliefs concerning gin or vodka to explain behavior.

Yet I believe that this line faces difficulties in handling explanations of linguistic behavior, about which we must ask: Is the *explanandum* to be specified semantically or nonsemantically? Physicalists who have propounded versions of belief as reliable indication give intentional and semantic characterizations of the behavior that they want to explain. For example, Fred Dretske, a prominent proponent of belief as reliable indication, notes:

> [B]eliefs and desires are not (typically) invoked to explain physical movements. They are brought into play to explain what we *do*: why we moved our finger, pressed the key, turned off the lights, or insulted our host. And though we don't do these things without some associated movement, what we do must be carefully distinguished from whatever movements are required for the doing.[20]

It is difficult to think of a more intentional description of an *explanandum* than 'insulted our host.' Although this suggests that the *explanandum* may be specified semantically, consider the following example.

[20] Fred I. Dretske, "The Explanatory Role of Content," in *Contents of Thought: Proceedings of the 1985 Oberlin Colloquium in Philosophy*, ed. Robert H. Grimm and Daniel D. Merrill (Tucson: University of Arizona Press, 1988) (emphasis his).

Suppose that, in order to have adequate amounts of beverages on hand, the caterer for the embassy party took a poll of the new young people invited. The multilingual caterer, who asked each what he or she had been advised to drink, reported that the English-speaking girl, along with her fellow citizens, responded that she had been advised to drink vodka and that the non–English-speaking girl, along with her fellow citizens, responded that she had been advised to drink gin.

Suppose that we describe the behavior to be explained like this: The English-speaking girl said that she had been advised to drink vodka; the non–English-speaking girl said that she had been advised to drink gin. These are distinct *explananda*, which require distinct *explanans*. But since the girls are molecular duplicates who have always been in molecularly identical environments, the physicalist must give their responses the same explanation. Thus, such semantic specifications of the *explananda* seem ruled out by (P').

Perhaps we can move to a nonsemantic description of the behavior, which would allow a single explanation of both responses. For example:

x believes that she has been asked what she was advised to drink at embassy parties.

x believes that she was advised to drink a certain clear alcoholic beverage at embassy parties.

x believes that the clear alcoholic beverage is called (what sounds like) 'vodka.'

x wants to cooperate with her interlocutor, and so on.

Therefore, x emits the sound 'vodka.'

I have a number of comments regarding this suggestion. First, even with its nonsemantically specified *explanandum*, the proposed explanation is no stopping place for a physicalist; as it stands, it requires the theorist to invoke semantically described phenomena in specifying a belief about what the terms denote in the languages. We have seen that the nonintentional and nonsemantic conditions required by the physicalist for semantic claims have so far not been forthcoming.

Second, the strategy behind the proposed explanation seems to allow the recasting of too many beliefs as metalinguistic. Is there a reasonable principle that allows reinterpretation of the belief ascribed in the third premise as metalinguistic that does not also allow reinterpretation of the belief ascribed in the first and second premises as metalinguistic?

Third, what gets explained is not of particular psychological interest. Typically, we do not classify linguistic behavior by the way it sounds— and for good reason. If we did, we would miss relevant similarities and differences in what people say. (Unless he classified behavior in terms of what is said, the caterer would be unable to order the right beverages.)

It might be thought that this difficulty could be easily remedied by adding something to the explanation, separate from intentional attributions. The further *explanans* would be, in the one case, "In x's native language, 'vodka' designates vodka," and in the other case, "In x's native language, 'vodka' designates gin." But, of course, these are explicitly semantic specifications that fail to meet physicalistic standards.

Most of the details of the picture that takes belief to be reliable indication have yet to be filled in, so I am only guessing as to how they may be sketched. Nevertheless, I think that we have grounds to doubt that completion of the project is imminent. One way to put the general dilemma facing a physicalist is this: If *explananda* are described nonsemantically and nonintentionally, we seem to miss, at the least, what we set out to explain; and, indeed, it becomes unclear why appeal to belief is needed at all. (See Chapter Six for further discussion.) But if *explananda* are described semantically or intentionally, then beliefs conforming to (P') do not seem explanatory.

THE GENERALITY OF THE RESULTS

We have looked at physicalistic construals of content both in individualistic versions (in the discussion of methodological solipsism in Chapters Two and Three) and in nonindividualistic versions (in the discussions of narrow content relativized to context and of belief as reliable indication in Chapters Four and Five).[21] The thought experiments raise a series of doubts about the enterprise of specifying nonintentional and nonsemantic conditions for intentional states. (1) Content identified by 'that'-clauses does not conform to the (physicalistic) formality condition. (2) Narrow content, insofar as it does conform to the physicalistic constraint (P), does not determine a function from context to truth conditions. (3) The minimal physicalistic constraint on belief—namely, (P')—seems beyond satisfaction by a construal of belief as reliable indication. Indeed, consideration of (P') in light of the case of the embassy party suggests that no concept of content can satisfy that minimal physicalistic constraint.

Now let us consider how widespread are the consequences of these

[21] Recall that I am using 'individualistic' in Burge's sense and, hence, that any view that takes environmental factors into consideration is nonindividualistic. Also, since the discussion centers on physicalistic construals of belief, and since Putnam and Burge do not seek to specify nonintentional and nonsemantic sufficient conditions for intentional states, their views are not under consideration here.

doubts for physicalism of both individualistic and nonindividualistic varieties.

Individualism: Physicalism That Ignores Environment

Consider two widely held individualistic assumptions that are called into question. First, the doubts raised here cover any view that needs, overtly or covertly, the assumption that brain states, considered in isolation, have content. Two rather disparate examples follow.

A. John Searle has been a vigorous opponent of what he calls 'strong AI' and cognitive science. He emphasizes mental activities as biological phenomena and says: "Consciousness, intentionality, subjectivity and mental causation are all a part of our biological life history, along with growth, reproduction, the secretion of bile, and digestion."[22] But, I believe that Searle is firmly committed to the kind of individualistic psychology that, we have seen, precludes content, for he takes intentional states to be both caused by and realized in the (individual) human brain:

> The brain is all we have for the purpose of representing the world to ourselves and everything we can use must be inside the brain. Each of our beliefs must be possible for a being who is a brain in a vat because each of us is precisely a brain in a vat; the vat is a skull and the 'messages' coming in are coming in by way of impacts on the nervous system.[23]

We have seen that individuals with molecularly identical brains may differ in their beliefs, regardless of the construal of content; so, if "everything we can use must be inside the brain," then beliefs must not be things we can use. Indeed, the foregoing arguments suggest that brains in vats—individuals who have never been embedded in a natural or social environment—do not enjoy contentful states.

B. A number of writers have attempted recently to forge a synthesis between Freudian views and neuroscience.[24] (Freud himself early gave up the effort to discover in the brain a localization of mental proc-

[22] John Searle, *Minds, Brains and Science* (Cambridge, Mass.: Harvard University Press, 1984), 41.

[23] John Searle, *Intentionality: An Essay in the Philosophy of Mind* (Cambridge: Cambridge University Press, 1983), 230. I find Searle's criticisms of strong AI much more persuasive than his positive views. Indeed, it would seem that an argument parallel to his Chinese room argument, deployed masterfully against strong AI, could be aimed at his suggestion that we are brains in vats.

[24] See, for example, B. A. Farrell's critique of two such attempts. "Snails on the Couch," *New York Review of Books* 32 (1985), 36–40.

esses.)[25] But unless relatively simple, contentful phenomena are realized in the brain—unless, that is, brain states per se have content—there is little hope of identifying neural states with such complex phenomena as repression and transference.

The second individualistic assumption called into question by the doubts raised here is this: The way that one represents things to oneself or conceives of things is wholly in the head, independent of one's physical and social environment. This assumption seems to lie behind methodological solipsism, as the following two examples suggest.

A. Among others, Fodor explicitly takes *de dicto* attitudes, the way we represent states of affairs to ourselves, to be wholly internal. He says, for example, that "the *de re*/*de dicto* distinction seems to *be* the distinction between what is in the head and what is not."[26] But the argument in Chapter Two showed that *de dicto* attitudes are not wholly in the head. How one conceives of things depends, in part, upon the language one speaks, and what language one speaks is not determined solely by what is in the head.

B. Daniel Dennett has proposed "notional worlds," fictional worlds devised by a theorist that are to represent the subject's point of view. The theorist aims to capture "a person's subjective world, Helen Keller's *The World I Live In*, or John Irving's *The World According to Garp*, for instance." A notional world can be supposed to contain "all the objects and events the subject *believes in*, you might say."[27] Notional worlds are to be the "organismic contribution" to propositional attitudes; they are to be shared by molecular duplicates. But, as we have seen, what the girls at the embassy party have in common is not the way they represent things to themselves: one represents a certain liquid as vodka, the other represents it as gin.

Nonindividualism: Physicalism That Appeals to Environment

The doubts raised here apply both to nonindividualistic versions of physicalism that aim to isolate a wholly internal determinant of meaning or truth conditions and to those that do not. For example, Ned Block's two-factor, conceptual-role semantics identifies two determi-

[25] Adolf Grünbaum, "Freud's Theory: The Perspective of a Philosopher of Science," *Proceedings and Addresses of the American Philosophical Association* 57 (1983), 6. See also Grünbaum's major study, *The Foundations of Psychoanalysis: A Philosophical Critique* (Berkeley: University of California Press, 1983).

[26] Fodor, "Cognitive Science and the Twin-Earth Problem," 114 (emphasis his).

[27] Daniel C. Dennett, "Beyond Belief," in *Thought and Object: Essays on Intentionality*, ed. Andrew Woodfield (Oxford: Clarendon Press, 1982), 38.

nants of wide meaning: an internal component (narrow meaning), characterized by conceptual role, which "is 'in the head,' in the sense of this phrase in which it indicates supervenience on physical constitution"; and an external component "that has to do with the relations between the representations in the head (with their internal conceptual roles) and the referents and/or truth conditions of these representations in the world."[28] The doubts raised earlier about narrow content are immediately and obviously applicable to such a conception.

Thus, the hope of isolating a component contributed systematically by an organism to the truth conditions (or other semantic features) of its attitudes seems frustrated. In that case, none of the "two-factor" approaches to meaning—according to which meaning has an internal component entirely "in the head" and an external component that concerns relations between representations in the head and truth conditions—is likely to succeed.

The other nonindividualistic approach to physicalistic belief does not try to isolate a wholly internal or "organismic" contribution to the truth conditions of beliefs. One example of this approach, belief as reliable indication, has been discussed in detail. Rather than survey other nonindividualistic approaches to physicalistic belief, I shall simply point out how the embassy party example may extend to any wide functionalism.[29] Recall that in Chapter Three we found classical functionalism to be committed to an inconsistent triad. The difficulty was that no construal of belief, regardless of how narrow, was narrow enough for beliefs to be identified with classical functional states. One way that a functionalist may reply is to revise the notion of a functional state, by giving up the classical conception for a "wider" conception of functional states, individuated by reference to conditions in the environment. In this case, inputs may be specified in terms of environmental causes, and functional states may be specified partly in terms of environmental conditions. Then the wide functionalist claim would be that beliefs may be identified with functional states in this wider sense.

The story of the embassy party, however, shows that any such wide functionalism encounters difficulties analogous to those faced by clas-

---

[28] Ned Block, "Advertisements for a Semantics for Psychology," in *Studies in the Philosophy of Mind*, ed. Peter A. French, Theodore E. Uehling, Jr., and Howard K. Wettstein, Midwest Studies in Philosophy, 10 (Minneapolis: University of Minnesota Press, 1986), 620.

[29] David Lewis, David Armstrong, and Sydney Shoemaker may be considered wide functionalists. Also see, for example, Patricia Kitcher, "Narrow Taxonomy and Wide Functionalism," *Philosophy of Science* 52 (1985), 78–97, and Robert van Gulick, "Mental Representation—A Functionalist View," *Pacific Philosophical Quarterly* 63 (1982), 3–20.

sical functionalism. In particular, the story suggests that molecular duplicates in the same contexts (nonintentionally and nonsemantically described) may have different beliefs. If so, then two tokens of a single wide functional type may be different beliefs. But if we add this result to wide functionalism, construed as (a')and (b') below, we get an inconsistent triad, analogous to the one—(a)–(c) in Chapter Three—generated by classical functionalism:

(a') Beliefs are psychological states.
(b') Psychological states are wide functional states.
(c') Two tokens of a single wide functional type may be different beliefs.

Statements (a')–(c') may be seen to be inconsistent by reasoning parallel to that offered against (a)–(c) in Chapter Three.

Thus, if the embassy party example and the other thought experiments work as they should (and at this point they at least stand as a challenge to the physicalist), then they apply to any physicalistic construal of content. They suggest not just that some particular concept of content is incoherent but also that *no* concept of content will satisfy both (S) and (P) or, even more minimally, (P') alone: Molecular duplicates in physically identical environments throughout their careers are simply not guaranteed to have in common beliefs or other attitudes identified by content. Thus, the concept of content seems unavailable for a science that satisfies (C) or any other physicalistic constraint.

The reason that the thought experiments threaten such a range of projects is that they show that belief/desire psychology, which is more or less continuous with the common-sense conception, is not physicalistic psychology. Consider again the "Argument from Physicalism" formulated in Chapter One:

ARGUMENT FROM PHYSICALISM

(1) Either physicalistic psychology will vindicate (in a sense to be specified) the common-sense conception of the mental, or the common-sense conception is radically mistaken.
(2) Physicalistic psychology will fail to vindicate (in the relevant sense) the common-sense conception of the mental.
Therefore,
(3) The common-sense conception of the mental is radically mistaken.

In the most robust sense of vindication, it appears that (2) is true. Attitudes constitutive of the common-sense conception of the mental are identified by content, but the concept of content resists incorporation into a physicalistic psychology. Thus, the conclusion of Part I is not just that a particular approach fails to vindicate the common-sense conception but that no psychology conforming to (C) will vindicate it.

We have been considering the possibility of a physicalistic construal of the concept of content attributable by 'that'-clauses. I shall not try to determine how closely akin to the concept of content are other concepts that may be employed; I merely note that the less recognizably related they are to concepts of what is attributable by 'that'-clauses, the less likely they are to vindicate the common-sense conception in any sense. In Part II we shall examine the consequences of nonvindication.

The result of Part I can be summarized as follows. In order for physicalistic psychology to vindicate belief in the robust sense that we are considering, the concept of content (or a recognizable successor) must be a physicalistically adequate concept. But no concept of content meets the physicalistic conditions of adequacy (such as the conjunction of (S) and (P), or even the weakest condition, (P')). Thus, the arguments suggest that the concept of content (or a recognizable successor) cannot be a physicalistically adequate concept.

But if physicalistic psychology fails to vindicate belief, what assessment should be made of the common-sense conception? Is belief obsolete?

PART II

IS BELIEF OBSOLETE?

· 6 ·

HOW HIGH THE STAKES?

Could it turn out that no one has ever believed anything? Underlying this question, of course, is the idea that a completed scientific psychology may impugn the common-sense conception of the mental, the framework in which concepts such as *belief, desire,* and *intention* are embedded. If the common-sense framework is exposed as a "false and radically misleading conception of the causes of human behavior and the nature of cognitive activity,"[1] then a concept like *belief* may be as empty as the concept of phlogiston.

Part I showed that neither cognitive science nor any other approach to physicalistic psychology is likely to vindicate belief in the robust sense of recognizing generalizations over states identified by content nor, indeed, in the sense of simply recognizing states identified by content. The difficulty is that no concept of content conforms to the strictures of a physicalistic science: nonintentional sufficient conditions for a state's having a certain content have eluded us.[2]

From now on, I shall take it for granted that the second premise in the argument from physicalism—that physicalistic psychology will fail to vindicate the common-sense conception of the mental—is true if vindication is understood in the robust sense intended by cognitive science. Since the argument from physicalism is valid, we have several options: (i) to show that physicalistic psychology vindicates the common-sense conception in some weaker sense of vindication; (ii) to accept the conclusion that the common-sense conception of the mental is radically mistaken; or (iii) to deny the first premise, the premise to which physicalists are committed. In this chapter I shall argue that the first option collapses into the second. Then, after pointing out ways in which the common-sense conception differs from an empirical theory, I shall explore what is at stake in attempted rejection of the common-sense conception. In Chapter Seven I shall suggest that the second option is not really available. That result leaves the third option, to deny physical-

[1] Paul M. Churchland, *Matter and Consciousness* (Cambridge, Mass.: MIT/Bradford, 1984), 43.

[2] The target of the argument is broader than what Burge calls 'individualism.' The conclusion is that even *nonindividualistic* sufficient conditions for having a belief with a certain content will not be forthcoming so long as the conditions are described nonintentionally and nonsemantically.

ism. Before exploring that option, I want to examine a view that looks like a way to salvage both physicalism and the common-sense conception without admitting even "reducible" intentional entities into the ontology. Such a position, as endorsed by Daniel C. Dennett, will be the subject of Chapter Eight. Finally, in Chapter Nine, I shall assess the results.

Although I have focused on the common-sense conception with respect to physicalistic psychology, the far-reaching consequences of eliminating the common-sense conception extend to semantic issues as well. If no one has ever had a belief or intention, it is unclear how to interpret any inscription to be a claim that such-and-such and, in particular, how to construe as meaningful a claim advancing the view that no one has ever had a belief. In the absence of some indication of how meaning would be possible without beliefs or intentions, one who denies the common-sense conception of the mental is akin to a logician who takes the moral of the semantic and logical paradoxes to be that all logic is wrong and just leaves it at that.[3] Or, to use another of David Austin's suggestive analogies, it is as if someone were to write on a blackboard, "The following sentences have no meaning or interpretation," and then, three or four sentences down, repeat that same sentence. We would be entitled to puzzlement. We can hardly assess a claim that takes away everything we possess to understand it.

This burden of proof is implicitly acknowledged by the philosophers who deny the common-sense conception of the mental when they mount extended discussions of the plausibility of their position. Here I want to consider whether that burden has been successfully discharged, especially in the writings of Stephen P. Stich and Paul M. Churchland. There are many different issues that might fruitfully be addressed—for example, the accounts of belief ascription, arguments against functionalism, proposals concerning *de re* and *de dicto*—but these I shall leave aside to focus on the argument from physicalism, versions of which may be found in the writings of both Stich and Churchland.

For example, Stich entertains the possibility that the common-sense conception of the mental "will have to go" (his phrase) when he says that either the common-sense conception of the mental, which he construes as a kind of folk theory, will be "vindicated by scientific theory," or "[s]tates and processes spoken of in folk psychology are . . . mythical posits of a bad theory."[4] He argues at length that it is a "serious possi-

[3] David F. Austin suggested this analogy.

[4] Stephen P. Stich, *From Folk Psychology to Cognitive Science: The Case Against Belief* (Cambridge, Mass.: MIT/Bradford, 1983), 9–10.

bility" that "ordinary folk psychological belief ascriptions will turn out, quite generally, not to be true."[5]

Similarly, Paul Churchland writes that the categories of the common-sense conception of the mental "appear (so far) to be incommensurable with or orthogonal to the categories of the background physical science whose long-term claim to explain human behavior seems undeniable. Any theory that meets this description must be allowed a serious candidate for outright elimination."[6]

Although Churchland envisages a science that types psychological states in terms of neurophysiological properties and Stich envisages a science that types psychological states in terms of "syntactic" properties, the two share a basic assumption: the psychological states that explain behavior are typed without regard to content. Thus, vindication of the common-sense conception by a scientific psychology, so conceived, will depend upon how "comfortable" (Stich's term) such a psychology is with attributions identified by content.

Both Stich and Churchland consider two possible outcomes for the common-sense conception: either a very weak kind of vindication or elimination. In neither case would physicalistic psychology recognize a property of believing that p or invoke beliefs or other attitudes. Roughly, the difference between weak vindication and elimination is that scientific psychology would weakly vindicate the common-sense conception if a sufficient number of statements licensed by the scientific psychology meshed with or matched up with or correlated with statements licensed by the common-sense conception; otherwise, the common-sense conception would be eliminated. So, although such a weak sense of vindication could be viewed as a kind of elimination (as I suggested in discussing weak reductivism in Chapter One), I want to distinguish between weak vindication and elimination because, on the views of Stich and Churchland, the propriety of attributions of attitudes hangs in the balance. Weak vindication would give a kind of warrant to attributions of attitudes; elimination would imply that all such attributions are false.

COLLAPSE OF A "MODIFIED PANGLOSSIAN VIEW"

On a syntactic theory of the kind advocated by Stich, psychological states are relations to uninterpreted sentence tokens. Stich stipulates that a scientific psychology must conform to what he calls "the auton-

[5] Ibid., 242.

[6] Paul M. Churchland, "Eliminative Materialism and Propositional Attitudes," *Journal of Philosophy* 78 (1981), 76.

omy principle," according to which "the states and processes that ought to be of concern to the psychologist are those that supervene on the current, internal, physical state of the organism."[7] The states of interest to scientific psychology have a "narrow causal role," in that molecule-for-molecule duplicates are in the same psychological states.[8] (The autonomy principle is a content-free analogue of (P); cf. Chapter Five.) We now know little more about the character of Stich's syntactic states than that they conform to the autonomy principle; they are narrow causal states.

On the other hand, Stich argues that belief ascriptions are sensitive to the "pragmatic surround."[9] Thus, it is no surprise that Stich holds that a token of a given syntactic type may be a belief that p and that another token of the same syntactic type may fail to be a belief that p.[10] Indeed, Stich argues convincingly against the view that content is correlated with syntactic type: "[A] full narrow causal profile will not enable us to characterize the content of the subject's belief states nor to determine the semantic properties of sentences in his mental code." Or again: "It is simply not the case that the content or truth conditions of those mental state tokens to which content or truth conditions can be ascribed correlate with the syntactic type or narrow causal profile of the tokens."[11]

Nevertheless, Stich suggests that, although 'belief' is unlikely to appear in laws, some syntactic states may be describable as beliefs by virtue of partial correlations between them and our intuitive ascriptions of belief. It seems, he says, "perfectly plausible to say that certain of these syntactic state tokens are, as it happens, beliefs that p." In that case, although predicates formed from 'believes that p' would not ex-

[7] Stich, *From Folk Psychology to Cognitive Science*, 164.

[8] Ibid., 164. No argument is given for adopting the autonomy principle. Stich simply states that it alone will allow for the generalizations of interest to cognitive scientists. If such a principle really were adopted, then cognitive science would have nothing to say about learning, about development generally, about language, or about action under ordinary descriptions. In light of such restrictions, it would seem that cognitive scientists reasonably may want generalizations that violate the autonomy principle.

[9] Stephen P. Stich, "On the Ascription of Content," in *Thought and Object: Essays on Intentionality*, ed. Andrew Woodfield (Oxford: Clarendon Press, 1982), 178; cf. *From Folk Psychology to Cognitive Science*, ch. 5. Stich's account of belief ascription is not relevant to the present concern. Assume that his account is correct; the pertinent question, which Stich himself raises, is whether or not concepts like belief are true of anything: "On my view it is up for grabs whether the terms of folk psychology denote anything at all. Perhaps the concepts of folk psychology . . . will turn out to be true of nothing; perhaps there are no such things as beliefs" (76).

[10] Stich, *From Folk Psychology to Cognitive Science*, 198.

[11] Ibid., 109, 207.

press the property of believing that p, they may be used, on occasion, to express truths. This is not quite a token identity theory for belief, since Stich denies that the expression " 'token of the belief that p' specifies some well-defined class or category." It is rather the view that "anything which, in a given context, may be appropriately described as a belief that p is identical with some belief-like syntactic state token."[12] So Stich's best hope, his "modified Panglossian prospect," is for a syntactic theory that "postulates states many of whose tokens turn out to be describable as the belief that p, the desire that q and so on."[13]

But in this case it is difficult to see why syntactic tokens should be describable as beliefs *at all*. One may as well "vindicate" attributions of spell casting to an accused witch by noting that quite often when the woman utters certain syntactic tokens, her hearers break out in a sweat and misfortune soon befalls them. The partial correlation between scientific descriptions of syntactic tokens and descriptions in terms of spell casting would hardly justify a theory of sorcery. It is simply no vindication of the claim that certain women cast spells to say that scientific psychology "postulates states many of whose tokens turn out to be describable as" the casting of a spell. And no more is it vindication of the common-sense conception to say that scientific psychology "postulates states many of whose tokens turn out to be describable as beliefs that p."

Setting aside qualms about the assumption, shared by Fodor and others, that 'belief' applies to internal tokens if it applies to anything, we may still wonder under what conditions, on Stich's view, a given *syntactic token* may be appropriately described as a belief that p. Stich's modified Panglossian view offers no justification for ever describing any syntactic token as a belief at all. Nor does Stich's consideration of our practices of belief ascription give direction here, for belief ascription has nothing to do with identifying particular syntactic tokens. Rather, Stich emphasizes the dependence of belief ascription on social factors and context, far removed from internal states, and suggests (mistakenly, I think) that we ascribe states lacking determinate content. Thus, so far as Stich has elaborated his modified Panglossian prospect, it does not offer a clear alternative to his darker suspicion that "ordinary folk psychological belief ascriptions will turn out, quite generally, not to be true."[14]

12 Ibid., 223.
13 Ibid., 224, 227. Stich comments that if 'reduction' is used in a "suitably loose sense," then his modified Panglossian prospect is a kind of reduction of the common-sense conception to a syntactic theory of the mind.
14 Ibid., 242.

Stich is prepared for such a result. Taking the common-sense conception of the mental to be on a par with folk astronomy, he observes:

> However wonderful and imaginative folk theorizing and speculation has been, it has turned out to be screamingly false in every domain where we now have a reasonably sophisticated science. Nor is there any reason to think that ancient camel drivers would have greater insight or better luck when the subject at hand was the structure of their own minds rather than the structure of matter or of the cosmos.[15]

Little wonder, then, that Stich is as ready to pronounce false any utterances purporting to be about mental states with content as he is any utterances purporting to be about the rotation of the celestial sphere.

THE DEAD END OF THEORETICAL REDUCTION

Churchland formulates a slightly heartier sort of vindication, one that requires at least a systematic correlation between generalizations concerning attitudes and generalizations concerning psychological states in the vocabulary of the scientific psychology. Vindication in this sense is a reduction of one theory (the common-sense conception) to another (neuroscience). As Churchland construes theoretical reduction, a new theory reduces an old theory if the new theory, together with appropriate limiting assumptions and boundary conditions, logically entails a set of theorems that is "relevantly isomorphic" with claims of the old theory. The reducing theory is a "roughly equipotent *image*" of the reduced theory, which is "just the target of a relevantly adequate *mimicry*." If the reduction is "sufficiently smooth"—if, for example, many of the principles of the old theory find analogues in the new theory— the reduction may "sustain statements of cross-theoretic identity."[16]

Whether the common-sense conception is reduced in this sense by a scientific psychology or eliminated altogether is taken by Churchland to depend upon whether or not the mature science of the mind will "include, or prove able to define, a taxonomy of kinds with a set of embedding laws that faithfully mimics the taxonomy and causal generalizations of *folk* psychology."[17] It would seem to be a condition of the relevant mimicry that generalizations of the common-sense conception

---

[15] Ibid., 229–230.

[16] Paul M. Churchland, "Reduction, Qualia, and the Direct Introspection of Brain States," *Journal of Philosophy* 82 (1985), 10–11.

[17] Ibid., 17 (emphasis his).

be at least materially equivalent to generalizations couched in the vocabulary of neuroscience.

Since Churchland sees such reduction to be the only alternative to outright elimination of the common-sense conception, consider the following variation on the "Argument from Physicalism":

VARIATION ON AN ARGUMENT FROM PHYSICALISM

(4) Either generalizations of attributions of attitudes identified by content will be materially equivalent to statements deducible from mature physicalistic psychology, or no one has ever had a belief or other attitude identified by content.

(5) Generalizations of attributions of attitudes identified by content will fail to be materially equivalent to statements deducible from mature physicalistic psychology.

Therefore,

(6) No one has ever had a belief or other attitude identified by content.

One may reasonably complain that mere material equivalence is still too weak to be called 'vindication' of the common-sense conception. (After all, even uniform regularity between ascriptions of spell casting and scientific descriptions of neurophysiological states would not bring back witchcraft.) Nevertheless, I think it doubtful that even this weak sense of vindication will be forthcoming. Thus, I share Churchland's (and Stich's) suspicion that (5) may be true.

Another thought experiment will tell against any claim of systematic correlation between particular attributions of attitudes and statements describing neurophysiological or other narrow states. This is so for the familiar reason that two individuals, in the same nonintentional states (whether "syntactic" or neurophysiological) and in the same physical environment, may still differ in their beliefs, construed as narrowly as possible. Although similar in structure to the previous thought experiment, this one is novel in that it shows that a single token, rather than two tokens of the same physical (and other nonintentionally specified) type, equally warrants description as two distinct beliefs.

Suppose that two combatants are brought to a Red Cross field hospital. The two not only have fought on different sides but are also from different cultures. One speaks English; the other speaks only his native language, a mythical dialect that by chance has an odd overlap with English. The non-English dialect is just like English, with a single exception: The non-English dialect has a word that is phonetically indistinguishable from the English word 'locusts' but that any competent translator would render into English as 'crickets.' It occurs in contexts that are unproblematically translated into English as 'The male x produces chirping noises by rubbing together parts of his forewings' and 'No plagues of x's are reported in the Bible.' Recall the analogy: Just as the Spanish word 'burro' means 'donkey' and the Italian word 'burro' means 'butter,' so the English word 'locusts' means 'locusts' and the mythical dialect word 'locusts' means 'crickets.' In all other respects, translation is homophonic.

Each combatant has lost his voice box; luckily, the hospital has artificial external voice boxes to which patients can be hooked up. Since the hospital does not have enough such devices, however, both combatants are attached to the same one. Each can activate the external voice box as if he were speaking naturally.

One day, while the combatants are recuperating in an atmosphere of excruciating boredom, the conversation in the hospital turns to the subject of insects. At exactly the same time, each of the combatants activates the artificial voice box, out of which comes a single token that sounds like 'Locusts are a menace.' But only for the English speaker does the token express his belief that locusts are a menace; for the non-English speaker, the token expresses his belief that crickets are a menace. There is nothing about either token per se that makes it (the expression of) the one belief rather than the other.

With only a slight enlargement of the story, we may suppose that the machine is more than an artificial voice box, that it performs a portion of the patients' neural processing as well. That is, suppose now that the machine is activated not by the muscles that would activate a natural, organic voice but by certain configurations of neural firings in the brain. Now, if the patients activate this more sophisticated machine at the same time, their shared speech token is caused by a shared neurophysiological token.

We may imagine the combatants to be as alike as we please. For example, we may suppose that the combatants also have eye injuries and that they can see only by being attached to a single machine that presents each with the same visual stimulation. We may even imagine that the two combatants came to have their beliefs about locusts and crickets, respectively, under the same sort of (nonintentionally described) circumstances. Suppose that neither had seen or heard of locusts or crickets until he joined his guerrilla group. During training, each was exposed to illustrations of insects that might be encountered. Making demonstrative reference to exactly similar drawings, the instructor of each group, entirely independently of the other, said what sounded like 'locusts' and then went on to give some information about the pictured insects, information that by chance pertains to both locusts and crickets. Both instructors may have pointed to their respective pictures and emitted the same sequence of sounds. Indeed, the training episodes by which each combatant acquired his beliefs may have satisfied all the same relevant nonintentional descriptions.

Nevertheless, there remain (intentional) differences between the two cases. One instructor intended to inform the recruits about locusts, the other about crickets. Locusts and crickets are sufficiently similar in appearance that visual stimulation provided by a single picture may equally well introduce a person to either type of insect; in any case, one may have beliefs about locusts in the absence of information about their appearance. Since both combatants, as well as their instructors, are competent speakers of their respective languages, and since there is nothing unusual about acquiring beliefs from what one is told and what one sees in pictures, it seems straightforward that one of the combatants acquired the belief that locusts are a menace and that the other acquired the belief that crickets are a menace.[18] The difference in their beliefs serves to illustrate the division of linguistic labor.

The example suggests that the hospitalized combatants may be in the same neurophysiological states (individuated either narrowly in terms of what is "in the head" or widely in terms of environmental causes). They are in the same physical environment; their relevant states are caused by the same environmental condition; they display the same linguistic behavior (nonintentionally described). Indeed, they may have been in the same sequence of mental states, described nonintentionally, all the way back to the acquisition of their beliefs and beyond. They may even be molecular replicas. Nevertheless, the English speaker, who has never heard of crickets, believes that locusts are a menace, whereas the non-English speaker, who has never heard of locusts, believes that crickets are a menace.[19]

---

[18] The example, like the previous ones, owes a great deal to Tyler Burge's work. See, for example, "Individualism and the Mental," in *Studies in Metaphysics*, ed. Peter A. French et al., Midwest Studies in Philosophy, 4 (Minneapolis: University of Minnesota Press, 1979), 73–122, and "Other Bodies," in *Thought and Object: Essays on Intentionality*, ed. Andrew Woodfield (Oxford: Clarendon Press, 1982), 97–120. The example is a kind of converse of Putnam's Twin Earth cases; see "The Meaning of 'Meaning,' " in Putnam's *Mind, Language and Reality: Philosophical Papers*, vol. 2 (Cambridge: Cambridge University Press, 1975), 215–271.

[19] As we saw in the gin/vodka case, the example does not require natural-kind terms. What the present example adds to the previous ones is that it requires only a single token, rather than two tokens of a single type. Both examples also tell against Daniel Dennett's claim that "perfect equivalence of program . . . is a sufficient but not a necessary condition for sharing intentional characterizations." See "A Cure for the Common Code?" in

The thought experiment shows that generalizations of attributions will not be materially equivalent to generalizations deducible from neurophysiology plus boundary conditions and limiting assumptions. If they were equivalent, then predicates of the form 'x has a token T of neurophysiological type Y in context C' would be true of all and only those individuals of whom predicates of the form 'x believes that locusts are a menace' are true. Yet the same predicates describing neurophysiological state and (physical) context are true of each combatant, though attribution of belief that locusts are a menace is true of one but not the other. Therefore, the candidate predicates are not even extensionally equivalent.

In the absence of the relevant materially equivalent statements, it seems doubtful that neurophysiology will have, in Churchland's words, "the resources to conjure up a set of properties whose nomological powers/roles/features are systematic *analogues* of the powers/roles/ features of the set of properties postulated by" the common-sense conception.[20] Lacking such "systematic nomological parallels," the common-sense conception will not reduce (in Churchland's sense) to neurophysiology.

If, as I have argued, Stich's modified Panglossian prospect offers no conditions under which to determine when a particular syntactic token is describable as a belief that p and when it is not, and if Churchland's reduction fails, then (5) may well be true. Such an eventuality would not disturb Churchland or Stich, who take the issue to be wholly empirical, contrary to the suggestion of my thought experiment. (Their arguments that the common-sense conception is a would-be empirical theory will be discussed in the next section.) In any case, if, as Stich fears, "the humanities, the social sciences, and the many social institutions which are so intimately interwoven with the conceptual framework of folk psychology" are in any danger from a scientific psychology at all,[21] they will not be rescued by the kind of psychology envisaged by either Stich or Churchland.

But (5) alone does not entail that there is anything amiss in the common-sense conception or that no one has ever had a belief. Statement (4) is also required for that bold conclusion. An interpretation of the premise of physicalism, (4) expresses the assumption that the common-sense conception will be either vindicated or eliminated altogether. Thus, if (4) is true, and if my arguments against Stich's modified Pan-

Dennett's *Brainstorms: Philosophical Essays on Mind and Psychology* (Montgomery, Vt.: Bradford, 1978), 105.

[20] Churchland, "Reduction, Qualia and the Direct Introspection of Brain States," 13.

[21] Stich, *From Folk Psychology to Cognitive Science*, 224.

glossian prospect and Churchland's theoretical reduction are correct, then no token of the form '*S* believes that *p*' expresses, or has ever expressed, a truth.

Is the Common-Sense Conception
an Empirical Theory?

Many philosophers readily countenance the possibility that no token of the form '*S* believes that *p*' expresses, or has ever expressed, a truth. Why have philosophers seen rejection of the common-sense conception as a live option? The answer, I think, is that many philosophers take the common-sense conception to be a kind of folk theory with pretensions to rival scientific theories. The relation between the common-sense conception and scientific psychology is often seen as simply a relation between concepts of two empirical theories.

Stich and Churchland, for example, have both argued that the common-sense conception is an empirical theory and, as such, subject to replacement *in toto* by a physicalistic psychology.[22] Consideration, however, of the arguments that they give for taking the common-sense conception to be an empirical theory will bring into focus *dissimilarities* between the common-sense conception and scientific theories and, hence, will begin to highlight what is at stake in abandoning the common-sense conception.

To make plausible the suggestion that the common-sense conception is just another folk theory, like folk astronomy, Stich and Churchland each offer historical analogies to show that the common-sense conception of the mental is no more secure than Ptolemaic astronomy. Just as no stone ever has sought its natural position in the earth, just as no celestial sphere ever has revolved around the earth, just as no phlogiston ever has had negative weight, so, the argument goes, it may turn out that the common-sense conception is radically wrong and that no one ever has had a belief.

But these analogies do not tell against the common-sense conception of the mental. The natural way to describe these historical episodes is in terms of change of belief—from Aristotelian to Copernican cosmology, from alchemy to elemental chemistry, and so on. If the common-sense conception is false, however, such natural descriptions are barred. If no one ever has had a belief or any other attitude identified

---

[22] Ibid., ch. 5. Paul M. Churchland, *Scientific Realism and the Plasticity of Mind* (Cambridge: Cambridge University Press, 1979), 114; Churchland, *Matter and Consciousness*, 64–65; Churchland, "Eliminative Materialism and Propositional Attitudes," *Journal of Philosophy* 78 (1981), 68–72.

by content, we cannot truly say that people used to believe that the celestial sphere revolved around the earth but that they turned out to be wrong and now almost no one has that mistaken belief. Until the purported historical analogies are described in terms independent of belief, they contribute nothing to the plausibility of displacing belief. If one aims to undermine concepts like belief by means of analogies, one must provide relevant descriptions of analogies that do not presuppose the very concepts to be undermined. No such descriptions are offered.

Indeed, there is a striking disanalogy between the present case and the cases of conceptual change produced by science. Historically, successor theories make it understandable both how the predecessors could reasonably have made the errors that they did and why the earlier views were erroneous. For example, after the discovery of oxygen, it is understandable how, on the available evidence, one may have postulated phlogiston with negative weight and also why such postulation was an error. From the point of view of Copernican astronomy, we can easily see how, from the observations, one may have postulated the increasingly complex systems of epicylces needed for Ptolemaic astronomy, and so on. But from the point of view of the eliminativist's denial of the common-sense conception, how is the error of the common-sense conception even to be intelligible?

Errors of the past can be described and explained easily enough from the viewpoint of the common-sense conception. One makes a cognitive error if such-and-such appears to be the case when it is not the case— for example, although the geocentric view of the universe turned out to be false, it did appear that the sun revolved around the earth. But, of course, the notion that such-and-such appears to be the case is as laden with content as the notion that one believes such-and-such to be the case.[23] So if the common-sense conception, with its attributions of content, is false, the normal contrasts between appearance and reality cannot be drawn.

Moreover, without attitudes identified by content, nothing has ever *seemed* to be one way rather than another. For it to *seem* to be the case that *p* cannot be understood or relevantly described without invoking attitudes identified by content; for it to *seem* to one that she has a certain belief is at least as "contentful" a thought as simply having a belief. Where physics applies, we say things like, "The universe has seemed to be Newtonian, but it really isn't." But this is exactly the contrast that

[23] Stich sets up the issue as one of the relation between the manifest and scientific images. But if there are no states with content, then there are no images, scientific or manifest. Nothing satisfies the open sentence '*x* is a conception of *y*.'

becomes problematic if mental states lack content. Without content, there is nothing to be mistaken about. We could no more describe current error by saying that it wrongly seems to people that they have beliefs than by saying that people falsely believe that they have beliefs. So if the common-sense conception is false, we are under no illusion that we believe one thing rather than another. Indeed, without content we are under no illusions at all.

What needs to be shown, and what has not been shown by anyone denying the common-sense conception, is how, in the absence of attitudes identified by content, physicalistic psychology can characterize cognitive error as error at all. So on the one hand, if the thesis denying the common-sense conception is true, then we all are mistaken. But on the other hand, from the point of view that denies the common-sense conception, there seems to be no mistake to be made.

Thus, far from supporting the view that the common-sense conception is an empirical theory, supplantable by a superior empirical theory, invocation of past conceptual changes generated by science suggests differences between the common-sense conception and outmoded scientific theories. Whereas the errors of outmoded scientific theories are explained by their successors, the "errors" of the common-sense conception are not even intelligible as errors without attitudes identified by content. Rather, at least, no one skeptical of the common-sense conception has furnished a clue about how, from his point of view, the entire human race could have been misled into uttering all those false ascriptions of beliefs, desires, and intentions. Thus, the analogies do nothing to show that the common-sense conception is an empirical theory.

Stich and Churchland, however, although they put heavy emphasis on the putative historical analogies, do not rely exclusively on them. Both have further arguments to show that the common-sense conception is a (would-be) empirical theory, subject to replacement by a better theory. Stich supposes the common-sense conception to rest on empirical assumptions, disconfirmation of which he takes to be fatal to the common-sense conception. He puts the most weight on a claim that "it is a fundamental tenet of folk psychology that *the very same* state which underlies the sincere assertion of 'p' also may lead to a variety of nonverbal behaviors," and he offers empirical evidence from self-attribution theory to prove this tenet false. "[O]ur cognitive system keeps two sets of books" in a way allegedly inconsistent with the common-sense conception: "In those cases when our verbal subsystem leads us to say 'p' and our nonverbal subsystem leads us to behave as though we believed some incompatible proposition, there will simply be no saying which we believe."[24]

But this point hardly forces abandonment of the common-sense conception—any more than Kripke's puzzle about belief does. Indeed, differences in what might be called "belief as behavioral cause" and "belief as opinion" are the source of issues of philosophical interest—for example, issues concerning weakness of the will and self-deception.[25] The discovery of puzzles generated by the common-sense conception presents a challenge to philosophers, just as discovery of logical and semantical paradoxes presents a challenge to logicians. To give up the common-sense conception in the face of them would be a drastic move with no more warrant than to give up logic.

Moreover, Stich looks to attribution theory to disconfirm the alleged empirical tenet of the common-sense conception. But experiments in attribution theory can hardly be adduced as evidence that there are no beliefs or other attitudes identified by content. In order to undermine the purported assumption about the gross architecture of the mind, the utterances by the experimental subjects must be taken to express their *beliefs* (albeit false ones) about the causes of their behavior. But if the hypothesis for which such utterances are to provide evidence is true— if, that is, there are no beliefs—then the utterances cannot be taken to express the subjects' beliefs. Since attribution theory, like most of social psychology, simply takes for granted the common-sense framework of attitudes identified by content, it is unlikely to provide empirical disconfirmation of that framework.

Churchland likewise regards the common-sense conception as an empirical theory up for grabs. His most potent argument is that the common-sense conception rests upon particular empirical generalizations, which may be readily abandoned. He argues that just as terms like 'acceleration' derive their meanings from their places in a network of lawlike statements, so too, terms like 'believes' derive their meaning from their places in a network of lawlike statements, in which case empirical falsification of the lawlike statements would discredit belief. Churchland discusses the following as an empirical lawlike generalization supporting action-explanations:

(L) $(X)(\phi)(A)(\text{If}\ [1]\ X\ \text{wants}\ \phi,\ \text{and}$

[2] X believes that A-ing is a way for him to bring about ϕ under those circumstances, and

---

[24] All of the quotations in this paragraph are from Stich's *From Folk Psychology to Cognitive Science*, 231 (emphasis his).

[25] This point was made by Tyler Burge.

[3] there is no action believed by X to be a way for him to bring about φ, under the circumstances, which X judges to be as preferable to him as, or more preferable to him than, A-ing, and

[4] X has no other want (or set of them), which, under the circumstances, overrides his want φ, and

[5] X knows how to A, and

[6] X is able to A,

then

[7] X A-s.)[26]

However, if (L) is an empirical generalization, it is false, even if the common-sense conception is generally correct, for it may have a true antecedent and a false consequent. Suppose that Jones, attending an APA convention, wants to get a job at State ([1]); she believes that having a chat with a senior faculty member at State is a way to bring about her landing the job under the circumstances ([2]); she can't think of any better way to get the job ([3]); and she has no wants, under the circumstances, that override her want to get the job ([4]). At the smoker, a friend points out to Jones some senior faculty members at State. Jones knows how to chat with a senior faculty member ([5]), is able to chat with a senior faculty member ([6]), and realizes that she is able to chat with one. (An extra clause, omitted by Churchland, is needed to ensure that the agent realizes that she is able to do A.) Hence, the antecedent of (L) is satisfied. Yet Jones fails to chat with a senior faculty member. Why? The friend has pointed to the wrong group, and Jones ignores the readily available faculty members in order to chat with an aging graduate student at State, who quickly sees Jones's mistake but is having too much fun to let on.

The simplicity and obviousness of this example suggest that our common-sense conception of psychology is not committed to any such generalization as (L) as an empirical regularity. My example is not aimed just at a particular formulation, which may be patched up to withstand other counterexamples; I believe that similar examples are available to defeat any such generalization as (L), whether cast as *de dicto*, as (L) is, or as *de re*.[27]

[26] Paul M. Churchland, "The Logical Character of Action-Explanations," *Philosophical Review* 79 (1970), 221.

[27] It may be objected that condition [5] of the antecedent is not satisfied by the counterexample, on the grounds that since Jones misidentifies an aging graduate student as a senior faculty member, she fails to know how to chat with a senior faculty member. Prima facie, I think this inference implausible. In any case, the objection would require interpreting [5] as *de re* and, as such, would be subject to the criticisms of *de re* belief in ex-

If the common-sense conception were committed to generalizations like (L) as empirical regularities, then it would have been falsified long ago by people innocent of neuroscience. The point is not that the common-sense conception is nonempirical but that it has greater resources than elminativists give it credit for. Indeed, the fact that disconfirmation of (L) is internal to the common-sense conception, with no appeal to scientific psychology, suggests that Stich and Churchland have underestimated the richness and complexity of the common-sense conception, which is worthy of more painstaking exploration than has been attempted by philosophers who are willing to reject it outright.

In any case, if the common-sense conception is an empirical theory subject to falsification, it is not easily falsified. And the considerations offered in Chapter Seven, which show ways in which the thesis denying the common-sense conception may be self-defeating, strongly suggest that the common-sense conception is not on a par with, say, the geocentric conception of the universe. It is for this reason that rejection of the common-sense conception is so problematic.

WHAT'S AT STAKE

All parties to the discussion of the status of the common-sense conception recognize that the stakes are high. I offer several examples.

Fodor, the ardent defender of intentional psychology, sees no alternative to invoking propositional attitudes: "[W]e have—or so it seems to me—no notion of behavioral systematicity at all except the one that makes behavior systematic under intentional description."[28]

Stich takes the social sciences to be at risk; the brightest prospect he sees is this:

> When suitably hedged, the economist's or sociologist's generalizations may be both true and useful, just as the chef's are. When (or if) a social science matures to the point where the vagueness and limitations of folk psychology become problematic, social scientists can begin to recast their theories . . . in the content free language forged by the [syntactic theory of mind] cognitive theorist.[29]

But if what Stich calls 'the modified Panglossian view' is not borne out as a genuine alternative to out-and-out repudiation of the common-

planations of action formulated in my "*De Re* Belief in Action," *Philosophical Review* 91 (1982), 363–387.

[28] Jerry A. Fodor, "Cognitive Science and the Twin-Earth Problem," *Notre Dame Journal of Formal Logic* 23 (1982), 102.

[29] Stich, *From Folk Psychology to Cognitive Science*, 228.

sense conception—and I have argued that it is not—then Stich would take all the social sciences, in their specific claims and their generalizations, to be simply false. Stich would greet such an outcome with regret: "One cannot but hope that *some* vindication of propositional attitudes will be forthcoming, since without them we hardly know where to begin in thinking about ourselves, our institutions, our history, and our values. . . ."[30]

Dennett, as indicated in Chapter One, also sees a great deal riding on exculpating attitudes: "[T]he validity of our conceptual scheme of moral agents having dignity, freedom, responsibility stands or falls on the question: can men ever be *truly* said to have beliefs, desires, intentions?"[31]

On the other hand, Churchland is fairly exuberant about the envisaged elimination of the common-sense conception:

> The magnitude of the conceptual revolution here suggested should not be minimized: it would be enormous. And the benefits to humanity might be equally great. If each of us possessed an accurate neuroscientific understanding of (what we now conceive dimly as) the varieties and causes of mental illness, the factors involved in learning, the neural basis of emotions, intelligence, socialization, then the sum total of human misery might be much reduced. The simple increase in mutual understanding that the new framework made possible could contribute substantially toward a more peaceful and humane society. Of course, there would be dangers as well: increased knowledge means increased power, and power can always be misused.[32]

Whether they see the common-sense conception as inevitable or in danger, however, these philosophers seem to me to have failed to appreciate just how high the stakes are. At issue are not only practical reasoning (as Fodor argues) and morality (as Dennett is aware) but also, as we shall see, language, rationality, truth—indeed, cognitive virtue generally.

Suppose that it made sense to assume that nobody ever has had a contentful state. (Of course, if mental states lack content, one cannot assume anything; one cannot even suppose that one can.) Suppose that all attributions of beliefs, desires, hopes, wishes, fantasies, intentions, and so on are false. I doubt that Churchland or Stich would flinch from

[30] Ibid., 194 (emphasis his).

[31] Daniel C. Dennett, "Skinner Skinned," in Dennett, *Brainstorms*, 63 (emphasis his).

[32] Churchland, *Matter and Consciousness*, 45. Cf. "Eliminative Materialism and Propositional Attitudes," 84ff.

the consequences. Again, as Stich states the issue: "Might it be the case that ordinary folk psychological ascriptions will turn out, quite generally, not to be true? The answer I have been urging is that this is a serious possibility. . . ." And he braces for the result: "If we had to renounce folk psychology, we should probably have to reject the notions of personhood and moral agency as well."[33] Consider just some of the consequences.

1. *Social practices that depend upon ordinary explanation and prediction of behavior would become unintelligible.*

a. Our ability to predict others' behavior would become inexplicable. Suppose that I dialed your phone number and said, "Would you join us for dinner at our house on Saturday at 7:00?" You replied, "Yes." On Saturday, I act in the way I should act if I believed that you were coming to dinner. But if neither of us had any beliefs, intentions, or other states attributed via 'that'-clauses, it would be amazing if I actually prepared dinner for you and if you actually showed up.

b. Commonplace interactions among people and what is said about such interactions would become mysterious. Although (what we now think of as) expectations about the behavior of others are constitutive of daily life, there would be no true statements of the form, "I expected him to pull back over to the right lane after he passed me." No one would ever have had any expectations, and without expectations, all would be free of disappointment as well.

c. Behavior could never go wrong. In the absence of contentful states, one could never do anything unintentionally, by accident or by mistake. Nor, of course, would anyone ever do anything deliberately or on purpose. Without distinctions between, for example, doing something deliberately and doing it accidentally, practices of excusing and justifying actions (and of not excusing or justifying them) could not sensibly be maintained.

2. *Moral and legal practices would become senseless.*

d. Almost every explanation that anyone has ever given for her action would be false. No sentence of the form "I fired because I thought my life was in danger" would ever express a truth, nor, of course, would any sentence of the form "I fired because I wanted her money."

---

[33] Stich, *From Folk Psychology to Cognitive Science*, 242.

Criminal proceedings and legal processes generally would simply make no sense.

e. There would be no distinction between what we now call lying and an honest mistake. Related phenomena, such as deceit and fraud, for which one now would be morally, if not legally, blameworthy would disappear.

f. Every moral judgment would be false or senseless. Moral judgments are in an obvious way parasitic on attributions of attitudes, specifically on attributions of attitudes that could figure in intentional explanations. The degree of Mrs. Harris's culpability for shooting the doctor is related to her mental states identified by content. But if all attributions of content were false, and if all intentional explanations, constituted by false attributions, failed to explain, then no moral assessment would be more appropriate than any other. If there were no difference between believing that one is doing A and not so believing, then it would be altogether inappropriate to praise or blame a person for doing A.

g. Nothing would ever have mattered to anybody. For example, nobody would ever have feared that she had cancer or wished that she were a movie star. One cannot value something in the absence of beliefs, desires, or other contentful states regarding it. A heartening corollary: Since even discerning that p is as contentful as believing that p, no one would ever regret doing one thing rather than another. We would all live without regrets, no matter what we said.

3. *Linguistic practices would become mysterious.*

h. It would be a total mystery why we say the things we do (though not why we emit the noises we emit) and why we give the explanations of our actions that we do. If no one had ever had a belief, then no one would ever even have thought that she or anyone else ever had a belief. It would never have seemed that anyone had ever had a belief. (I shall return to this point later.) Thinking that one has a belief is at least as content-ridden as any belief that one professes to have.

i. It would be a miracle that we are able systematically to utter truths. Ask a person on the street whether or not snow is white, the federal deficit is over a million dollars, nuclear war is dangerous, and so on. If the informant is offered enough money for correct answers, she will provide them. Assuming that there are true sentences that are uttered even if no one has ever intended to say anything—an assumption called into question in Chapter Seven—it would be a marvel that, in the absence of mental states with content, everybody has the ability to utter truths.

j. Reports of deliberation and decision would be false. For example, suppose that Jones goes through steps that she describes as trying to decide whether or not to accept a particular job offer and then announces what she (says she) decided. Since attitudes with content are what Jones reports as the materials of her practical reasoning, we could not accept her reports as straightforwardly true while denying that there were such attitudes.

k. What one does would be totally unrelated to what one reports that she thinks she is doing. Subsequent to her announcement that she will accept a new job, Jones's behavior changes; for example, she starts going to a different office. But if there were no contentful states, then what she (falsely) said she decided must be irrelevant to her changed habits. In order to discover why she now goes to a different office, we must look elsewhere than at what she says. People's reports on the sources of their behavior would be almost uniformly false.

4. Psychology would become problematic.

l. Most sorts of applied psychology, from market research to the various psychotherapies, would be bogus. No brand of existing psychotherapy would be superior to any other, since all presuppose that the client or subject has states with content—desires and fantasies, at least. The facts that market research (sometimes) does increase profits and that patients (sometimes) do report that they are better would become inexplicable. If the basic assumptions of these enterprises were false, why do they seem, as we should pretheoretically put it, as successful as they do?

m. The *explananda* of psychology would become problematic. If contentful mental states were denied, then much of what called for psychological explanation would evaporate. In the absence of beliefs, memories, or other states with content, what is psychology (including neuroscience) supposed to explain that is not better explained by physics?

The skeptic about the common-sense conception may claim to be prepared to swallow all these consequences. He may say, for example, that while believing and the rest are fictions, physicalistic psychology will provide successor concepts in which the truth of these matters will be expressible. If the skeptic is right, however, then the full truth of all these matters will be expressible without invoking content. So, whatever the proposed successors to 'believes that' and so on, they must be adequate for expressing the relations among mental states, language, and action generally without identifying mental states by 'that'-clauses.

Until the skeptic gives some substantive indication of how the phenomena of language and behavior can be dealt with in a content-free way, his profession of skepticism about the common-sense conception is just idle play.

In the next chapter, we shall explore further the enormity of the task facing the skeptic about the common-sense conception: No one who entertains denial of the common-sense conception has shown how, if there are no contentful states, there can be argument, or even language, as opposed to mere marks and audible emissions. The best that anyone has come up with are putative historical analogies, all of which fail until they can be described without presupposing content. It is difficult to see how the skeptic about the common-sense conception can avoid undercutting his own position; he seems on the brink of self-defeat.

· 7 ·

THE THREAT OF
COGNITIVE SUICIDE

To deny the common-sense conception of the mental is to abandon all our familiar resources for making sense of any claim, including the denial of the common-sense conception. It may be thought that the image of Neurath's ship being rebuilt at sea plank by plank, may be of service to those denying the common-sense conception. On the contrary, the image works the other way. Local repairs, in the common-sense conception, presuppose a concept of content, but content seems not susceptible to physicalistic formulation. Thus, physicalists are in no position to replace the common-sense conception plank by plank. From a consistent physicalistic point of view, what is at issue must be the entire framework of attitudes specified by 'that'-clauses.[1] If it is hazardous, as it surely is, to attempt to rebuild a ship at sea all at once, it is all the more hazardous to undertake rebuilding with no replacement material available.

On the other hand, in the absence of a replacement, it is literally inconceivable that the common-sense conception of the mental is false. But it is such a thought that, with a measure of trepidation, I next want to explore. I shall set out several ways in which denial of the common-sense conception may be self-defeating or otherwise pragmatically incoherent. If the thesis denying the common-sense conception is true, then the concepts of rational acceptability, of assertion, of cognitive error, even of truth and falsity are called into question. It remains to be seen whether or not such concepts (or suitable successors) can be reconstructed without presupposing the truth of attributions of content. Of the three kinds of incoherence I discuss, the first two may be familiar (though not, I think, sufficiently appreciated).[2]

---

[1] The arguments in this chapter are aimed at those prepared to relinquish attitudes specifiable by 'that'-clauses, whether or not they want to develop some other concept of content not specifiable by 'that'-clauses. Content in the common-sense conception is specified by 'that'-clauses.

[2] See, for example, Norman Malcolm, "The Conceivability of Mechanism," *Philosophical Review* 77 (1968), 45–77. Also, Lewis White Beck, *The Actor and the Spectator* (New Haven: Yale University Press, 1975), formulates a sense in which arguments for mechanism may be "self-stultifying."

Rational Acceptability at Risk

The first way in which the view denying the common-sense conception may be self-defeating is this: Anyone who claims that the thesis is rationally acceptable lapses into pragmatic incoherence because the thesis denying the common-sense conception undermines the concept of rational acceptability.

The skeptic about the common-sense conception has two, perhaps insurmountable, obstacles to overcome: one concerns the idea of *accepting* a proposition or theory; the other, the idea of *justifiably* accepting a proposition or theory. Obviously, if the common-sense conception is eliminated, no one is justified in believing anything; indeed, no one believes anything, justifiably or not. The skeptic who would salvage the idea of rational acceptability is then left with two problems. First, he must come up with some successor to the family that includes 'believes that,' 'accepts that,' and other such expressions, which will permit a distinction between, say, "accepting" (or whatever the content-free successor of accepting is) one thing and "accepting" another *without adverting to content*. The arguments of Part I, which reveal the difficulty, if not the impossibility, of providing nonintentional and nonsemantic sufficient conditions for a state's having a particular content give us reason to be dubious about making the correct distinctions in a vocabulary that does not attribute content.

Putting aside worries about how a content-free mental state can replace acceptance, the second difficulty here concerns the normative notions of rationality, justification, and good argument. If the thesis denying the common-sense conception is true, then it is unclear that there could ever be good arguments for it or that anyone could ever be justified in "accepting" (the successor of accepting) it. The thesis seems to undermine the possibility of good argument and justification generally.

In many cases, if a person is justified in accepting a thesis, then there exists evidence for the thesis, which the person appreciates. It is difficult to see how the ideas of evidence and of appreciating the evidence can be unpacked in the absence of states with content. Of course, the skeptic about the common-sense conception, reaching for consistency, may "agree" (or do whatever replaces agreement in a post–common-sense framework) that ideas of evidence and of appreciating the evidence are part of the common-sense conception, which is to be left behind. Then, if the skeptic holds that the thesis denying the common-sense conception can be rationally accepted, he owes us some other "account" (an appropriate successor of an account) of "justification" (an appropriate successor of a justification) that does not presuppose the repudiated ideas. The successor concepts must allow both for a distinction between being "justified" in "accepting" p and not being so "justified" and for a distinction between being "justified" in "accepting" p and being "justified" in "accepting" q, without presupposing that there are contentful states. But every skeptic about the common-sense conception freely uses ideas integral to the common-sense conception in his attack (another common-sense idea that the skeptic must replace) on it.

The language of accepting and denying, as well as of evidence, hypothesis, argument, is part and parcel of the common-sense conception. Before the skeptic about the common-sense conception has any claim on us, he must replace these ideas with successor ideas that make no appeal to states with content (or otherwise do without such ideas). What is at stake here, as all parties to the discussion agree, are all attributions of contentful states. If the successor concepts advert to content, then they do not avoid the common-sense conception that I am defending. But if they do not advert to content, it is difficult to see how they can make the needed distinctions between accepting (or rather its content-free successor) one thesis and accepting another. And the absence of such distinctions would make it impossible to accept any thesis at all.

Here, then, is a dilemma for the skeptic about the common-sense conception: From the perspective that denies the common-sense conception, either he can distinguish being "justified" in "accepting" that p from being "justified" in "accepting" that q or not. If not, then no one is "justified" in "accepting" the thesis that denies the common-sense conception of the mental or any other thesis. But if so, then, in light of the arguments of Part I, the skeptic must absolve himself of the charge that he is covertly assuming contentful states by producing relevant content-free successors to concepts of acceptance and justification. If the skeptic declines on grounds that absolving oneself of charges is part of the common-sense conception that is to be discarded, then he is playing into the hand of the critic who says that the skeptic jeopardizes any standards of rational acceptability.[3]

On the face of it, one can hardly see how to free rich concepts, like that of being justified in accepting a particular thesis, of layers of content. At least, the challenge is there for the skeptic about common sense to come up with replacement concepts that permit distinctions like those between accepting and not accepting a thesis and between being

---

[3] Suppose that a skeptic tried a kind of *reductio ad absurdum* of the common-sense conception by using, say, the notion of rational acceptability in order to show that that notion has insurmountable internal problems; from this, he concludes, so much the worse for the idea of rational acceptance. It would remain unclear how any such argument could have a claim on us. We obviously could not rationally accept it.

justified and not being justified in accepting a thesis—replacement concepts that make the needed distinctions without presupposing that any attribution of content has ever been true.

Churchland has taken the tack of urging the rational acceptability of denying the common-sense conception by proposing as an alternative to states with content an account of what constitutes a cognitive economy. Regardless of what alternative account he proposes, however, this move is not available to him. In order to be an *alternative* account to the common-sense conception, the successor must at least allow scientists to identify certain systems as cognitive; and in order to be an alternative *account* of cognition, the successor must allow scientists to hypothesize that cognitive states have such-and-such a character. But no one has shown how concepts like those of *identifying* something as a cognitive system or *hypothesizing* that cognitive states lack content have application in the absence of content. Indeed, it is difficult to see how anything could count as advancing an alternative to the common-sense conception in the absence of contentful states. Without contentful states, what makes it *p* rather than *q* that one "advances"? What makes an audible emission one of advancing at all?[4]

Indeed, it is difficult to see how to construe what scientists are doing generally when they engage in research if they lack mental states with content. The ideas of evidence, hypothesis, and experiment at least seem to presuppose content. (Or that is the only way I know to put it, even though I do not see how 'seems to presuppose something' could be true of anything if we have no contentful states.) It would help to see an account (or rather, a content-free successor to an account) of these ideas or of successor ideas in terms of which science could be practiced without presupposing states with content. The common-sense conception pervades the language of rational acceptability in scientific activity as well as in everyday affairs.

To sum up: The first threat of self-defeat for the thesis denying the common-sense conception of the mental stems from the consequences for the concept of rational acceptability. Without a new account of how there can be rational acceptability in the absence of belief and intention, we have no way to evaluate the claim denying the

---

[4] An objection that I do not meet the thrust of the eliminativists' arguments would seem to presuppose the common-sense standpoint. If eliminativism is correct, then in what sense do anyone's bodily movements qualify as arguments at all? Arguments about the allegedly self-defeating character of anything are, I think, frustrating to people on both sides of the issue. People on each side think that those on the other miss the point. From my side, it seems that I ask straightforward questions (like that above), which require answers but receive none.

common-sense conception. This first threat suggests that, apart from the common-sense conception, we may not be able to say much about our so-called rational practices. The next kind of pragmatic incoherence suggests that, apart from the common-sense conception, we may not be able to say anything at all.

Assertion at Risk

The second way in which the thesis denying the common-sense conception may be self-defeating is this: Anyone who asserts that view lapses into pragmatic incoherence because the thesis undermines the concept of assertibility; at least, he must offer some indication of how there can be assertion without belief.[5] Both Patricia Churchland and Paul Churchland have denied charges that, if a certain thesis is true, it cannot be asserted. Paul Churchland has aimed to rebut the claim that eliminative materialism—a corollary of the view that the common-sense conception is radically mistaken—is self-refuting. Here is how he sets out the argument that he intends to undermine:

> [T]he statement of eliminative materialism is just a meaningless string of marks or noises, unless that string is the expression of a certain *belief*, and a certain *intention* to communicate, and a *knowledge* of the grammar of the language, and so forth. But if the statement of eliminative materialism is true, then there are no such states to express. The statement at issue would then be a meaningless string of marks or noises. It would therefore *not* be true. Therefore it is not true. Q.E.D.[6]

Churchland finds this argument question-begging and illustrates his point by presenting an argument against antivitalism, which, he claims, is both parallel to the above argument against eliminative materialism and obviously question-begging. The argument that he claims to be parallel is this:

> The anti-vitalist says that there is no such thing as vital spirit. But this claim is self-refuting. The speaker can expect to be taken seri-

---

[5] It should be clear that I am not asking for a reduction of speech to thought; in particular, I do not suppose that thought exhibits intrinsic intentionality and speech exhibits derived intentionality. I do not think that a reduction either way—from language to thought to brain, or from thought to language to physicalistic theory of meaning—is promising.

[6] Paul M. Churchland, "Eliminative Materialism and Propositional Attitudes," *Journal of Philosophy* 78 (1981), 89; cf. his *Matter and Consciousness* (Cambridge, Mass.: MIT/Bradford, 1984), 48 (emphasis his).

ously only if his claim cannot. For if the claim is true, then the speaker does not have vital spirit and must be *dead*. But if he is dead, then his statement is a meaningless string of noises, devoid of reason and truth.[7]

But the arguments fail to be parallel in two crucial respects. First, the pairs of imaginary disputants differ in the presuppositions they share. The antivitalist would agree with the vitalist that being alive is a necessary condition for making a claim; he simply differs in his account of what it is to be alive. The eliminative materialist, on the other hand, could not consistently agree with his opponent that having beliefs or other attitudes identified by content is a necessary condition for making claims. The eliminative materialist is not offering a different account of what it is to have beliefs; he is denying that anyone has beliefs. The parallel to an eliminative materialist would be an antivitalist who held that dead men make claims. Therefore, the silliness of the argument against antivitalism has no bearing on the argument against eliminative materialism.

Second, the error in the argument against antivitalism has no echo in the argument against eliminative materialism. It is a mistake to charge the antivitalist with being dead on account of lacking a vital spirit *either* on the assumption that antivitalism is true *or* on the assumption that antivitalism is false. If antivitalism is true, then the lack of a vital spirit is irrelevant to death; if it is false, then the antivitalist, who mistakenly denies vitalism, has a vital spirit and is not dead.

But the argument against eliminative materialism, stated more carefully than Churchland concedes, challenges the eliminative materialist to show how there can be assertion without belief or other states with content. It begs no question to assume, as the argument against eliminative materialism does, that eliminative materialism is true.[8]

Churchland explains his rejection of the argument that eliminative materialism is self-defeating by claiming that the argument assumes a certain theory of meaning, one that presupposes the integrity of the common-sense conception. But only to a minimal extent is a particular theory of meaning assumed; issues that divide theorists like Frege, Davidson, Kaplan, Montague, and Grice are wholly irrelevant to the argument that eliminative materialism is self-refuting. The argument

---

[7] Churchland, "Eliminative Materialism and Propositional Attitudes," 89 (emphasis his).

[8] This point was also made by Karl Popper in "Is Determinism Self-Refuting?" *Mind* 92 (1983), 103, a reply to Patricia Smith Churchland, "Is Determinism Self-Refuting?" *Mind* 90 (1981), 99–101.

against eliminative materialism makes the minimal assumption that language can be meaningful only if it is possible that someone mean something.

Of course, history is full of received views that turn out to be false. That a hot object heats up a cold object when caloric fluid flows from one to the other or that knowledge is justified true belief are two examples.[9] Unlike the assumption about meaningful language, however, these examples are instances of explicitly formulated theories. Moreover, the superseding theories make it intelligible why people said (false) things like "The sun revolves around the earth." But from the perspective that denies the common-sense conception, it would be a mystery why anybody would ever say (false) things like "I ran inside because I thought I heard the phone ring." (Of course, the emission of the noises would have a physical explanation.) Not only would thinking that one heard the phone ring fail to be either reason for or cause of one's rapid house-entering behavior, but worse, one would never have *thought* that she heard the phone ring. Nor, if the common-sense conception is false, did anyone ever *seem* to think that she heard the phone ring. As noted earlier, a mental state of seeming to think that *p* would be, if anything, more content-laden than one of merely thinking that *p*.

It is clearly incumbent upon anyone who wants to deny the near-platitude that language can be meaningful only if it is possible that someone mean something to show how there can be meaningful language even if no one has ever meant anything, even if no one has ever intended to say anything. The claim of the syntactic theory—that mental activity consists of relations to uninterpreted sentences—just begs for an account of what those who advocate the syntactic approach are doing when they write; without such an account, the sentences that they write can have no more claim on us than do crevices etched into the Rock of Gibralter by the weather.

Suppose someone were to say: On a speech-dispositional view, assertion does not require belief or any other state with content. So we can have assertion and language, even without contentful states. But, we should reply, a satisfactory speech-dispositional view has yet to be developed.[10] Since assertion *simpliciter* is sincere assertion, an alterna-

[9] These examples were suggested by Charles Chastain, who commented on an earlier version of this chapter at the Oberlin Colloquium in Philosophy, April 12–14, 1985.

[10] Quine's view, for example, seems susceptible to arguments similar to those Chomsky deployed against Skinner. See Noam Chomsky, "A Review of Skinner's *Verbal Behavior*," in *Readings in the Philosophy of Psychology*, vol. 1, ed. Ned Block (Cambridge, Mass.: Harvard University Press, 1980), 48–63. In addition, Alan Berger has argued that Quine's account presupposes ideas to which he is not entitled. See Berger, "A Central

tive to the common-sense view, speech-dispositional or otherwise, would have to distinguish assertion from "noise" on the one hand and from lying on the other. Such an alternative account of assertion would be called on to do three things:

(i) Without appeal to the content of mental states, the alternative account of assertion must distinguish assertion from other audible emission. Perhaps the account would distinguish between kinds of causal history.

But it is difficult to guess how to specify the right causal history without attributing to the speaker some state with the content of what is asserted. (This difficulty will be discussed further in the next section.) Notice also that a speech-dispositional account presupposes an answer to the question of which audible emissions manifest speech dispositions and hence provides no answer to it.

(ii) The alternative account of assertion, again without appeal to the content of mental states, must distinguish sounds that count as an assertion that p rather than as an assertion that q.

This would require a physicalistic reduction of semantics much stronger than, say, Davidson's, which takes for granted the availability of an interpreted metalanguage and takes the truth predicate as a primitive. The arguments in Part I are easily modified to suggest that the difficulties in supplying nonsemantic conditions for application of semantic notions may be insurmountable.

(iii) The alternative account of assertion must at least have conceptual room for a distinction between sincere assertion and lying.

Since the distinction between sincere assertion and lying is made by reference to whether or not one believes what one is saying or whether or not one intends to mislead, it is less than obvious, to say the least, how to make out a comparable distinction without presupposing mental states with content. Certainly no one has offered any evidence that a concept like sincerity can be reconstructed without appeal to the content of mental states.

Thus, I think we have substantial reason to doubt that any alterna-

Problem for a Speech-Dispositional Account of Logic and Language," in *Studies in the Philosophy of Language*, ed. Peter A. French, Theodore E. Uehling, Jr., and Howard K. Wettstein, Midwest Studies in Philosophy, 14 (Minneapolis: University of Minnesota Press, forthcoming). In any case, a speech-dispositional account does not seem to meet (i)–(iii) below; nor, as we shall see, can it accommodate the locust/cricket case.

tive account of assertion that is free of appeal to contentful mental states will be forthcoming.[11]

Although Churchland has offered several scenarios in which he imagines the actual displacement of the common-sense conception by neuroscience, they all bypass the question raised here. For example, Churchland asks: "How will such [post–common-sense conception] people understand and conceive of other individuals? To this question I can only answer, 'In roughly the same fashion that your right hemisphere "understands" and "conceives of" your left hemisphere—intimately and efficiently, but not propositionally!' "[12] At this level of description, the analogy is unhelpful, as Churchland signals by his use of scare-quotes around 'understands' and 'conceives of.' One's right hemisphere does not conceive of one's left hemisphere at all. Not only does the idea of nonpropositional "understanding" remain mysterious, but a strictly neurophysiological account of understanding would seem to leave us in the dark about how anything, including putative denials of the common-sense conception, could have meaning.

To sum up: The second threat of self-defeat for the thesis denying the common-sense conception stems from the consequences for assertion. Without a new "account" of how there can be assertion in the absence of belief and intention, we have no way to interpret the claim denying the common-sense conception.[13]

[11] Since Stich has explicitly linked the notion of sincere assertion to belief, I should expect that he would let sincere assertion go the way of belief. He says that it is difficult to see how the notion of 'sincere assertion of p' "could be unpacked without invoking the idea of an utterance *caused by the belief that p." From Folk Psychology to Cognitive Science: The Case Against Belief* (Cambridge, Mass.: MIT/Bradford, 1983), 79 (emphasis his).

[12] Churchland, "Eliminative Materialism and Propositional Attitudes," 88. Churchland thinks that with the resources of a future scientific psychology, we could "manage to construct a new system of verbal communication entirely distinct from natural language," which everyone may actually come to use. In that case, the categories of natural language, along with propositional attitudes, would disappear (87). I can imagine the disappearance of natural language, along with the disappearance of the human race as the result of a nuclear war, say; but neither I nor anyone else has the ability to imagine business as usual without natural language or propositional attitudes. Imagining is itself a propositional attitude. Of course, I can imagine a world without propositional attitudes; but from the fact that I imagine it, it follows that such a world is not ours.

[13] It is no criticism that I presuppose the common-sense conception in discussing, for example, the possibility of a surrogate "denial." All we now have are common-sense ways to understand what, for example, a denial is; we cannot very well dispense with common sense and keep even a surrogate for denial, unless we have some idea of what that surrogate is. What is it? Is it just a prejudice of common sense that a denial is always a denial *of* something?

Truth at Risk

The third way that the view denying the common-sense conception may be self-defeating is this: If the thesis is true, it has not been shown to be formulable. We can formulate a thesis if and only if we can specify what would make it true. In addition to undermining concepts of rational acceptability and of assertibility, the thesis denying the common-sense view may make incoherent the concepts of truth and falsity, as applied to mental states and language, in which case neither it nor any other thesis would be formulable.[14]

In the interest of reducing obscurity, let me make some observations. Content is attributable by 'that'-clauses. Just as a mental state has content if and only if it is correctly identifiable as, for example, a believing that p, so an utterance or inscription has content if and only if it is correctly identifiable as a saying that p. At this point, however, the contours of the terrain blur. Although these terminological matters may be carved up differently without detriment to my argument, related issues—for example, whether or not the (alleged) impropriety of 'believes that' carries over to 'says that'—are no mere matters of terminology.

I hope to avoid begging any substantive questions by joining the skeptic of the common-sense conception in his main contention, namely, that mental states have no content, that is, they are not correctly identified by 'that'-clauses. I shall urge that this contention comes to grief on the question: Can such content-free mental states have truth value? Case 1: If so, what makes mental state tokens that are not identifiable by 'that'-clauses true or false? Case 2: If not, what makes utterances and inscriptions true or false?

Anyone who denies the common-sense conception on the basis of the argument from physicalism is a scientific realist who cannot beg off these questions. Even so, since I see no reason to suppose that thought may be reduced to language or language to thought, adequate answers to these questions do not require anything resembling a scientific theory, only an indication that there is space, as it were, for answers. It is difficult to see how insistence that cognition requires a distinction between truth and falsity (or at least between being right and being wrong) could be written off as dogmatism or mere prejudice.

Case 1: Suppose that the skeptic about the common-sense conception says that, yes, mental state tokens may be true or false even without content. In this case, the skeptic must answer the question: By vir-

[14] If one endorses a redundancy theory of truth, then the problem raised in this section about truth would reduce to the problem raised about assertibility.

tue of what is a mental state token, identified without 'that'-clauses, true?

On the horizon are only two approaches to truth available to the skeptic who denies the common-sense conception. One is to try to account for the truth of a true mental state (identified in wholly nonintentional terms) by means of a correspondence between it and a particular state of affairs. The other is to try to account for the truth of a true mental state in terms of the way that the state was caused or the way that such mental states typically are caused. I find neither of these approaches promising.

First, in the absence of attitudes identified by content, a mental state token, as identified by a physicalistic psychology (syntactic or neurophysiological), may be true if it "corresponds" in the right way to states of affairs. But how are mental states to be mapped on to states of affairs? Which correspondence is the right one?[15]

Given only the syntactic or neurophysiological properties of mental state tokens and the physical properties of contexts, any token may be mapped on to any state of affairs. (Indeed, it is difficult to see why any molecular configuration is to count as one mapping as opposed to another if there are no mental states with content.) A natural way to select an appropriate mapping—one that plausibly has a claim to securing truth—would be to identify mental states by content. But if mental states could be identified by content, then the skeptic about the common-sense conception would be refuted. Thus, I do not see how the truth of mental state tokens can be explained in terms of correspondence between mental state tokens and states of affairs without invoking content.

The second way to characterize the truth of mental state tokens without presupposing attitudes identified by content would be in terms of the causes of one's mental states. Truth could then be understood in terms of standard causal chains. To take an oversimplified example, snow's being white may cause, in some standard way to be specified, a certain mental state m, which in turn contributes to an utterance, 'Snow is white.'

But this proposal, too, as we saw in Chapter Five, has difficulties. It is unlikely that the notion of a standard causal chain can be filled out satisfactorily. The problem of specifying standard or normality conditions simply arises once again. Moreover, as the cricket/locust example

---

[15] Tarski's theory of truth is of no help here. That Tarski has not formulated a "materialistically adequate" concept of truth has been argued by Hartry Field in "Tarski's Theory of Truth," *Journal of Philosophy* 69 (1972), 347–375. For further criticisms, see Robert C. Stalnaker's *Inquiry* (Cambridge, Mass.: MIT/Bradford, 1984), ch. 2.

indicated, two routes may be indistinguishable as long as they are described nonintentionally; yet one may lead to a belief that p and the other to a belief that q, where 'p' and 'q' differ in truth conditions. Finally, in many cases, a belief that p is not connected with the state of affairs that p in any obvious way.

Therefore, I do not think that the notion of correspondence or of cause will secure the distinction between truth and falsity of mental state tokens lacking content. So let us turn to case 2.

Case 2: Suppose that the skeptic about the common-sense conception says that, no, mental state tokens without content may not be true or false. In this case the skeptic must answer the question: By virtue of what are inscriptions and utterances unmoored to mental states that are true or false themselves true or false?

Before addressing these issues directly, consider the rather drastic consequence of having to conclude that, without content, mental states also lack truth value.[16] It would follow that no one is, or ever has been, in cognitive error. Still assuming for the moment that the skeptic about the common-sense conception is correct, all those false attributions or would-be attributions of belief, desire, and intention cannot be the product of any mistake on our part.

One may rather relinquish the possibility of describing anything as cognitive error before letting go of a preferred theory. Still, the difficulty of a distinction between truth and falsity, even the truth or falsity of particular inscriptions, would remain. One may utter sentences, some presumably true and some presumably false; but the truth or falsity of the sentences that one utters would have nothing to do with any semantic value of one's mental states. The falsity of any utterance would be no reflection on the speaker, whose mental states are free of any taint of error. Indeed, the fact that certain sounds we emit are true (if they are) can only be fortuitous. It would be as if we were simply transmitting sounds, whose truth or falsity is beyond our ability to appreciate. This point alone raises suspicions about how audible emissions, swinging free of semantically evaluated mental states, can be true or false. So, to return to the development of case 2, if there is no such thing as cognitive error, if mental states lack not only content but also

---

[16] Denying truth value to mental states would have several further unfortunate consequences. One could not reasonably be held accountable for the truth or falsity of one's statements if their truth or falsity is in no way connected to one's mental states. One would have no duty to speak the truth and avoid falsity. Indeed, it would be a mystery how falsity and error could even be of concern to us if our mental states lacked truth value. (If mental states lack content, one could not even think that one is saying something true or that one is saying something false.)

truth value, by virtue of what are inscriptions and utterances true or false?

Truth or falsity attaches to items that are semantically interpreted. But any arbitrary mapping of symbols on to states of affairs is an interpretation. What distinguishes the mapping that pairs symbols with their truth conditions? By virtue of what does an inscription signify one state of affairs rather than another, or signify anything at all?

By now, the line is familiar. A causal account is no good: Snow's being white cannot cause 'snow is white' to express that fact. A "use" account is no good: To say that 'snow is white' is used to express the fact that snow is white just smuggles in contentful states—for example, that people intend to express such facts. A speech-dispositional account is no good: Such an account must suppose that many people assent when queried, "Is snow white?" But that supposition leaves the fundamental question without a hint of an answer: What makes the investigator's audible emission a query or the respondent's audible emission an assent?

In addition, a speech dispositional account would return the wrong verdict on cases like the cricket/locust example. Suppose that a radical translator comes to the ward where our two combatants languish. Since the two combatants have exactly the same dispositions, they assent to exactly the same stimulus sentences. So on a speech-dispositional analysis, their utterances should receive exactly the same translation into the translator's language. But that would be a mistake. Each is a competent speaker of his language, in which syntactically and acoustically similar tokens differ in content. In jointly producing a single token, one says that locusts are a menace; the other says that crickets are a menace.

No matter how hard the bullet one is prepared to bite, cases 1 and 2 are exhaustive: Either mental states without content can have truth value or they cannot. If they can, then we have not even a sketch of how; if they cannot, then we have not even a sketch of how inscriptions and utterances can be true or false. But without a distinction between truth and falsity, neither the thesis denying the common-sense conception nor any other is even formulable.[17]

To sum up: The third threat of self-defeat for the thesis denying the common-sense conception of the mental stems from the consequences

[17] Invocation of possible worlds is of no help. Suppose that one says: assign 'snow is white' the value 1 in all possible worlds in which snow is white; assign 'grass is green' the value 1 in all possible worlds in which grass is green, and so on. Such a procedure begs the question now at issue. If mental states lack content, by virtue of what does 'assign' mean assign? What makes '1' mean 'true' rather than something else?

for the distinction between truth and falsity. Without a new "account" of how there can be truth and falsity in the absence of true attributions of content, we have no way to formulate the claim denying the common-sense conception.

Thus, in light of the considerations just presented, it seems that we can neither rationally accept nor assert nor even formulate the thesis denying the common-sense conception of the mental. Indeed, if the thesis is true, it is at least problematic whether we can rationally accept or assert or even formulate any thesis at all.[18] This seems ample reason to deny the conclusions of the arguments from physicalism.

The Upshot

If the denial of the common-sense conception is self-defeating in any of the ways that I have suggested, then we must consider again the valid arguments that led to such a conclusion.

ARGUMENT FROM PHYSICALISM

(1) Either physicalistic psychology will vindicate (in a sense to be specified) the common-sense conception of the mental or the common-sense conception of the mental is radically mistaken.
(2) Physicalistic psychology will fail to vindicate (in the relevant sense) the common-sense conception of the mental.
Therefore,
(3) The common-sense conception of the mental is radically mistaken.

If the conclusion cannot be accepted, we must reject at least one of the premises.[19] Since the second premise may well be true—since, that is, it is a real possibility that science will fail minimally to vindicate the common-sense conception—the culprit is likely the first premise, the commitment to physicalism. In that case, we should have to reject the

---

[18] One may want to respond that all that has been shown is that denial of the common-sense conception is not *currently* formulable or conceivable and that we cannot predict what enlarged conceptual resources there may be in the future. But in order for the thesis *ever* to be conceivable (or formulable, and so on), we would have to have a new conception of conceiving without content—that is, a conception of conceiving that did not distinguish between conceiving that *p* and conceiving that *q*. As vague as our current concept of conceiving is, it is difficult to see how it could be replaced by any concept that failed to distinguish between conceiving that *p* and conceiving that *q*.

[19] From a significantly different angle, Terence Horgan and James Woodward have also defended folk psychology from the criticisms of Stich and Churchland. See their "Folk Psychology Is Here to Stay," *Philosophical Review* 94 (1985), 197–226. I did not see their article until after I had presented the arguments given here.

assumption that physicalistic psychology will either vindicate or eliminate the common-sense conception of the mental.

Less an empirical theory than a condition of intelligibility, the common-sense conception may not be an option for us. One need not be any kind of Cartesian dualist (certainly, Davidson and Wittgenstein are not dualists) to hold that physicalistic science is in no position either to vindicate or to eliminate the common-sense conception of the mental. Since cognition without content is empty, denial of the common-sense conception may be a kind of cognitive suicide that we are constitutionally unable to commit. Thus, we may have to reject the physicalistic dichotomy.

There may yet remain an alternative to the rejection of physicalism. It may be possible to accept the argument from physicalism as sound and, at the same time, to blunt the impact of its conclusion. Instead of supposing that the resistance of the common-sense conception to accommodation with scientific theory robs the common-sense conception of legitimacy, we may take the common-sense conception to be practically indispensable, even if, strictly speaking, it is false. Its usefulness may be thought to confer on it a kind of legitimacy, even a kind of instrumental truth.

Such, I take it, is Dennett's view, a bold attempt to reconcile eliminative materialism with the unavoidability of intentional explanations. If Dennett's project fails, then we seem left with the stark options of either rejecting the premise of physicalism or of rescuing the skeptic about the common-sense conception from self-defeat. It is to Dennett's promise of a way out that we now turn.

· 8 ·

INSTRUMENTALISM:
BACK FROM THE BRINK?

A physicalist who doubts that physicalistic psychology will vindicate beliefs and other attitudes identified by content may yet be loath to risk cognitive suicide. A natural approach is to distinguish various levels of description and to claim that, although the level at which scientific theories describe and explain phenomena delivers the ultimate truth, still the "higher" levels of intentional attribution are practically necessary for less than omniscient beings. Hence, attributions of beliefs, desires, and intentions may be justified by their heuristic value.

Daniel C. Dennett is the philosopher who has most effectively exploited such intuitions.[1] Dennett is a physicalist who tries to avoid both the unfortunate alternatives: either taking beliefs to be scientific entities or concluding that no one has ever had a belief.[2] Although a genuinely explanatory psychology, on Dennett's view, invokes no beliefs or other attitudes, we need not banish ascriptions of belief as false or as scientifically outmoded. The trick is to show how, in the context of eliminative materialism, ascriptions of belief may be legitimized by a certain strategy for predicting behavior.

On the one hand, Dennett would agree with philosophers like Stephen Stich that concepts like belief are unpromising as scientific concepts. As ordinarily understood, not only are "*beliefs* and *pains* not good theoretical *things* (like electrons or neurons), but the state-of-believing-that-p is not a well-defined or definable theoretical *state*."[3] On the other hand, the "validity of our conceptual scheme of moral agents having dignity, freedom and responsibility stands or falls on the ques-

---

[1] Since Dennett continues to develop his position, he may no longer hold all the views that I attribute to him here. See his *The Intentional Stance* (Cambridge, Mass.: MIT/ Bradford, 1987). Nevertheless, these views well illustrate the difficulties of working out the details of an instrumentalism about belief.

[2] Dennett has explored "the relationship between our vision of ourselves as responsible, free, rational agents and our vision of ourselves as complex parts of the physical world of science," with the aim of showing how the vision of ourselves as persons is not threatened by a mechanistic understanding of the mind. Daniel C. Dennett, introduction to his *Brainstorms: Philosophical Essays on Mind and Psychology* (Montgomery, Vt.: Bradford, 1978), x.

[3] Dennett, introduction to *Brainstorms*, xx (emphasis his).

tion: can men ever be *truly* said to have beliefs, desires, intentions?"[4] Dennett's aim is to vindicate, *within the context of physicalism*, our view of ourselves as rational and moral agents—despite the facts that our view of ourselves as rational and moral agents depends upon our having beliefs and that beliefs will not figure in a scientific theory. His attempt to insulate attributions of attitudes from scientific disconfirmation lies in his *instrumentalism* regarding beliefs, desires, and intentions, an instrumentalism worked out in his concept of an intentional system.

INTENTIONAL SYSTEM THEORY

Dennett's concept of an intentional system depends upon what Dennett calls 'stances,' strategies that one may adopt to predict the behavior of a person or machine. From the physical stance, objects are described and their behavior predicted on the basis of physical constitution. From the design stance, objects are described and their behavior predicted in terms of normal operation or function; such predictions assume no breakdown or malfunction. From the intentional stance, objects are described and their behavior predicted by attributing rationality to them, that is, "by ascribing to the system *the possession of certain information* and supposing it to be *directed by certain goals*, and then by working out the most reasonable or appropriate action on the basis of these ascriptions and suppositions."[5] In addition to assuming no breakdown or malfunction, predictions from the intentional stance assume that the agent will select an optimal strategy to reach his or her or its goals.

Although in principle the moves of a chess-playing computer may be predicted from the physical stance on the basis of physics or from the design stance on the basis of program (assuming that the program is not an evolving one and that there is no breakdown), the best strategy for a player who hopes to defeat the computer, practically speaking, is to treat the computer as one would an intelligent human opponent. That is, "one assumes not only (1) that the machine will function as designed, but (2) that the design is optimal as well, that the computer will 'choose' the most rational move."[6]

Ascription of beliefs and intentions to the computer has obvious heuristic value, regardless of the internal states of the computer. Even if there is nothing in the computer that could plausibly answer to the description 'plan to get the Queen out early,' ascription of such a plan might pay off. But it is only for the player's convenience that he ascribes

[4] Dennett, "Skinner Skinned," in *Brainstorms*, 63 (emphasis his).
[5] Dennett, "Intentional Systems," in *Brainstorms*, 6 (emphasis his).
[6] Ibid., 5.

intentional states; and having ascribed them, he finds that they do have predictive value. The computer, considered apart from the predictive strategies of its chess-playing opponent, may be fully described without invoking intentional states at all. With respect to intentional states, there is no difference among sophisticated computers, normal adult humans, and (perhaps) extraterrestrial beings—all alike are "intentional systems."

An intentional system is one whose behavior is predictable from the intentional stance, from which attitudes like belief are attributable. To have a belief is to have it predictively attributable: "[A]*ll there is* to being a true believer is being a system whose behavior is reliably predictable via the intentional strategy, and hence *all there is* to really and truly believing that *p* (for any proposition *p*) is being an intentional system for which *p* occurs as a belief in the best (most predictive) interpretation."[7] Since intentional explanations exhibit behavior as reasonable, attributions of belief presuppose the rationality of the believer. Common-sense psychology, then, "is *idealized* in that it produces its predictions and explanations by calculating in a normative system; it predicts what we *will* believe, desire and do, by determining what we *ought* [rationally ought] to believe, desire, and do."[8] Finally, attributions of belief and other attitudes are holistic in that a single belief could not be attributed in isolation from all other attitudes. An ascription of a particular belief or desire is false if, when conjoined with others, it fails to be predictive of behavior.

In sum, "being rational is being intentional is being the object of a certain stance."[9] Dennett's instrumentalism is explicit:

> The success of the stance is of course a matter settled pragmatically, without reference to whether the object *really* has beliefs, intentions, and so forth; so whether or not any computer can be conscious, or have thoughts or desires, some computers undeniably *are* intentional systems, for they are systems whose behavior can be predicted, and most efficiently predicted, by adopting the intentional stance toward them.[10]

[7] Daniel C. Dennett, "True Believers: The Intentional Strategy and Why It Works," in *Scientific Explanation*, ed. A. F. Heath (Oxford: Oxford University Press, 1981), 68 (emphasis his).

[8] Daniel C. Dennett, "Three Kinds of Intentional Psychology," in *Reduction, Time and Reality*, ed. Richard Healey (Cambridge: Cambridge University Press, 1981), 45–46 (emphasis his).

[9] Daniel C. Dennett, "Conditions of Personhood," in *Brainstorms*, 271.

[10] Daniel C. Dennett, "Mechanism and Responsibility," in *Brainstorms*, 238 (emphasis his).

CHAPTER EIGHT

Since "the choice of stance is 'up to us,' a matter of *decision*, not discovery,"[11] a system has beliefs and other attitudes attributed from the intentional stance only by virtue of its relation to the (possible) predictive strategies of someone else. On intentional system theory, then, systems have beliefs; and attributions of beliefs may be unproblematically true. But—and here is the instrumentalism—what makes such attributions true is not any property intrinsic to the believer but rather just the believer's succumbing to a certain strategy or stance.

An intentional explanation, for all its heuristic value, is never more than an intermediate step on the way to an explanation in terms of design or physical constitution. "Intentional theory is vacuous as psychology because it presupposes and does not explain rationality or intelligence."[12] Although it is a free decision to adopt the intentional stance for convenience, the business of a scientific psychology is to illuminate mentality from the deeper, more explanatory stances: "if one wants to predict and explain the 'actual, empirical' behavior of believers, one must . . . cease talking of belief, and descend to the design stance or physical stance for one's account."[13] In short, the intentional stance, which presupposes neither of the "lower" stances, is only a resting place on the way to the "lower," more mechanistic stances, from which genuine explanations are advanced.[14]

It will be useful in what follows to make explicit a distinction implied by Dennett. I shall use the term 'feature' with next to no ontological commitment: A system *S* has a feature *F* if and only if sentences of the form '*S* is *F*' are true. Dennett's program invites contrast between those features that a system has by virtue of (possibly) being the object of a stance and those features that a system has that are independent of (the possibility of) anyone's taking any stance toward it. For example, al-

[11] Ibid., 239 (emphasis his). Hilary Kornblith has pointed out that, although Dennett seems to take the fact that the intentional stance works to be evidence for instrumentalism, others may take the fact that it works to be evidence for the reality of entities posited from it.

[12] Dennett, "Intentional Systems," 15.

[13] Ibid., 22.

[14] Dennett, "Mechanism and Responsibility," 240. Some readers may find such compatibility, born of instrumentalism of intentional explanations and realism of mechanistic explanations, a "sham . . . and mere word play." John Haugeland, "The Mother of Intention," *Noûs* 16 (1982), 616. As Robert Cummins has remarked, "[A]n instrumentalist treatment of propositional attitudes will ultimately undermine their explanatory value. (Actually, this should come as no surprise: if there are not any, how can they explain anything?)" Cummins, "What Can Be Learned from *Brainstorms*?" *Philosophical Topics* 12 (1981), 88. And Stephen Stich has characterized Dennett's project as "patently disreputable." Stich, *From Folk Psychology to Cognitive Science: The Case Against Belief* (Cambridge, Mass.: MIT/Bradford, 1983), 245.

though one may correctly predict that a certain glass of water will freeze at 0 degrees Centigrade, the water's having the property of freezing at 0 degrees Centigrade does not depend on anyone's (possible) predictive strategies. On intentional system theory, on the other hand, the feature that someone has of *believing* that water freezes at 0 degrees is relative to the (possible) predictive strategies of others.

So let us distinguish between features that are *stance-dependent* and features that are *stance-independent* as follows. Suppose that x has a feature F. Then F is a stance-dependent feature of x if and only if x's having F is relative to (possible) strategies, attitudes, or ascriptions toward x of some y; otherwise, F is a stance-independent feature.

Stance-dependent features are those features that a system has only by virtue of its (possibly) being an object of a certain stance. The expression 'stance-dependent feature' may be eliminated in favor of the more cumbersome but more explicitly Dennettian 'feature possessed only in relation to someone's strategies.' Compare: A "particular thing is an intentional system only in relation to the strategies of someone who is trying to explain and predict its behavior."[15]

The distinction between stance-dependent and stance-independent features is motivated by Dennett's ontology. About putative entities like beliefs, experiences, and pains, Dennett is an eliminative materialist.[16] At the same time, Dennett is at pains to argue that sentences of the form 'S believes that p' have truth value and that not all are false.[17] As Dennett remarks, "Attributions of belief and desire are not just 'convenient fictions;' there are plenty of honest-to-goodness instrumentalist *truths*."[18] The innocuous construal of 'feature' permits the distinction between stance-dependent and stance-independent features to accommodate both aspects of Dennett's view. On the one hand, in line with eliminative materialism, we may deny that beliefs are stance-independent features. But on the other hand, we may understand the truth of sentences of the form 'S believes that p' in terms of stance-dependent features of the systems that have them.

The point of distinguishing between stance-dependent and stance-in-

[15] Dennett, "Intentional Systems," 3–4. Not only is my formulation of the relevant distinction shorter, but it will also make plain the unity of my objections. All the arguments point to a single, central flaw in Dennett's conception, namely, an inconsistency in the use of the idea of being a feature possessed only in relation to someone's strategies, or, more briefly, of stance-dependence.

[16] Dennett, introduction to *Brainstorms*, xix.

[17] Ibid., xvii. Cf. "True Believers."

[18] Daniel C. Dennett, "Intentional Systems in Cognitive Ethology: The 'Panglossian Paradigm' Defended," *Behavioral and Brain Sciences* 6 (1983), 380 (emphasis his).

dependent features is to contrast Dennett's instrumentalism about the intentional with his realism about the physical. Because he is explicitly committed to what I call the 'stance-dependence' of features attributed from the intentional stance, Dennett could reject the formulation of the stance-dependent/stance-independent distinction only by rejecting the stance-independence of features attributed from the nonintentional stances. And since to do that would be to abandon realism about physical phenomena, I think that the distinction is unavoidable for Dennett—so long as he remains in any sense a realist.

It is important to see that the distinction between stance-dependent and stance-independent features is, in the first instance, not between the characteristic vocabularies of the stances but between the kinds of features that make descriptions in those vocabularies true.[19] On Dennett's official view, what makes it the case that x has F, where F is a physical feature, is not relative to anyone's strategies (that is, F is stance-independent); but what makes it the case that x has F', where F' is an intentional feature, is relative to someone's (possible) strategies (that is, F' is stance-dependent).

The stance-dependent/stance-independent distinction should not be confused with other distinctions in the literature, such as intrinsic/extrinsic or intrinsic/relational distinctions. Velocity is relative to inertial frame and hence is not an intrinsic feature of bodies. But it is not thereby a stance-dependent feature: The velocity of an object is not relative to anyone's possible predictive strategies any more than its temperature is. (To insist here that velocity depends upon someone's *choice* of frame would be misleading.) Not all relational features are stance-dependent, only those whose possession is relative to someone's strategies.

Further elaboration of exactly what stance-dependence is would require explication of what strategies are and would take us afield. (I have characterized stance-dependence as sharply as Dennett has characterized the intentional stance.) What matters for the arguments that follow is that Dennett is explicitly committed to the idea of stance-dependence (if not to the phrase) and that the stance-dependence/stance-independence distinction is exhaustive and hence can ground the premise common to a series of dilemmas.

---

[19] Dennett's view may be constrasted with Davidson's here. On Davidson's view, mental events are simply physical events described in a special (mentalistic) vocabulary. If this were Dennett's view, as we shall see in the discussion of rationality below, his instrumentalism would collapse. See my discussion in the last section.

Belief, Rationality, and Design

Dennett puts his intentional system theory to two distinct uses: one broadly ethical and the other protoscientific. He uses intentional system theory to vindicate our view of ourselves as persons, as moral and rational agents acting on beliefs and desires; and he uses it as a vehicle of discovery, a source of testable hypotheses in psychology and biology. As we shall see, neither of these purposes is well served by instrumentalism.

Belief and Other Attitudes

On the official view, believing that *p* and other attitudes are stance-dependent features of systems. When discussing ethical issues, however, Dennett often implies that the features attributed from the intentional stance are more than mere stance-dependent features. Let me give a few examples.

Dennett says, "a belief is essentially something that has been *endorsed* (by commission or omission) by the agent on the basis of its conformity with the rest of his beliefs."[20] Although endorsement by the agent is eminently plausible as a requirement of belief and is necessary in many contexts of ethical evaluation, it goes well beyond the view that belief is what is predictively attributable. Since what is predictively attributable to an individual need not coincide with what that individual endorses (think of a chess-playing computer), Dennett is not entitled to this claim.

A natural move for an intentional system theorist here is to point out that to endorse is no less intentional than to believe and that the intentional system approach to belief extends to all intentional concepts worth preserving. So, one may counter, a person endorses something if and only if endorsement of it may be predictively attributed to the person. This interpretation may have the merit of rendering the account consistent by treating intentional concepts like endorsement in terms of intentional system theory—but at the price of robbing Dennett's claims about agency and decision making of all plausibility. If endorsement were taken as no more than what can be predictively attributed, then the difficulties that we find in belief understood in terms of intentional system theory would simply accrue to endorsement.

Time and again, especially in discussion of ethical issues, Dennett treats features that are officially stance-dependent as if they were in fact stance-independent. To cite another example, he agrees with Ans-

---

[20] Dennett, "Mechanism and Responsibility," 252 (emphasis his).

combe: "*If I am to be held responsible for an action* (a bit of behavior of mine under a particular description), I must have been *aware* of it under that description."[21] This is so because one can give reasons for her action only under a description that she is aware of, and "only those capable of participating in reason-giving can be argued into, or argued out of, courses of action or attitudes, and if one is incapable of 'listening to reason' in some matter, one cannot be held responsible for it."[22] Although Dennett is surely correct that the capacity to give reasons for what one does is a condition of responsibility, it is difficult to see how an instrumentalistic account of giving reasons—which is even more intentional than merely believing something—can satisfy the condition. Officially, giving a reason is stance-dependent and cannot be understood apart from predictive strategies. To give a reason, on intentional system theory consistently applied, would be no more than to succumb to a certain predictive strategy. But succumbing to a certain predictive strategy seems too anemic an account of reason giving: giving reasons seems to be something that I do (with no conceptual dependence on a would-be ascriber).

Or again: "One must *ask oneself*," Dennett says, "what one's desires, motives, reasons really are, and only if one can say, can become aware of one's desires, can one be in a position to induce oneself to change."[23] But what one's desires, motives, reasons really are amounts only to what can be predictively attributed; to be aware of one's desires is only to be subject to more complex predictions. It is difficult to see how one could understand not only one's desires but also one's *awareness* of one's desires as a matter of predictive attribution. So, at least on occasion, Dennett appears to have in mind intentional concepts that at least seem to fail to conform to the intentional system analysis of intentional phenomena as what is predictively attributable.

Moreover, throughout *Elbow Room*, Dennett takes beliefs to provide reasons that cause us to behave one way rather than another.[24] But if beliefs have such causal efficacy, they can hardly be merely stance-dependent features of believers. On the one hand, it is difficult to see

[21] Dennett, "Conditions of Personhood," 282–283 (emphasis his).
[22] Ibid., 283. Hilary Kornblith has pointed out that one may be responsible for an action even if one was unaware of it under the relevant description at the time of the action. Cf. J. L. Austin's example of treading on a baby: One cannot evade responsibility by pleading ignorance of the relevant description.
[23] Dennett, "Conditions of Personhood," 285 (emphasis his).
[24] Daniel C. Dennett, *Elbow Room: The Varieties of Free Will Worth Wanting* (Cambridge, Mass.: MIT/Bradford, 1984), ch. 2. See also in this volume Dennett's "Just So Stories."

how an eliminative materialist can suppose that features whose possession depends upon the (possible) predictive strategies of others can
cause anything at all. On the other hand, one who takes beliefs to have
causal powers is in no position to be an instrumentalist with regard to
belief (unless he is also an instrumentalist with regard to causation).

Dennett does suggest a way to gloss causal claims about belief. He
draws a distinction between core elements ("the concrete, salient, separately stored representation tokens") and virtual beliefs ("only implicitly stored or represented"). Although he says that "there is no reason
to suppose the core elements . . . will explicitly represent (or *be*) a sub-
set of our *beliefs* at all," it is the core elements that have causal efficacy:
"[The] core elements, whatever they may be, can be cited as playing the
causal role, while belief remains virtual." To believe that p is to be in
"some one of an indefinitely large number of structurally different
states of type B that have in common just that each one of them licenses
attribution of the belief that p."[25]

This line of thinking illustrates the tension in instrumentalism. On
the one hand, core elements may not explicitly represent beliefs at all.
Yet they "license" attributions of belief: By virtue of what does a physical state license an attribution of p, rather than of q or of nothing at
all? (See the discussion of the "Modified Panglossian View" in Chapter
Six.) On the other hand, if to attribute a belief that p is to attribute one
of a large class of physical states, where is the instrumentalism?

The plausibility of Dennett's *rapprochement* of the physical and the
intentional seems to require sleight-of-hand deployment of intentional
system theory, deployment that conflicts with the theory's official instrumentalism. The conflict is unresolvable because consistent instrumentalism is inadequate to bear the weight of the ethical claims.

Rationality

Officially, rationality is attributed from the intentional stance, and
features attributed from the intentional stance are stance-dependent.
Yet much of Dennett's discussion suggests that rationality is as stance-
independent as a design feature like vision. For example, he advises that
we think in terms of design "*all the way in*—not just for eye-design, but
for deliberation-design and belief-design and strategy-concoctor design."[26] And, since Dennett offers an explicitly design-level model of
practical reasoning, he further implies that rationality is a design fea-

[25] Dennett, "Three Kinds of Intentional Psychology," 49–50 (emphases his).
[26] Ibid., 43 (emphasis his).

ture.[27] Finally, Dennett accounts for the success of the intentional stance by appeal to adaptation. In evolved organisms, rationality is produced by mechanisms of natural selection.[28]

So, quite often, Dennett emphasizes his construal of rationality as part of a system's design.[29] He sounds as if the intentional stance, with its presupposition of rationality, simply offers a handy alternative vocabulary to designate those design features that make a system predictable in a certain way. But if the intentional stance offered only a convenient vocabulary for designating certain design features, then attributions of rationality and of design would designate a single set of features, and rationality and design features would both be stance-dependent or both be stance-independent.

Rationality, like belief, cannot be stance-independent without aborting intentional system theory: If ascriptions of rationality simply ascribed features equally (or better) describable from the design or physical stance, they would be true by virtue of the obtaining of some actual (that is, physical) state of affairs. In that case, the grounds for instrumentalism would be thoroughly eroded. So rationality is *not* a stance-independent feature of systems that have it.

On the other hand, Dennett often seems to hold that design features, at least in evolved organisms, *are* stance-independent: The possession of features produced by natural selection is not relative to anyone's (possible) predictive strategies.[30] For example, whether or not a plant undergoes photosynthesis seems independent of anyone's possible predictive strategies. So it seems that features produced by natural selection are stance-independent and that rationality is stance-dependent. But in that case, Dennett cannot consistently explain rationality as the product of natural selection.

One may be tempted to object: A feature is stance-dependent just in case its attribution allows prediction from the intentional stance. Although mechanisms of natural selection are stance-independent, they may produce features that make an organism predictable from the in-

[27] Dennett, "On Giving Libertarians What They Say They Want," in *Brainstorms*, 295.

[28] See Dennett's "Just So Stories" in *Elbow Room*. For discussion of the similarities and dissimilarities between intentional system theory in psychology and adaptationalism in biology, see Dennett's "Intentional Systems in Cognitive Ethology," with open peer commentary and Dennett's replies.

[29] Dennett, "Intentional Systems," 5–6.

[30] Dennett suggests that the design stance belongs with the physical stance as the "mechanistic" stances, and he contrasts these "lower" stances with the intentional stance, from which stance-dependent features are attributed. See Dennett, "Mechanism and Responsibility" and "Intentional Systems," 22. Later, I shall consider the possibility that Dennett may take features attributed from the design stance to be stance-dependent.

tentional stance. So, the objection may go, there is no contradiction in supposing that stance-independent features may also be stance-dependent features.

The objection is misguided because it construes stance-dependence in a way that undercuts Dennett's instrumentalism: If stance-dependence were merely a matter of an alternative vocabulary for designating features that a system has independently of anyone's taking a stance, then there would be a physical fact of the matter as to whether or not the system had the feature, specified in a stance-dependent way; and ascriptions of rationality would be true or false in exactly the same way as physical descriptions. In that case, construing the intentional stance as intrumentalistic but the physical stance as realistic would be wholly unmotivated, and, again, the instrumentalism would dissolve.

An objector may go on to claim that, at least, there is a strong similarity between optimality of design (at the design level) and rationality (at the intentional level): They both have survival value. But, I should reply, the appearance of similarity here is vitiated by an equivocation on 'has survival value.' Assuming (for the moment) realism about the design level and instrumentalism about the intentional level, to say that optimality of design has survival value is to say that the design causally contributes to an organism's survival; but to say that rationality has survival value is only to say that certain attributions have predictive power.

Dennett treats rationality inconsistently. Although rationality is officially a stance-dependent feature, Dennett often implies that it is a stance-independent feature, a feature that an organism has per se, without regard to the predictive strategies of others. And this shift to suggesting that rationality is a stance-independent feature is nowhere more prominent than when Dennett invokes evolution; he almost always speaks of rationality as something that an organism has per se. Indeed, the "creation and improvement of intelligence is one of evolution's most impressive products."[31] But possession of a feature that an organism has per se does not depend upon the predictive strategies of others. It is a stance-independent feature.

To sum up the discussion of rationality: On the official theory, rationality cannot be understood as a feature that an organism has per se, apart from predictive strategies. Officially, "being rational is being intentional is being the object of a certain stance."[32] But when Dennett

---

[31] Dennett, *Elbow Room*, 37. Cf. Dennett, "Making Sense of Ourselves," *Philosophical Topics* 12 (1981), 63–81.

[32] Dennett, "Conditions of Personhood," 271.

links rationality to design in the various ways, he treats rationality as a feature that an organism has per se, as opposed to a feature that an organism has by virtue of its (possibly) being the object of a certain stance. One cannot consistently suppose that rationality is acquired by natural selection if one is a realist about the products of natural selection but an instrumentalist about rationality.

Design

Just as the concept of rationality seems to wobble back and forth between the intentional and design stances, the design stance itself wobbles between stance-independent features attributed from the physical stance and stance-dependent features attributed from the intentional stance. This latter instability, I believe, has obscured the inconsistency in the treatment of rationality.

In keeping with Dennett's scientific realism and the status of theories of natural selection as scientific, I have been supposing that, officially, Dennett takes design features to be stance-independent.[33] Since descriptions from the design stance assume absence of breakdown or malfunction, however, it is time to question that supposition: Can the relevant concept of malfunction or breakdown be understood in a stance-independent way?

For artifacts familiar to us, the answer is no. As a simple-minded illustration, suppose that someone presses the brake pedal of an automobile and there is no response. One natural way to describe this episode is as a malfunction of the brakes. Yet there is no fact of the matter, in terms of stance-independent features, as to whether an occurrence should be described as a breakdown or, more neutrally, as a reorganization or change of disposition. The "failure" of the brakes is clearly a malfunction or breakdown only relative to someone's (probably the designer's and/or user's) intentions. But on intentional system theory, beliefs, desires, and intentions are stance-dependent. Therefore, to describe an event as a malfunction or breakdown, in the case of artifacts, is to attribute to it a stance-dependent feature.[34]

Dennett has observed that Darwin did not dethrone design as an ex-

[33] In "Evolution, Error and Intentionality" (in *The Intentional Stance*), Dennett extends his view in a way that indicates that he does not take design features to be stance-independent.

[34] It may be thought that we can avoid regarding brake failures as dependent on intentions if our theory about cars is an idealization that permits identifying nonresponsive brakes as breakdowns relative to that idealization. Which idealization is the correct one, however, will be determined in part by the intentions of the designers.

planatory concept but rather showed that design need not be construed anthropomorphically.[35] Thus, to say that a feature is part of the design of a system is not to imply that the system was designed by an intelligent being. Nevertheless, the facts remain that malfunctions are relative to design, that artifacts are designed by intelligent beings, and that what design an artifact has is relative to the intentions of the designer. What warrants the description 'breakdown' or 'malfunction' depends upon such stance-dependent features as intentions. Therefore, at least in cases of artifacts, features attributed from the design stance cannot be understood in a stance-independent way.

Are malfunctions in evolved organisms also stance-dependent features? If malfunctions in evolved organisms are *not* stance-dependent features, then the fact that malfunctions in artifacts are stance-dependent features puts Dennett's goal of a general theory of intelligence that applies equally to organisms and artifacts permanently out of reach. If, on the other hand, malfunctions in evolved organisms *are* stance-dependent features, then there remains nothing in the design stance untainted by the intentional.

Suppose that Dennett takes design features generally to be stance-dependent. This position would seem to allow for a unified view of humans and artifacts: Functions of a machine are relative to the intentions of the designers (namely, humans), and functions of evolved organisms are relative to the intentions of Mother Nature. But to say that Nature has intentions is to say no more, officially, than that attribution of intentions is predictive. Thus, the cost of taking design features to be stance-dependent seems to be instrumentalism about theories of natural selection.

Dennett seems faced with a deep dilemma regarding the design stance. If design features are stance-independent, then there is no place for malfunction, at least in the case of artifacts (since having brakes, and the like, is not stance-independent). But if design features are stance-dependent, then theories of natural selection, as theories explaining design features of evolved organisms, must be construed instrumentalistically. In the first case, the design level tends to collapse into the physical; in the second case, the design level tends to collapse into the intentional. The result is that the design stance is inherently unstable.

The unavoidable inconsistencies in the treatment of belief, rationality, and design suggest that instrumental intentionality is an illusion.

[35] Daniel C. Dennett, "Why the Law of Effect Will Not Go Away," in *Brainstorms*, 73.

This suspicion will be further confirmed as we consider the status of the physical and intentional stances.

THE STATUS OF THE STANCES

Suppose that Dennett were to fend off the difficulties of design. Still, the problems would persist. The one that I shall focus on concerns another aspect of the relation between the physical and the intentional stances: Is the intentional stance dispensable without cognitive loss? Attempts to answer this question lead, I believe, to another dilemma, which has been obscured by inconsistent treatment of the intentional stance.

Apart from the difficulties engendered by ambiguity, the attempt to render physical and intentional explanations compatible leads, I believe, to a kind of metaphysical dilemma, one that can be resolved within a physicalist framework (if at all) only at the expense of the vocabulary of the intentional stance that Dennett aims to preserve. On the one hand, if there is something that eludes the physical stance, then Dennett's instrumentalism is imperiled; on the other hand, if nothing eludes the physical stance, then Dennett's intentionalism cannot play its assigned role.

If Dennett is correct, then any system, human or not, may be described exhaustively and its operations explained wholly in terms of its physical constitution. Dennett points out that "if some version of mechanistic physicalism is true (as I believe), we will never *need* absolutely to ascribe any intentions to anything. . . ."[36] This statement seems to imply that the intentional stance is in principle (even if not in practice) dispensable.

On the other hand, Dennett has suggested, to fail to take an intentional stance is, in some cases, to miss certain "objective patterns." Surely this claim, which would help give the intentional stance the weight it needs to be more than a "sham," leads straight to a dilemma for Dennett; for the existence of *objective* patterns that would be missed by a physical stance would seem to falsify Dennett's instrumentalism concerning the intentional level.

Consider, for example, Dennett's superior Martians, who can predict all our behavior, every physical movement, from the physical stance. Despite this ability, "if they did not also see us as intentional systems, they would be *missing something* perfectly objective: the *patterns* in human behavior that are describable from the intentional stance, and only from that stance, and which support generalizations

[36] Dennett, "Conditions of Personhood," 273 (emphasis his).

and predictions."[37] If Dennett's view is that the Martians would miss something objective about us by failing to take the intentional stance, he would seem to have revised his earlier view that "a particular thing is an intentional system only in relation to the strategies of someone who is trying to explain and predict its behavior."[38] This example purports to show that our being intentional systems is something perfectly objective apart from the strategies of the ascribers, which, *ex hypothesi*, are wholly served by the physical stance. What might be missed from the physical stance?

> Take a particular instance in which the Martians observe a stock broker deciding to place an order for 500 shares of General Motors. They predict the exact motions of his fingers as he dials the phone, and the exact vibrations of his vocal cords as he intones his order. But if the Martians do not see that indefinitely many *different* patterns of finger motions and vocal cord vibrations—even the motions of indefinitely many different individuals—could have been substituted for the actual particulars without perturbing the subsequent operation of the market, then they have failed to see a real pattern in the world they are observing.[39]

But whether or not the pattern Dennett indicates requires the intentional stance for discerning it depends upon how the expression 'perturbing the subsequent operation of the market' is understood. If it is cashed out in physical terms, then he has not shown any "perfectly objective" pattern that is missed by the physical stance. On the other hand, if it cannot be cashed out in physical terms, then the claim would have to be that there are things that elude the physical stance.

Either way, the example illustrates the dilemma suggested earlier: If there is something intentional that eludes the physical stance, then Dennett's instrumentalism about the intentional is endangered; if there is nothing that eludes the physical stance, then the intentional stance seems, in principle, dispensable without cognitive loss, in which case Dennett's intentional stance is "just a sham and a word game."[40]

Ersatz Intentionality

Dennett's instrumentalism concerning intentionality does not deliver the goods. If intentional system theory is genuinely instrumentalistic, if

[37] Dennett, "True Believers," 64 (emphasis his).
[38] Dennett, "Intentional Systems," 3–4.
[39] Dennett, "True Believers," 64 (emphasis his).
[40] Haugeland, "The Mother of Intention," 616.

the features that are designated from the intentional stance are stance-dependent features, then the theory cannot play either the ethical or the protoscientific role that Dennett assigns to it. It cannot play the ethical role unless inconsistently applied, and it cannot play the protoscientific role because, as mere "interpretation," the intentional stance swings free of the design and physical stances.

On the other hand, if Dennett means the intentional stance to offer a special vocabulary for describing features equally well described in the vocabulary of the design or physical stance, and if he remains a realist about entities posited from these other stances, then the intentional stance is not even instrumentalistic. To attribute a belief that p would be to attribute a design or physical property (that is, a stance-independent feature) in a special vocabulary. This would be a straightforward reduction, to which appeals to hermeneutics are irrelevant.

These critical points have been submerged, in part because Dennett has not been altogether consistent in his construal of instrumentalism. Throughout *Brainstorms*, he understands attitudes solely in terms of predictive attributability, and it is on this basis that I distinguished between stance-dependent and stance-independent features. Elsewhere, however, in comparing beliefs to centers of gravity, he implies that all he means by his instrumentalism is that beliefs are not to be identified with any particular inner physical state. But clearly, nonidentity with a particular inner state is only a necessary, not a sufficient, condition for an instrumentalistic account of belief. One could be a realist about belief and still identify a belief with a complex state of a subject and the environment.

In addition, if the aim is to give an instrumentalistic account of attitudes, the analogy between beliefs and centers of gravity is off the mark. Although we do not identify an object's center of gravity with any inner state or particle, we do not take attributions of centers of gravity to be instrumentalistic, and for good reason: An object's center of gravity is fully determined by the physical properties of the object (near Earth); it is not a matter of "interpretation." Like the use of exponents in mathematics, employment of the concept of a center of gravity provides a kind of shorthand for genuine properties (stance-independent features) that an object really has. Centers of gravity, unlike beliefs on Dennett's view, are not relative to someone's (possible) attitudes, ascriptions, or strategies.

The analogy is further vitiated by the fact that the idea of a center of gravity is ensconced in a genuine theory, while the idea of belief is not. As Dennett says, he derives his conclusions about intentional systems from what "seems . . . to be a slapdash, informal sort of thinking that I explicitly deny to be a theory in the strict sense of the term."[41] Thus, the comparison of the concept of a belief to that of the concept of a center of gravity is likely to mislead and to obscure the deep dilemma of Dennett's instrumentalism.

It has been easy to see from the outset that, on a consistent intentional system theory, too many things (such as game-playing computers, perhaps even lecterns) have beliefs and have them in the same sense that we do. Officially, beliefs are nothing but stance-dependent features whose attribution enables the attributor to predict behavior described in certain ways. Although there is little predictive advantage in attributing beliefs to a lectern (since its behavioral repertoire is so limited), it cannot be deemed an error to do so by intentional system theory. Moreover, to be consistent on intentional system theory, one must regard one's own beliefs as no more than aids for predicting behavior, and even the regarding of them must be cashed out in terms of predictive attributability. Although not emphasized here, the wildness of the consequences of the theory should not be overlooked.

Quite apart from its counterintuitive consequences, however, Dennett's instrumentalism is beset, as we have seen, by difficulties. It is plagued by a series of inconsistencies in the treatment of the concepts of belief, rationality, and design, and it is caught in a dilemma concerning the epistemic completeness of the physical stance. For these reasons, I think it unlikely that intentional system theory will be made coherent.

At first glance, instrumentalism seems more promising for a physicalist than it turns out to be. As it happens, it is extraordinarily difficult, perhaps impossible, to be an eliminative materialist and to give a coherent account of attributions of attitudes that permits them to be true. The moral is that the ideas of different stances or levels of description are not simply available to the physicalist for the taking; it is more difficult than may be suspected to show how such ideas can be intelligible in the context of eliminative materialism.

The argument against instrumentalism here has been directed toward the view that construes belief solely in terms of predictive attributability. Nevertheless, I suspect that the criticisms may be extended to any physicalistic view that holds that to have a belief is no more than to be interpretable as having a belief, that to work out a rationale is just

---

[41] Dennett, "Intentional Systems in Cognitive Ethology," 382. If, as Dennett says (380), there are "physical facts in virtue of which a monkey believes what it believes," and if those facts (whatever they are) fully determine the monkey's beliefs in the way that the comparison to centers of gravity suggests, then there remains little point in calling the position instrumentalistic. (Moreover, as the thought experiments have shown, such a position is unlikely to be sustained.)

to be interpretable as working out a rationale, and so on. In addition, the idea of interpretation is problematic in this context. Any adequate account of what it is for something to be interpreted in a certain way would seem to require a more robust idea of interpretation than Dennett's view has room for. The labeling of an episode as one that gives an interpretation itself seems to be to give an interpretation, and we are back on the merry-go-round. Thus, I am no more sanguine about the prospects for other versions of instrumentalism concerning attitudes than I am about Dennett's.

Instrumentalism concerning attitudes seems helpless to soften the significance of the conclusion of the argument from physicalism. Therefore, instrumentalism concerning attitudes does not offer a genuine alternative to one who would avoid the austere dichotomy of vindicating attitudes by physicalistic psychology or repudiating attributions of attitudes as radically false altogether.

· 9 ·

WHERE WE ARE NOW

At the end of Part I we concluded that *belief* resists treatment by physicalistic psychology; and now, at the conclusion of Part II, we find that *belief*, nonetheless, is not obsolete. The common-sense conception of the mental, in terms of attitudes identified by content, neither needs nor will receive a foundation in physicalism.[1] Many philosophers would endorse the conclusion of Part I or the conclusion of Part II; few, as I mentioned in Chapter One, would be eager to embrace both. Before looking at some implications of this pair of conclusions, let me summarize the results in slightly greater detail.

In Sum

Much of Part I was aimed at showing that physicalistic psychology will not save belief or other attitudes. Belief is not amenable to physicalistic treatment because physicalistic psychology cannot make room for the requisite concept of content: no content, no belief. And the reason that physicalistic psychology cannot make room for the requisite concept of content is that it is committed to a physicalistic condition of adequacy, in the form either of (P) or of (P'):

(P) Molecular duplicates necessarily share their narrow contents: If C is a given narrow content, and S has a belief with narrow content C, and S' is a molecule-for-molecule duplicate of S, then S' has a belief with narrow content C.

(P') There are no differences in content between molecular duplicates who have been in the same types of contexts, described nonintentionally and nonsemantically, throughout their existences.

(P) and (P') are special cases of the general requirement of physicalism, which, until this chapter, we have assumed to be a scientific psychology to honor. A psychology is physicalistic if it individuates psychological states in conformity with the following condition:

[1] Although I hope to have extended the Putnam-Burge tradition in Part I, philosophers working in that tradition may not find the arguments in Part II congenial. In particular, I would not attribute to either Putnam or Burge agreement with my general conclusions.

(C) Molecular duplicates necessarily make the same contribution to their psychological states: For some level of description in the vocabulary of the scientific psychology, if S is in a state of that description, and S' is a molecule-for-molecule duplicate of S, then S' is in a state of that description.

If my diagnosis has been correct, then no physicalistic theory—that is, no theory committed to (C)—can admit belief. On the other hand, as I argued in Part II, we cannot dispense with belief and other attitudes identified by content without courting cognitive suicide.

Let us put the conclusions in the context of the 'Argument from Physicalism.' In Chapter One, physicalism was taken to be the product of a thesis about science together with a particular conception of scientific theory. The thesis is scientific realism, and the conception is that scientific theories are to be physicalistic in the sense of conforming to (C). To give up either component is to give up physicalism as I have construed it.

ARGUMENT FROM PHYSICALISM

(1) Either physicalistic psychology will vindicate the common-sense conception of the mental or the common-sense conception is radically mistaken.
(2) Physicalistic psychology will fail to vindicate the common-sense conception of the mental.
Therefore,
(3) The common-sense conception of the mental is radically mistaken.

The incompatibility of physicalism and the common-sense conception—the failure even of extensional equivalence of attributions of attitudes and descriptions governed by (C)—shows that the second premise of the argument from physicalism is true: In no sense will physicalistic psychology vindicate belief. Since the argument is valid and (2) is true, then either (3) is true or (1) is false. The arguments in Chapters Six and Seven were aimed at exposing the difficulties of holding (3) true. In the absence of the common-sense conception, it is unclear that anything could be affirmed or denied, or even that the distinction between truth and falsity could remain intact. The argument of Chapter Eight was aimed at showing that the dire conclusion of Chapter Seven could not be avoided by construing the common-sense conception instrumentalistically. Thus, denial of the common-sense conception seems a serious threat to intelligibility generally. Certainly, no one who has entertained denying it has shown how normative concepts (like those of reason and justification) or semantic concepts (like those of truth and interpretation) can survive in the absence of attitudes identified by content.

In light of the evidence for (2) and the untenability of (3), we seem pushed to abandon (1). In that case, the proper conclusion is that intentionality, without which we have no conception of science or of anything else, stands in no need of vindication at all. Trying to vindicate intentionality in nonintentional terms is like trying to disappear up one's own sleeve.

The incompatibility of the common-sense conception with physicalism is not, in any ordinary sense, an empirical matter. It stems rather from differences in schemes of individuation. Beliefs, desires, and other attitudes are identified by content, and *content* is a semantic notion par excellence, as Fodor noted. But individuation by semantic features simply fails to coincide with individuation by physical, functional, causal, or other nonsemantic features, as the thought experiments aimed to show. Thus, the conflict is unlikely to admit of empirical resolution.

But now we must ask: What are the implications of conjoining the conclusion that physicalistic psychology will not save beliefs or other attitudes identified by content with the conclusion that attribution of such attitudes is indispensable? Does this pair of conclusions jeopardize prospects for a science of the mind?

PROSPECTS FOR A SCIENCE OF THE MIND

Assuming now that physicalism cannot accommodate intentionality, there seem to be two alternatives for an aspiring science of the mind: either (i) embrace the physicalistic conception of theories and eschew attitudes, and recognize the inherent incompleteness of such a science; or (ii) forgo the physicalistic conception of theories and abandon the endeavor generally to provide nonintentional conditions for intentional states. Both alternatives part with physicalism as I have construed it. The first gives up scientific realism; the second gives up commitment to (C) as a restriction on what can count as a scientific psychology.

A science of the mind that embraces the physicalistic conception of theories and eschews attitudes will not be a comprehensive account of mentality inasmuch as it is blind to attitudes identified by content. A physicalistic psychology that aspires to completeness would have the odd consequence that, if it is true, it could not have been thought of, for in eliminating intentionality, a physicalistic theory eliminates the possibility of thinking *of* anything. If a physicalistic theory of the mind is true and comprehensive, by virtue of what would the cognitive states of its formulators be about the theory? To be consistent with physicalism, the answer is: nothing. A consistent physicalistic theory cannot admit intentionality, and a theory that cannot admit intentionality is not entitled to invoke the "aboutness" of cognitive states. This point is independent of any particular theory of thinking; it relies only on the insight that it is inconsistent to avail oneself of what one denies.

Therefore, a physicalistic theory of the mind, insofar as it can be thought of, must be incomplete. Physicalistic theories may be quite useful, however, as long as they are not taken to be comprehensive. But once they are seen not to be comprehensive anyway, the motivation to require that theories be committed to (C) fades. In this case, the second alternative for a science of the mind, or rather for sciences of the mind, becomes quite attractive.

That second alternative is to forget the physicalistic commitment to (C) and abandon the endeavor generally to provide nonintentional conditions for psychological states. The latter course seems the more promising and more in line with the reigning pluralism of research programs.[2] To embrace physicalism would be to diminish the domain of psychology to a fraction of its original province and to deprive it of its original interest. Indeed, barring intentionally described phenomena from scientific inquiry would leave out most of what was initially puzzling. Recall that if we insist on physicalism, the behavior of the experimental subjects in Chapter Two would have to receive the same psychological (now, nonintentional) explanations.

As we saw at the end of Chapter Six, if we banish attributions of attitudes identified by content, it becomes unclear why psychology is needed at all. We could not explain a person's behavior in terms of her beliefs, desires, or intentions; we could not distinguish what a person actually does from what she thinks she is doing. To justify such impoverishment of psychological explanation, there should be some powerful motivation (if the concept of motivation can survive physicalism) springing from requirements of progressive research programs, not from metaphysical allegiances.

Suppose that we abandon physicalism. May we then hope for a comprehensive nonphysicalistic science of the mind, comparable in scope to physical theories of fundamental forces? At this point, it would be rash to guess. It should be noted, however, that one may remain skeptical

[2] Tyler Burge has argued that current psychological theories, such as Marr's theory of vision, in fact do not conform to the individualistic physicalistic conception of theories. See his "Individualism and Psychology," *Philosophical Review* 95 (1986), 3–46.

without suggesting that anything is beyond the reach of science—as long as we take the tolerant view of science as systematic investigation governed by research programs and avoid the overly stringent demands of physicalism. Indeed, I should suppose that there can be fruitful theories of any aspect of mental life under some illuminating description. But to say that there can be a theory of anything is not to say that there can be a single theory of everything completely. Piecemeal theories that account for various ranges of mental phenomena need not all fit together or even be compatible with a comprehensive theory.

The arguments presented here do not indicate doubts about neuroscience or psychology; still less should they suggest that the intentional is insulated from the nonintentional. Who, for example, could doubt that the main hope for victims of stroke and Alzheimer's disease lies in brain research? Surely it is methodologically unassailable to look for structural abnormalities in the brain to account for various kinds of bizarre behavior. But far from dispensing with intentionality, such research, like any other research, is itself an intentional activity. Pretheoretically, we may describe an investigator as one who formulates and tests hypotheses, but it is unclear how to give nonintentional conditions even for confirming a hypothesis that p, not to mention how (relevantly) to characterize such activities in terms uninfected by intentional assumptions.

Not only the conduct of scientific inquiry but also the phenomena investigated by neuroscientists seem riddled with intentional assumptions. Many, if not most, of the phenomena that neurology is concerned with would be invisible in the absence of the common-sense conception. This is particularly clear in the case of identifying neurological disorders. The symptoms of senility, for example—say, that a particular patient thinks she is back in Fredericksburg—are simply indescribable without content. The intentional and the nonintentional seem so interwoven as to be inextricable.

What I want to reject is any requirement that precludes irreducibly intentional psychology. For example, Dennett has said, "Intentional theory is vacuous as psychology because it presupposes and does not explain rationality or intelligence."[3] I hope to have suggested that if psychology proper really did not presuppose rationality or intelligence, it would be in danger of disappearing.

Fortunately, the contributions of psychology and the social sciences do not depend upon the physicalistic program that has been found

---

[3] Daniel C. Dennett, "Intentional Systems," in his *Brainstorms: Philosophical Essays on Mind and Psychology* (Montgomery, Vt.: Bradford, 1978), 15.

wanting here. Their contributions stem from research programs that set problems and provide criteria for solutions without any particular regard for physicalistic probity. Much of the research simply assumes the intentionality of the experimental subjects, as we saw in the case of attribution theory. And the main contribution even of those who repudiate intentionality has not lain in their repudiation. Skinner's influence, for example, is traceable, not to his metaphysical commitments but to the fact that he provided a flexible and fruitful research paradigm. The amalgam of interdisciplinary efforts by psychologists, linguists, philosophers, and computer scientists who work on and solve specific problems will (and should) continue to develop. Models of language acquisition, of vision, and of other cognitive activities are useful and illuminating whether they conform to physicalism or not.

The rampant pluralism that marks current research can only be a good thing. If we evaluate research programs by their fruits, then there is no need to insist on the metaphysical purity of physicalism. Indeed, it is difficult to see how actual research could be well served by a rigid commitment to physicalism. So a challenge to physicalism is no challenge to psychology as actually practiced. Everything, as Wittgenstein said for different effect, remains exactly as before.

Naturalism Without Physicalism?

The burden of this antireductive and antieliminative argument has been to reveal the poverty of physicalism. Perhaps because physicalism is the dominant expression of the impulse to see mind as part of the natural order, philosophers have not widely acknowledged that one can deny physicalism without denying that mind is part of the natural order.

For example, as different as the approaches of Fodor and Stalnaker are, Fodor would agree with Stalnaker when he says, "The challenge presented to the philosopher who wants to regard human beings and mental phenomena as part of the natural order is to explain intentional relations in naturalistic terms."[4] Stalnaker intends to meet that challenge by explaining the intentionality of language in terms of the intentionality of mental states and then by explaining the intentionality of mental states without reference to semantic properties of language. Fodor, by contrast, intends to meet that challenge by showing how the intentional properties of mental states derive from the semantic properties of mental representations and then by giving a "naturalistic" account of the semantic properties of mental representations. Stalnaker

[4] Robert C. Stalnaker, *Inquiry* (Cambridge, Mass.: MIT/Bradford, 1984), 6.

and Fodor proceed from different directions, but both aim to arrive at the same kind of physicalistic destination: certification of the naturalistic credentials of intentionality by specifying nonsemantic conditions for intentional and semantic phenomena. Although reductive physicalism is clearly naturalistic, we may question whether, conversely, naturalism requires physicalism.

Historically, naturalism has been construed as the view that there is nothing, in principle, beyond the scope of scientific investigation.[5] Although naturalism has been confused with materialism (and now physicalism), it is distinct from it and does not entail it. Naturalism places no restriction on what kinds of principles are appropriate for science, as long as they have testable consequences. Since the mark of science lies in its experimental, self-corrective methods and not in commitment to any particular ontology, science no more needs a foundation in physicalism than does belief. On this interpretation, naturalism is an ontologically neutral, methodological principle. Interpreted in this methodological way, as the view that there are no intrinsic limits on what can be naturally explained, naturalism can survive rejection of physicalism.

In that case, there is no reason to assume that naturalism requires a *theory* of intentionality in any sense that requires specification of nonintentional sufficient conditions for intentional states. The situation here bears a certain resemblance to Hume's problem of induction. Induction, Hume argued, cannot be justified deductively, but any inductive argument for induction is circular. Likewise, intentionality, it seems, cannot be justified in terms of nonintentional conditions, but any intentional account is circular.

Although neither induction nor intentionality can be justified in standard ways, neither is eliminable. The "justification" of each lies in its indispensable contribution to the cognitive enterprise. Indeed, if I have been correct in arguing that without intentionality science would be impossible, then one cannot (consistently) reject intentionality without rejecting science. Or, to put it another way, the legitimacy of whatever is required for science—induction, intentionality, or anything else—is assured by the legitimacy of the science that it underwrites.

We seem left with a need for something analogous to Hume's "skeptical solution" to the problem of induction: Intentionality does not need what is not available for it, namely, any kind of physicalistic vindication. The next step, one that would raise issues different from the

---

[5] See Arthur Danto, "Naturalism," in *The Encyclopedia of Philosophy*, which was the source of the characterizations in this paragraph.

critical ones here, would be to work out the details of such a "skeptical solution" to the problem of intentionality. At this point, I hope to have established the antireductive and antieliminative conclusion and thus to have cleared the way for a "skeptical solution"—a solution that drains the initial plausibility out of the terms that seem to force upon us an unachievable goal.

INELIMINABLE INTENTIONALITY

As long as we can make distinctions like the one between the manifest and scientific images, as long as there is scientific inquiry, as long as cognition is about anything at all, we have not eliminated the intentionality of the common-sense conception. So we literally cannot imagine that we enjoy cognition without content. But is there some inconsistency in supposing, as anyone who is a physicalist in life as well as in philosophy must suppose, that we can abandon the common-sense conception of mentality constituted by attributions of attitudes identified by content? Can we do what we cannot conceive of having done?

Such a question, as Dennett has pointed out,[6] is tantamount to asking whether or not we can give up being persons. With a somewhat heartier notion than Dennett has of what it is to be a person, I should agree but urge that to give up being persons would not be simply to give up the point of view from which ethics, value, and culture may be maintained. If within our power at all, it would be to give up the point of view from which thinking about anything, meaning anything, or doing anything intentionally is possible. To abandon the common-sense conception of the mental would be to relinquish the point of view from which the idea of making sense makes sense. Even if psychologically possible, wholesale surrender of our cognitive resources is, fortunately, rationally unwarranted.

[6] Daniel C. Dennett, "Mechanism and Responsibility," in *Brainstorms*, 254.

INDEX

Amarel, Saul, 47n
Armstrong, D. M., 33n, 108n
Austin, David F., 31n, 41n, 71n, 114

Bach, Kent, 27n
Baker, Lynne Rudder, 28n, 54, 62n
Beck, Lewis White, 134n
belief, 15–20; *de dicto/de re*, 63, 70–71, 82–83, 107, 127; narrow individuation of, 50–53; and physicalism, 167; as stance-dependent, 155–157. *See also* restricted semantic type
belief/desire psychology, 23, 38, 41, 61, 82–83, 99, 109
Berger, Alan, 54n, 57n, 140n
Block, Ned, 4n, 8n, 33n, 34n, 45n, 107, 108n
Brady, Mike, 49
Burge, Tyler, 71n, 72n, 105n, 126n, 167n; on individualism, 4, 32n, 121n, 170n

Cartesian interactionism, 33–34
Chastain, Charles, 140n
Chisholm, Roderick, 71, 79n
Chomsky, Noam, 140n
Churchland, Patricia S., 77n, 90n, 138, 139n
Churchland, Paul M., 10–13, 19n, 61n, 90n, 113n, 114–115, 142, 147n; on eliminative materialism, 138–139; on folk psychology, 125–127, 129; on theoretical reduction, 118–123
cognitive error, 124–125, 144–145
cognitive science, 14, 23–24, 37–38, 41
common-sense conception, 15–20; and assertibility, 138–142; consequences of rejection of, 128–133; as empirical theory, 123–128; and normative concepts, 135–138; and truth, 143–144
computer metaphor, 43, 45–51; artificial intelligence, 44, 50; computational processes, 24. *See also* functionalism
content, 15–20. *See also* narrow content

context, 91–96
Cummins, Robert, 45n, 152n

Danto, Arthur, 29, 173n
Davidson, Donald, 7, 20, 154n
Dennett, Daniel C., 6, 12, 13, 28n, 33n, 36n, 46, 48n, 77n, 114, 121n, 129; on belief, 155–157; and cognitive status of stances and instrumentalism, 149–166; on design, 160–162; and intentional system theory, 150–154, 162–163; on notional worlds, 107; on rationality, 157–160; and stance-(in)dependent features, 152–154; and stances described, 150–153, 171n, 174n
Devitt, Michael, 93n
Dretske, Fred I., 10n, 100n, 101n, 103
Dreyfus, Hubert, 62n

Eco, Umberto, 29n
eliminative materialism, 13, 134–147. *See also* physicalism
Evans, Gareth, 95n

Farrell, B. A., 106n
Feldman, Fred, 97n
Field, Hartry, 7n, 85n
Fodor, Jerry A., 5, 8–12, 46n, 86n, 93n, 101n, 102n, 107, 128, 172–173; on computer metaphor, 45; on form and content, 23–28, 34n, 37–38; on modularity, 65–68; narrow content, 52, 85–86; and observation/theory distinction, 63–66, 68–77; on opacity, 24n, 25, 26n, 28n, 55, 63; on propositional attitudes, 24n, 38, 41n. *See also* language of thought; methodological solipsism; phenomenological accessibility
folk psychology, 6, 15–16, 118–119, 123–128
formality condition, 24, 37–38. *See also* narrow states
Freud, Sigmund, 106

175

63; and narrow states, 53–62. *See also* belief
Rey, Georges, 57
Rorty, Richard, 43
Rosenberg, Alexander, 7n

Samet, Jerry, 68n
Sanford, David, 41n
Schiffer, Stephen, 71n
scientific psychology, 3, 14, 47–48, 113
scientific realism, 4, 168–169
Searle, John, 14n, 62n, 106
Sellars, Wilfrid, 4
semantic concepts, 168–169
semantic constraint (S), 66, 86, 87n
semantic counterparts, 81
semantic theories: conceptual role, 36n, 78; truth-conditional, 60; two-factor, 87, 92, 107–108. *See also* meaning; truth
Shoemaker, Sydney, 41n, 108n
Simon, Herbert A., 47n
Smart, J.J.C., 33n
Stalnaker, Robert C., 9, 10n, 101n, 144n, 172–173
Stampe, Dennis W., 10n, 100n
Stich, Stephen P., 28n, 45n, 61n, 90n,

124n, 142n, 152n; on folk psychology, 6, 122–123, 125–126, 129–130; on a modified Panglossian prospect, 12, 114–118, 128; on the principle of autonomy, 27n, 116; on weak reductivism, 10, 11

thought experiments: case concerning provoked assault/aggravated assault, 30–36; case concerning red things/gray things, 74–76; cases concerning Twin Earth, 64, 69–70, 77, 121n; cricket/locust case, 119–122; gin/vodka case, 88–100
truth, 143–144; redundancy theory of, 143n; Tarski's theory of, 144n

van Gulick, Robert, 51n, 108n
van Inwagen, Peter, 71n
vitalism analogy, 138–139

White, Stephen, 80–81
Winograd, Terry, 47n, 52n
Winston, Patrick Henry, 49
Wittgenstein, Ludwig, 7, 172
Woodward, James, 147n

Library of Congress Cataloging-in-Publication Data

Baker, Lynne Rudder, 1944–
Saving belief.

Includes index.
1. Belief and doubt. I. Title. II. Title:
Physicalism.
BD215.B27 1987   121'.6   87–25926
ISBN 0–691–07320–1 (alk. paper)